Alexander The Great And The Conquest Of The Persians

A Reconstruction Of Cleitarchus

by

Andrew Michael Chugg

2013

First Edition

ISBN 978-0-9556790-7-0

Riding on a cotton cloud, his victims to espy,
Zeus flings all his thunderbolts out of a clear blue sky,
For I have seen electric storms cross sunny Summer days
And shivered as I fell beneath that god's almighty gaze.

Alexander the Great
and the
Conquest of the Persians

Contents

1. Introduction

*In spite of the objections of Tarn, I regard it as certain that whatever source Diodorus used, it
was the same as that employed by Curtius. Schwartz assembled a formidable list of parallels
between the two writers, without exhausting the subject. It is adequate to prove the point. To
reconstruct this source would be a useful task.*

C. Bradford Welles[1]

*Cleitarchus, then, is elusive. Is he also irretrievable? My feeling is that it is possible to
reconstruct something of his work, but the exercise of doing so is particularly arduous.*

A. B. Bosworth[2]

This volume presents the fourth and penultimate stage of an ongoing project to
reconstruct the most influential of all the ancient accounts of the career of
Alexander the Great: the history of his reign compiled by Cleitarchus of
Alexandria, which has been lost since antiquity. I began this reconstruction with
the three Indian books of Cleitarchus (books ten to twelve), which have been
published together as *Alexander the Great in India*. Thereafter I reconstructed the
final book of Cleitarchus' work (book thirteen), which treated events from the
end of *Alexander the Great in India* through to the king's death and its aftermath.
This has been published under the title of *The Death of Alexander the Great*.
Subsequently, in 2011 I published my reconstruction of books seven, eight and
nine, constituting a reconstruction of all the Cleitarchan material between the
death of Darius and the opening of *Alexander the Great in India*, covering the
three year period between July 330BC and May 327BC under the title *Alexander
the Great in Afghanistan*. This latest extension of the project presents books four
to six of the reconstruction relating events between the Battle of Issus in
November of 333BC and the death of Darius in July of 330BC.

The successive highlights of the events recounted in this volume are therefore:
the Battle of Issus; Alexander's audience with the Persian queens; the treasures
found at Damascus; the first letter from Darius; the appointment of a new king
for Sidon; the siege of Tyre; the second peace offer from Darius; the siege of
Gaza; the occupation of Egypt; Alexander's expedition to Siwa; the foundation
of Alexandria; the march back to Byblos; the preparations of Darius;
Alexander's advance into Mesopotamia; the fording of the Tigris; the death of
Stateira; the third peace offer from Darius; the Battle of Arbela; the flight of
Darius and the capture of his treasure at Arbela; Mennis and its cave of
naphtha; the occupation of Babylon; the seizure of Susa; the capture of the
Susian Gates; a meeting with mutilated Greeks; the burning of Persepolis; the
pursuit of Darius and his murder by Bessus.

---

[1] C. Bradford Welles, *Loeb edition of Diodorus Siculus*, Vol. 8 (Harvard, 1963), Introduction, 12.

[2] A.B. Bosworth, *From Arrian to Alexander* (Oxford, 1988), Introduction, 13.

Alexander the Great and the Conquest of the Persians

It is my intention ultimately to produce as complete a reconstruction of Cleitarchus as may prove feasible and so supporting material already published in *Alexander the Great in India* has the scope of the entire work. However, the next section of this volume particularly provides a more detailed analysis of some key issues pertaining to the reconstruction of books four to six. The reconstruction itself comprises sections three to five. Then section seven provides a tabulation of the source references against each episode (revised from previously published versions of this Table). Finally, there is an updated bibliography, a few acknowledgements and an index for this volume.

Virtually every sentence and phrase of my reconstruction of Cleitarchus is derived directly from text in the antique source manuscripts of the so-called Vulgate tradition. That is to say that it has manuscript authority and indeed I have often eschewed emendations of the source manuscripts by modern editors, who often seem deficient in empathy with the perspective of Alexander's early historians in the context of their times and have not always cross-checked the sense of their modifications relative to the full range of surviving material on Alexander. The sense of my words in reconstructing Cleitarchus is therefore not invented and there is no fiction to be found here, unless that fiction had already become established as fact two thousand years ago, when the Vulgate tradition became fixed in the state that it has reached us. However, my reconstructed text is not merely a simple translation of passages from the surviving secondary sources. Instead it has been necessary to meld together overlapping and intersecting accounts and continually to assess which source should have pre-eminence in the case of (usually slight) disparities. Furthermore, I have thought it fitting to attempt to echo the evidently flowery literary style of Cleitarchus to some extent, especially in the case of speeches and descriptive passages. To this end I have sometimes employed poetical devices including rhythmic or metrical passages, incidental rhyming or simple assonance and alliteration. However, it would also be true to say that some of this embroidery is already reflected in the surviving Latin and Greek texts of Curtius, Diodorus and even Justin and Plutarch. In this sense my own text is not merely a reconstruction, but also an evocation of the original. It is especially fitting that the reconstruction should retain Cleitarchus' colourful sensationalism and prurience in contrast to the dull propriety and outright censorship of Arrian's *Anabasis Alexandrou*.

Different passages may be attributed to Cleitarchus with widely varying degrees of confidence. Therefore, I have indicated the approximate confidence level using a textual hierarchy running from lowest to highest (the latter being defined as attributed fragments of Cleitarchus from surviving ancient texts). This is implemented as follows: *italic*; plain text; ***italicized bold***; **simple bold**; **<u>underlined simple bold</u>**. Although grey text has been reserved for connecting passages, where the Cleitarchan version is unfathomable, it has not been necessary to resort to its use for books four to thirteen. Subject to a few minor exceptions, it is possible to read the reconstruction at a variety of confidence levels by ignoring all text below the desired level of fidelity.

Introduction

This reconstruction is particularly founded on the premise that Curtius and Diodorus (Book 17 & Book 18.1-4) are largely abridgements of the History of Alexander by Cleitarchus, whereas Justin (Books 11 to 13.4) and Plutarch's *Life of Alexander* are considered to contain substantial Cleitarchan elements (this has been argued in detail in *Alexander the Great in India* – the interrelationship between various of the lost and extant ancient sources is summarized in Figure 1.1). Although I cannot be absolutely sure that Curtius did not employ another major source, the process of performing the reconstruction to date has had the incidental consequence of accumulating many minor points of evidence so as to formulate a cumulatively strong case that Curtius is in fact substantially (though not entirely) a Latin translation of a moderately abridged version of Cleitarchus' Greek text. In particular, it has thus far transpired that this hypothesis resolves virtually all difficulties without generating significant inconsistencies.

However, reconstructed text solely based on material from only one of Curtius or Diodorus 18.1-4 or Justin 12-13.4 is indicated at a relatively lower level of confidence. Higher confidence is assigned to material exclusively derived from Diodorus 17. Still higher confidence is vested in cases where there are detailed matches between these sources and the highest confidence rests with the attributed fragments of Cleitarchus, although they are sadly sparse.

If the premise of a common source for the surviving texts were correct, then it would be expected that a relatively smooth and cogent version of the prototype could be reconstructed by merging them. However, if any of the extant sources had employed a significant secondary source, then it would be anticipated that the attempt to define a prototype that explained all the material in each of them should encounter numerous contradictions. It is a conclusion of the present research that it has been possible to reconstruct all ten years of Alexander's reign from the Battle of Issus without encountering significant contradictions when integrating all the appertaining material in Curtius, Diodorus and the *Metz Epitome* (with the obvious exception of a few passages in Curtius where that author is clearly offering his own comments and one instance, where he attacks Cleitarchus by name with reference to Ptolemy's version in a matter that concerned Ptolemy.) This is an important result, because it tends to reinforce the premise that Curtius, Diodorus and the *Metz Epitome* at least are essentially abridgements of Cleitarchus. Such an inference is not at all obvious in reading those sources individually.

In the case of Justin, we know from his manuscripts that he epitomised Trogus, although the latter probably used Cleitarchus (or else Timagenes who in turn used Cleitarchus). More difficulties tend to arise in reconciling his words with the tradition from the other Vulgate texts, as might reasonably be expected for such indirect transmission. A straightforward example is that Justin is more negative about Alexander's treatment of Philotas and Parmenion than either Curtius or Diodorus. Another example from the scope of the present volume would be Justin's assertion (11.10.14) that Tyre fell through treachery, which does not appear to be the Cleitarchan line. Yet in fact these incongruities are easily explained as either incidental consequences of successive stages of epitomisation via Trogus or else as among the many misunderstandings and over-simplifications, which are plainly attributable to Justin's rather careless epitomisation of Trogus. The process of reconstruction has also indicated significant amounts of Cleitarchan material in Plutarch, by virtue of some striking parallels between my text (reconstructed from Curtius and Diodorus) and some of Plutarch's anecdotes. But it is equally obvious that Plutarch used many early sources (as too did Cleitarchus himself), so I have used Plutarch's material sparingly and at low confidence.

Neither do I intend that this should be the final and immutable version of the reconstruction, but rather hope that it may evolve and be revised in the light of new evidence or arguments as they emerge.

Finally, I would also commend the account of Cleitarchus to those readers who have little interest in the technical niceties of source research for Alexander studies. Cleitarchus' account rested on its literary merits for centuries in winning its place as the most popular version of Alexander's campaigns among the Hellenistic Greeks and the Romans. I believe that it retains good measures of readability, atmosphere, coherence and accuracy even in the present metamorphosed and imperfect form, sufficient anyway that it may be read in isolation as an authentic breath of the distant past by readers who are relatively unfamiliar with the particulars of the history of the most glamorous king who ever reigned.

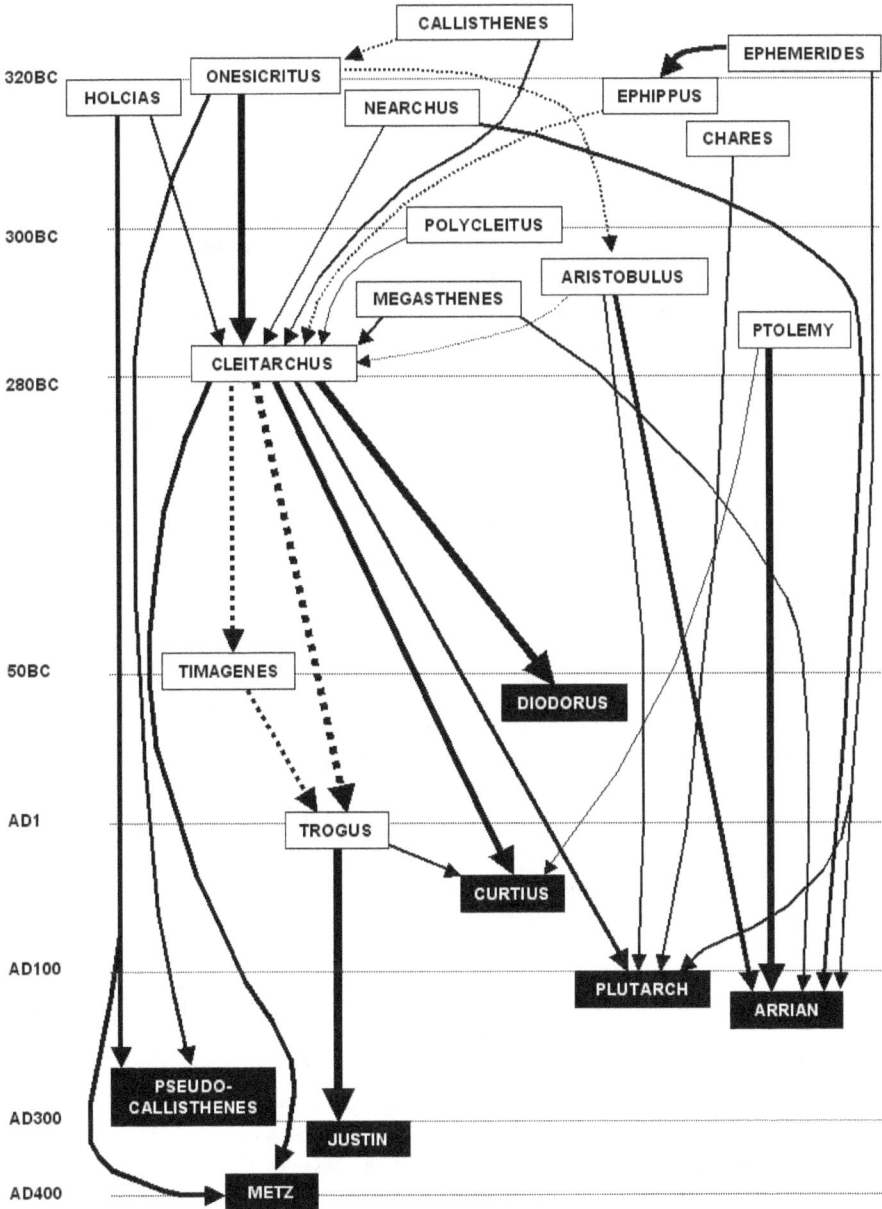

Figure 1.1. Relationships between ancient authors on Alexander's campaigns especially pertaining to Cleitarchus (white in black box = extant; and vice versa).

2. Matters of Historical Relevance

Is Arrian Reliable?

For many present and past aficionados of Alexander's story the infallibility of the "Official" tradition of Alexander historiography as represented by Arrian and the *Itinerarium Alexandri* has been and continues to be an article of faith. Since the Vulgate tradition, and Cleitarchus in particular, represents the main source of evidence for challenging this conviction, the particular question of Arrian's reliability is a cogent issue in pursuing the reconstruction of Cleitarchus, as he is the Vulgate's archetype.

Consequently, I have begun to formulate a list of cases where evidence from the Vulgate and elsewhere might appear to cast serious aspersions on Arrian's credibility. As a strong believer in the prioritisation of evidence over opinion, I am pleased to present this list here with some preliminary discussion of each point in the hope of at least chipping, if not cracking, the veneer of Arrian's plausibility. My objective is to rescue my readers from the trap that ensnares those faithful to the concept of Arrian's infallibility. Practitioners of this creed are progressively and inexorably compelled to disparage the accuracy of every other source of evidence, even and indeed often when they all agree. Those who adhere to this faith find themselves in the uncomfortable position of having to assert that Arrian alone managed to dissociate himself from a hideous conspiracy utterly to mislead posterity regarding Alexander's motivations and behaviour, which embroiled every other surviving authority from ancient times, despite that they wrote independently over a period of many centuries and were spread geographically right across the Graeco-Roman world.

However, the alternative view is not that Arrian is a bad source, for it is overly simplistic to describe any source as exclusively good or bad. Rather, to be specific: (a) he deliberately censored information concerning Alexander's personal life; (b) he had a rather poor grasp of the geography of Alexander's itinerary and the chronology of his campaigns; (c) he sometimes missed key strategic features in battles and sieges and misunderstood Persian and Macedonian terminology through sheer remoteness from the context of the events. He was afterall more distant from Alexander in time than we are from the era of Elizabeth 1 and some of the things he read in his sources were as obscure to him as much of the language used by Shakespeare is to us: what are bilboes, bolters and bombards, for example? Neither are all his flaws Arrian's alone. As I have suggested elsewhere (originally in *Alexander the Great in India*, p.39), there are reasons to suppose that the account of Alexander's campaigns by Arrian's most important source, Ptolemy Soter, was substantially censored by the Ptolemaic regime in the aftermath of his death and prior to its posthumous publication.

1)   Arrian gives an incorrect lifespan for Alexander at *Anabasis* 7.28.1

The facts are straightforward. Arrian, *Anabasis Alexandrou* 7.28.1 asserts: "According to Aristobulus, Alexander lived thirty-two years and eight months; his reign lasted twelve years and the same eight months." He had previously introduced his *Anabasis Alexandrou* at 1.1.1 with the words: "We are told that the death of Philip occurred in the archonship of Pythodelus at Athens; then around about twenty, Alexander succeeded, as Philip's son, and arrived at the Peloponnese."

The date of Alexander's death is well known: Plutarch, *Alexander* 76.4 relates that the king's own journal, known as the *Ephemerides* and kept by his secretary, Eumenes of Cardia, stated that Alexander died towards evening on the 28th day of the Macedonian month Daisios. Because this is a lunar date, which can be back-calculated astronomically, we are certain that this was 10th June 323BC in the Julian calendar (or 5th June 323BC in the Gregorian calendar).[3] Plutarch also mentions that Aristobulus stated that Alexander died on the 30th Daisios. Because a lunar month is 29.53 days long on average, nearly half the months in Greek lunar calendars only had 29 days. In such months, the Greeks gave the 29th day the name of the 30th day (i.e. thereby indicating that it was indeed the last day of the month). It appears that Daisios in 323BC was just such a "hollow" month, so Aristobulus meant that he heard of Alexander's death on 11th June 323BC. Similarly, a contemporaneous Babylonian astronomical record has been shown to give 11th June 323BC for Alexander's death. The proper inference is that Alexander died late on 10th June and that Eumenes, being a member of Alexander's inner circle of Friends, was aware of this and recorded it in the *Ephemerides*. However, the news was not made public until the next day. It is quite credible that it was concealed for a matter of hours by Alexander's Friends and Bodyguards, because we are also told (Plutarch, *Alexander* 76.4 and Arrian, *Anabasis Alexandrou* 7.26.1) that a few days beforehand the troops had insisted on being let in to see Alexander, **because they believed that news of his death was being suppressed by his Friends and Bodyguards**.

Thus, if Arrian were correct about Alexander's lifespan of 32 years and 8 months, Alexander would have to have been born in October of 356BC. But in fact this is flatly contradicted by a considerable weight of evidence from elsewhere. In particular, Plutarch, *Alexander* 3.2 provides an explicit date for Alexander's birth that is at odds with Arrian: "Alexander was born on the sixth day of the month Hecatombaeon, which the Macedonians call Loüs, the same day on which the temple of Artemis at Ephesus was burnt down." Hecatombaeon was the first month of the Attic year, which began at the first New Moon after the Summer solstice. The Julian calendar date can therefore

---

[3] That Plutarch really is using a very old citation from the *Ephemerides* is amply supported by the fact that he uses an antique Athenian format for specifying the days of the month, which fell out of fashion within a quarter of a century after Alexander's death.

easily be reckoned (e.g. from modern calculations of Lunar eclipses, which necessarily occur at Full Moon) to have been 20th July 356BC.

The burning of the Temple of Artemis at Ephesus was very much an historical event in the Summer of 356BC. An arsonist called Herostratus set it ablaze in a bid to immortalise his name amongst posterity: an objective that he achieved at the cost of his immediate execution. The incident was related in some detail by Theopompus in his lost work on *Hellenics* and the circumstances are also mentioned in some surviving ancient texts (e.g. Strabo 14.1).

Both Plutarch, *Alexander* 3.4-5 and Justin 12.16.6 tell the story that news of Alexander's birth reached his father, Philip, whilst he was besieging Potidaea on the isthmus of the westernmost peninsula of Chalcidice. They note that two other pieces of good news reached Philip at about the same time: a Macedonian victory over the Illyrians and the triumph of Philip's team in the Olympic four-horse chariot race.

Fortunately, there is now a basis to date the Olympic victory quite closely. A. E. Samuel concluded that "we are probably safe in accepting the evidence that the festival culminated with the full moon"[4] and subsequently Stephen G. Miller[5] argued convincingly that the Olympic festival culminated with religious ceremonies at the second full moon after the Summer solstice. That can be accurately calculated as 30th July (Julian calendar) in 356BC (the solstice was on about 26th June in that era). The contests would most probably have preceded this date by a few days.

We should suppose that the event that instigated the story of the triple news in Plutarch and Justin was Philip's announcement of the three happy happenings to his troops at Potidaea. He would have done this partly to boost morale, but also because the occurrences were all public events that would have become known by other avenues of communication within a month at the outside. Furthermore, the troops would have known that Philip had had news of all of them directly. As a matter of trust therefore, Philip needed publicly to announce the news before it leaked out. Otherwise his troops would have thought he was keeping secret things that they had a right to know from him: the succession, for example, was a matter of keen concern to all Macedonians.

It follows that the credibility of the triple news story requires principally that the events actually occurred sufficiently close together that there was not enough time for news of one to leak out before another had happened. This was necessary for Philip to be able to announce all three together as news items. If any event took place more than about a month from any other, this criterion could not be met (and even a separation of two weeks would be dubious). This is a stringent criterion. For example, it is completely broken by Arrian's implied

---

[4] A E Samuel, Greek & Roman Chronology, Munich 1972, p.194.

[5] Stephen G Miller, "The Date of Olympic Festivals" MDAI(A) 90 (1975) 215-31.

autumnal date for Alexander's birth: it is quite impossible that Philip's Olympic victory could have been considered news three months after the event. But it is closely obeyed by Plutarch's date, because the gap between Alexander's birth and the subsequent Olympic victory does seem to be only about one week.

Innumerable satisfactory reasons might be postulated for the simultaneous announcement of Alexander's birth and the Olympic victory despite the former preceding the latter by a week. Here are some (not exhaustive) examples: (a) we don't know exactly where Alexander was born – if it was somewhere remote or isolated then news of it might have been delayed; (b) a weather event might have flooded or otherwise damaged the highways in Macedonia; (c) Olympias may have wished to wait to ensure that the child was healthy before sending a messenger or some post-natal crisis may have delayed the dispatch of a messenger; (d) Philip may have wished to await confirmation that the boy was healthy before announcing his birth (since the announcement would also have constituted his official acknowledgement of the boy as his heir and he may have had a cautionary experience in this respect with his mentally defective son, Arrhidaeus, previously); (e) Philip may have expected good news from the Olympics and deliberately delayed announcing Alexander's birth and his other victory for a few days in the hope of having a triple good news story for the sake of the extra boost to morale; (f) something untoward may have befallen the first messenger carrying the news of Alexander's birth... this list could be extended endlessly. The point is that exact simultaneity is not necessary for the story to be true, but the story does constrain the time range sufficiently to show that Plutarch's date is the correct birthday for Alexander.

If Justin and Plutarch used different primary sources, then Arrian's error is quite certain. However, supposing that Cleitarchus (the acknowledged common source of Plutarch and Trogus, whom Justin was epitomising) was the source of both of our accounts of the triple news story, is it at all likely that he made it up or got it from a bad source and failed to check it? He was probably writing in Alexandria just after 280BC. Given that it is inconceivable that the triple news was not publicly announced to the army (either directly by Philip or via briefing of his officers who in turn briefed their men), it would have to have been a famous event from recent history with some Macedonians still alive who had been at Potidaea. In these circumstances a complete invention stretches credulity. Cleitarchus cannot reasonably have been so careless of his credibility as to publish inventions that were so easily refuted.

Aelian, *Varia Historia* 2.25 also supports Plutarch's date. He discusses famous events that occurred on the sixth day of the month. He means the sixth day after the New Moon, because he references the Attic month of Thargelion, which strictly speaking began with the New Moon. Aelian concludes with a remark that Alexander's life both began and ended on that day of the month. He would seem to be wrong about Alexander's death (although a story was told that Alexander's body still seemed lifelike when the embalmers came to deal with it seven days after his death, which would have been the sixth day after a New Moon), but Aelian's comment accords well with Plutarch's date of the sixth day of the Attic month Hecatombaeon for Alexander's birth.

There is even a third strand of evidence that bolsters Plutarch's date for Alexander's birth. There are circumstantial reasons to believe that Plutarch probably got many of his dates directly or indirectly from a famously pedantic Greek chronologist and historian of the late 4th and early 3rd centuries BC: Timaeus of Tauromenium. Though originally from Sicily, Timaeus was educated in Athens and spent most of his life there, so dating by the Attic calendar is to be expected of him. Diodorus and Polybius record his special attention to matters of accurate chronology.[6] There is strong evidence from elsewhere that both Cleitarchus and Plutarch were virtual disciples of the work of Timaeus. N. G. L. Hammond has argued that Plutarch's date of 6th Hecatombaeon for Alexander's birth comes from Timaeus, because Cicero gives many of the same details when he mentions the stories about Alexander's birth and he names Timaeus as his source in one instance.[7] Cleitarchus himself definitely used Timaeus, since Fragment 7 of Cleitarchus couples him with Timaeus as its co-source and it mentions the Heracleidae, Alexander's putative ancestors.[8] Then Fragment 36 of Cleitarchus from the Suda seems to make Cleitarchus a follower of Timaeus and Anaximenes.[9] This secondary path of association makes it quite likely that Plutarch got 6th Hecatombaeon from Cleitarchus (although Plutarch did also use Timaeus directly, for example, in his Life of Timoleon.) It should be noted that Plutarch also gives the correct Attic lunar date of 26th Boedromion for the Battle of Arbela/Gaugamela in his Life of Camillus (confirmed by eclipse evidence), so he is verified to be trustworthy on Alexander's dates. Conversely, Arrian thought that Arbela took place in the next Attic month of Pyanepsion (although he might be following a special festival version of the Attic calendar that was tampered with by the Athenian archon.)

Thus, firstly, Plutarch is supported by Aelian and, secondly, only his date is consistent with the simultaneous announcement of Alexander's birth and Philip's Olympic victory. Thirdly, the evidence suggesting that Timaeus was the ultimate source of Plutarch's date bolsters its credibility. Finally, the only other implied date for Alexander's birth from Arrian is not only non-specific in merely suggesting the month and at odds with all the other evidence, but it is also inherently flawed, because Arrian should not have stated that Alexander was "around about twenty" at his accession, but exactly twenty to the nearest

---

[6] Diodorus 5.1.3 & Polybius 12.11.1.

[7] N. G. L. Hammond, Sources for Alexander the Great (Cambridge 1993) 19-20; Jacoby 566 F150a of Timaeus (Cicero, N.D. 2.69); Cicero, Div. 1.47; Hammond also believed that Timaeus was born in the same year as Alexander.

[8] Jacoby 137 F7 (Clement of Alexandria, Strom. 1.139.4).

[9] Jacoby 137 F36 (Suidas s.v. εχετον).

month. The last point actually tells us what may in fact have occurred: Aristobulus, Arrian's source for these chronological details, probably stated that Alexander was "around about twenty" at his accession and separately noted that he reigned for twelve years and eight months. Both of these statements are correct. But Arrian misleadingly took the initiative to combine the two statements together to reach a lifespan for Alexander of thirty-two years and eight months, when the truth is thirty-two years ten months and twenty days.

In a last ditch defence of their idol, some Arrian disciples have even tried to argue that birthdays did not matter in Alexander's time, so that all our information on Alexander's birthday was compiled a long time after the event and may therefore be doubted in favour of Arrian's non-sequiter. However, this too is untrue. The date of birth always mattered greatly to the ancients not so much for the purpose of the celebration of birthdays as due to the need to be able to cast horoscopes accurately! You needed to know the configuration of the heavens at the time of birth to be able to do this. For this reason the date of birth was even more crucial to them than it is to us for modern birthday anniversary celebration purposes.

2)   Arrian suppresses the existence of Barsine, Alexander's mistress.

Arrian never mentions the existence of Barsine the daughter of Artabazus in either his *Anabasis*, his *Indica* or in his *Events after Alexander*. It is however beyond reasonable doubt that she existed, that she became Alexander's mistress after her capture at Damascus and that she had the very special distinction of being the mother of Alexander's elder (though illegitimate) son, Heracles. Both she and her son are widely referenced in the rest of the antique historical sources covering the period.

Arrian does mention Alexander's marriage to a daughter of Darius, whom he calls Barsine at *Anabasis* 7.4.4, but it is clear that this is actually a reference to the princess named Stateira in all other sources.

It is particularly astonishing that Arrian seems to have managed to maintain his silence on the existence of Barsine in the aftermath of Alexander's death. Admittedly we have only the summary by Photius of his *Events after Alexander* together with a few other fragments, but it is probably still significant that neither Barsine nor Heracles gains any mention at all. Other sources (Nepos, Strabo…) speak of the children (plural) of Alexander (i.e. Alexander IV, the son of Alexander and Roxane, *and* Heracles). Curtius (very probably following Clcitarchus) provides a gripping blow-by-blow account of the Macedonian Assembly held after Alexander's death at which Alexander's admiral, Nearchus, urged that Heracles should be made king.

Thirteen years later, after Alexander IV had been murdered on the orders of Cassander in 310BC, Polyperchon led another attempt to award Heracles the crown, which ended with Cassander bribing Polyperchon to do away with his protégé.

Devoid of these key elements the history of the era lacks proper coherence. It is as though the Civil War period had been edited out of English history. This constitutes an appalling degree of economy with the truth on the part of Arrian.

Why did he do this? Seemingly, as a matter of principle, Arrian believed that history should remain silent on the "private" lives of public figures and he determinedly maintained this stance, even when their "private" activities had major ramifications on the public stage. Such censorship should have no place in the work of an authoritative historian, because it completely undermines the balanced treatment of historical subjects.

3) Arrian suppresses the existence of Bagoas, Alexander's eunuch lover.

Parallelling his treatment of Barsine, Arrian similarly omits all mention of Bagoas, the Persian eunuch, except that he includes "Bagoas the son of Pharnuches" in his list of trierarchs of the major vessels in the Indus river fleet (*Indica* 18.8). As I have explained in detail in *Alexander's Lovers*, "Bagoas the son of Pharnuches" was probably actually "Bagoas the Eunuch" in the original list, which Arrian appears to have transcribed from Nearchus's lost account. It would seem that Arrian stopped short of summarily editing out a name on the list, but nevertheless it may have been Arrian himself who disguised the identity of the individual by adapting his epithet into a patronymic (in Greek the two are fairly similar).

There is no appreciable doubt that Bagoas became a senior courtier and Alexander's lover shortly after his first meeting with Alexander in Hyrcania just after the murder of Darius. Bagoas was subsequently influentially involved in some significant historical events. Curtius 10.1.22-37 names him as the prosecutor and executioner (under Alexander's orders) of Orsines in 324BC. Arrian, *Anabasis* 6.29.2 also records the execution of Orsines, whom he calls Orxines, but deliberately avoids naming Bagoas by instead refering to Orsines having been hanged by "persons appointed by Alexander".

The start of Alexander's liaison with Bagoas more or less coincided with the beginning of the "orientalising" phase of Alexander's career. If, gentle reader, you are, as Arrian intended, denied all knowledge of this steamy love affair with Darius' most beautiful eunuch, you are, I fear, placed in a very poor position to comprehend and assess Alexander's ensuing behaviour!

4) Arrian deliberately understates the relationship between Alexander and Hephaistion

As well as censoring the existence of Barsine and Bagoas, key characters in Alexander's personal life, Arrian is highly economical in his comments on the relationship between Alexander and Hephaistion. He never actually mentions in his works on Alexander that they had been lovers. The closest Arrian gets to revealing the amorous aspect of their relationship is to draw a parallel between Alexander & Hephaistion and Achilles & Patroclus at *Anabasis* 7.16.8. Yet he does refer to the lover (*eromenos*) of Alexander in his *Discourses of Epictetus* 2.22.17 and he demonstrably means Hephaistion. He writes that Alexander burnt down the Temple of Asclepius when his lover died, whereas Arrian also confirms in his *Anabasis* 7.14.5 that Alexander razed this sanctuary at the time of Hephaistion's death. This shows that Arrian deliberately avoided being clear about the relationship in his *Anabasis*, since he clearly knew the truth. The Chiliarch was such an important figure on the public stage that Arrian could hardly avoid mentioning his career and the fact that he and Alexander were close, but anyone reading Arrian in isolation from the Vulgate sources and other incidental records of the relationship would receive a misleadingly understated impression of the affair.

5)   Arrian completely confuses the order of events in 328-327BC

There is a magnificent article by Bosworth that cogently argues the case for Arrian's account of Alexander's campaigns having become completely confused for the year beginning in the middle of 328BC.[10] Bosworth points out that Curtius gives a coherent account of that year's activities, provided we avoid the temptation to emend Curtius 7.10.15 to read *Marginanum*, where the manuscripts read either *Marganiam* or *Marginiam*, and thereby send Alexander off on a wild goose chase to Margiana (modern Merv) some 450km westwards, when Curtius and the Metz Epitome actually appear to be suggesting that the king was marching eastwards from Bactra. Then in Section III of his article, Bosworth shows that all sources other than Arrian treat the three great Rocks (that of Ariamazes, that of Sisimithres and that of Chorienes) similarly and that the sieges of two of them should be placed in the campaigning season of 328BC rather than in the spring of 327BC as in Arrian. He concludes that Arrian has become confused due to switching between his main sources, Ptolemy and Aristobulus, and that Ptolemy confused Chorienes with Sisimithres. He summarises the issue as follows: "Ptolemy has confused two different native leaders, who were both confirmed in their dominions by Alexander. It is a disturbing testimonial to the erratic nature of this contemporary source, and Ptolemy's deficiencies are made worse by Arrian's method of switching from source to source without any critical discussion of variants or contradictions. The errors and exaggerations of the one are compounded by the uncritical and negligent approach of the other."

6)   Arrian repeatedly misinterprets the title Chiliarch used for Hephaistion and others in that role by terming it a cavalry command

The Chief Minister of the Persian Great King was known as the *Hazarapatis* (or *Hazarapatish*), which roughly translates from the Persian as "commander of a thousand". The Greeks in turn rendered this title fairly literally as *Chiliarch* on translating it into their own language. The incumbent was second only to the

---

[10] A. B. Bosworth, A Missing Year in the History of Alexander the Great, The Journal of Hellenic Studies, Vol. 101, 1981, pp. 17-39.

Great King himself in rank and prestige and he is stated to have been responsible for the running of the royal court, including admissions to audiences with the king. Cornelius Nepos, *Conon* 3.2-3 gives Tithraustes the title of Chiliarch serving the Persian King Artaxerxes II at the time of the audience of Conon early in the 4th century BC and Nepos goes on to assert that "without him, none could gain audience". Aelian, *Varia Historia* 1.21 describes probably the same Tithraustes as the court official "who took messages to the king and presented petitioners" in the context of the embassy of Pelopidas in 367BC. Furthermore, a decade before Alexander's conquest, a eunuch called Bagoas had for a while virtually ruled the Persian Empire, whilst bearing the title of Chiliarch. The eunuch Bagoas is assigned the title of Chiliarch (e.g. by Diodorus 17.5.3) in the context of his kingmaking in Persia in the years 338-336BC: initially poisoning Artaxerxes III Ochus and placing his youngest son, Arses, on the throne, then in turn murdering Arses and replacing him with Darius III.

It is quite certain that Alexander appointed Hephaistion to this exalted rank, probably sometime after Gaugamela, though the exact date is uncertain. Arrian accords Hephaistion the title of Chiliarch in his *Anabasis*, but he associates it with Hephaistion's command of the senior regiment of the Companion Cavalry, which is odd, since the proper title for such an appointment was Hipparch.[11] It is likely that Arrian is mistakenly conflating Hephaistion's separate (and separately awarded) offices of Chiliarch (of the empire) and Hipparch of the senior regiment of the Companion Cavalry (the latter seems also to have entailed overall command of the Companion Cavalry, for Hephaistion is so described by Appian, *Syrian Wars* 57.)[12] However, Photius has provided an epitome of Arrian's lost *Events after Alexander*, which states that, after Alexander's death, Perdiccas was appointed "to command the Chiliarchy which Hephaistion had originally held" and that this "entrusted him with the entire kingdom" in the context of the joint-kingship of Alexander's infant son and imbecilic half-brother, who were of necessity mere puppets.[13] It looks as though Arrian knew that Hephaistion had commanded the senior regiment of the Companion Cavalry *and* had acted as Alexander's Chief Minister in his court by virtue of his title of Chiliarch, but that he failed to distinguish clearly between the two roles, perhaps because he did not understand the Persian origins of the title and consequently thought that "lord of a thousand" had to refer to Hephaistion's cavalry command in some way. In other contexts the Greeks did

---

[11] Arrian, *Anabasis* 7.14.10.

[12] NGL Hammond, Sources for Alexander the Great, Cambridge 1993, pp.296-7 reaches this conclusion and is supported by Jeanne Reames in her treatise on Hephaistion; James Romm notes in the Landmark Arrian in respect of Arrian, *Anabasis* 7.14.10 that, "It seems possible that Arrian has confused this newly created Chiliarchy with a separate office, command over the Companion cavalry…"; PA Brunt reaches the same conclusion in App. XXIV.4 of the Loeb Arrian, II p.511.

[13] This is Photius 92, Epitome of Arrian's Events after Alexander; Photius 82, Summary of Dexippus' Events after Alexander also mentions this (it is likely that Dexippus used Arrian's work or that they had a common source).

use the word chiliarch to mean the commander of a military unit of a thousand men, so there exists some real potential for confusion.

Happily Diodorus 18.3.4 removes any possible ambiguity by stating that Perdiccas, when he became Chiliarch after Alexander's death, relinquished command of the Companion Cavalry in favour of Seleucus:

[Perdiccas] placed Seleucus in command of the cavalry of the Companions, a most distinguished office; for Hephaestion commanded them first, Perdiccas after him, and third the above-named Seleucus.

This makes it unambiguously clear that the cavalry command (Hipparchy) and the ministerial role at court (Chiliarchy) cannot have been indissolubly one and the same, as Arrian seems to have believed. Furthermore Diodorus explains:-

Antipater also made his own son Cassander Chiliarch and second in authority. The position and rank of Chiliarch had first been brought to fame and honour by the Persian kings, and afterwards under Alexander it gained great power and glory at the time when he became an admirer of this and all other Persian customs.   Diodorus 18.48.5

Obviously, Alexander's Chiliarch can only have been Hephaistion. Furthermore, Diodorus' statement that Alexander revived this title at the same time as he embraced other Persian customs makes it difficult to date Hephaistion's appointment later than the time of the proskynesis experiment (i.e. 328BC). His court management responsibilities as Chiliarch would also help to explain why it was Hephaistion who organised this experiment. It might further be argued that Hephaistion seemed already to be acting with the authority of a Chiliarch in the case of the Philotas affair. The common source of Diodorus 17.77.4 and Curtius 6.6.1-8 on the subject of Alexander's imitation of the kings of Asia[14] was Cleitarchus and it is clear from their accounts that Cleitarchus placed Alexander's main phase of "Persianisation" in the immediate aftermath of the death of Darius in around August 330BC. This was also the period in which the previous Chiliarch, Nabarzanes,[15] surrendered to Alexander in Hyrcania, so this was the most opportune occasion for the appointment of Hephaistion as his replacement, since Nabarzanes was sent off into retirement.

However, as already noted, Arrian, *Anabasis* 7.14.10 erroneously suggests a combination of the Chiliarchy with Hephaistion's cavalry command in the immediate aftermath of the Chiliarch's death:

Alexander made no one else chiliarch of the Companion cavalry in Hephaestion's place so that Hephaestion's name would not disappear from that unit. The Chiliarchy was still called Hephaistion's, and the standard went before it which had been made by his order.

---

[14] Cf. Plutarch, *Alexander* 45; Justin 12.3.8-12.

[15] Arrian, *Anabasis Alexandrou*, 3.21.1 & 3.23.4; Curtius 6.5.22-3.

Note that Arrian had previously termed Hephaistion a Hipparch at *Anabasis* 3.27.4, when he was appointed to joint command of the Companion Cavalry with Cleitus.

However, Plutarch, *Eumenes* 1.2 records that during Alexander's lifetime, just after the death of Hephaistion:

...[Eumenes] received the command in the cavalry which Perdiccas had held, when Perdiccas, after Hephaestion's death, was advanced to that officer's position.

This must mean that, whilst Alexander still reigned, Perdiccas received the command of the senior hipparchy (regiment) and thereby became overall commander of the Companion Cavalry, whilst Eumenes took over Perdiccas' original hipparchy. Consequently, it is clear that Hephaistion's cavalry command was filled by Alexander, but it does seem to be true that Hephaistion's *ministerial role* as Chiliarch was never filled until after Alexander's death.

Arrian repeats his association of the Chiliarchy with a cavalry command in his work on *Events After Alexander*,[16] where he speaks of Cassander having been granted the title of Chiliarch "of the cavalry". Similarly, in *Anabasis* 3.21.1 Nabarzanes is described as "Chiliarch of the cavalry" (and as Darius' Chiliarch at 3.26.4). It is therefore quite clear that the mistake is Arrian's, rather than being due to an error in transcription of some archetypal manuscript of his works. A transcriptional error is unlikely to have occurred three times in two different works. The double meaning of the term chiliarch must have confused Arrian. The alternative would be that the reports of a separation of the command of the Companion Cavalry from the Chiliarchy are inventions and that the completely consistent description of the Chiliarchy independently provided by all the other surviving ancient sources on the subject is wrong.

A recent scholarly article on the Chiliarchy potently illustrates the danger of trying to maintain that this obvious misunderstanding by Arrian concerning the nature of the Chiliarchy was in fact the correct view.[17] The author is led to infer that Arrian's epitomiser, Photius, flagrantly misrepresented the *Events after Alexander*, which had just read in stating that the Chiliarchy entailed the rule of the whole empire (in circumstances where the joint kings were not capable of exercising power in their own right). Furthermore, he invents the existence of two different Chiliarchies among the Persians, though the many ancient sources on the Persian Chiliarchy always refer to a single person. He makes the Chiliarchy basically a military command of cavalry, though all sources save Arrian describe it essentially as a court position. And he maintains Arrian's confusion between the Chiliarchy and command of the Companion Cavalry and in so doing makes Seleucus the Chiliarch when he led them after Alexander's

---

[16] F1.38 epitomised by Photius 92 [72a or 9.38].

[17] Alexander Meeus, Some Institutional Problems Concerning the Succession to Alexander the Great: Prostasia and Chiliarchy, Historia, Band 58, Heft 3, 2009, pp. 287-310.

death, though no source awards Seleucus the title. In other words, he infers many and varied mistakes and distortions concerning the Chiliarchy by practically every other source and invents several different sorts of Chiliarchy in order to avoid even contemplating the possibility of an understandable single point error by Arrian. He fails even to point out that, without Arrian's unilateral association of the Chiliarchy with a cavalry command, everything else available from all the other sources on the subject of the Chiliarchy is in complete agreement to the effect that the Chiliarch was a court official in both the Achaemenid and the subsequent Macedonian regimes, who acted as the deputy of the monarch and controlled the running of the monarch's court.

7)   Arrian's location of the homeland of the Mallians/Oxydracae south of the confluence of the Acesines with the Indus is dubious and his account of Alexander's chest wound is misleading

There is a direct contradiction between Vulgate sources and Arrian regarding the location of the war between Alexander and the Mallians in alliance with the Oxydracae. The Vulgate tradition reports that the Oxydracae mounted their resistance from the foothills of a mountain (*sub radicibus montis castra posuit*, Curtius 9.4.24) located south of the confluence of the River Acesines (modern Chenab) with the River Indus, whereas Arrian places Alexander's near fatal chest wound to the north of the same confluence. The proximity of the mountains during this confrontation is an important geographical clue. The nearest substantial hills to the part of the Acesines just north of the confluence are of the order of 80km west of the Acesines and well beyond the Indus itself. However, about 50km downstream of the confluence the mountain foothills come withn a couple of tens of km of the western bank of the river. Furthermore, Arrian, *Anabasis* 6.6.1 has Alexander march his troops through a waterless country to launch a surprise attack on the Mallians. Although there are arid areas to the east of the confluence, the dry country approaches the river most closely between 50km and 100km downstream of the confluence. Also in this war, Alexander was struck in the chest by an arrow. Arrian, *Anabasis* 6.10.1 cites Ptolemy for the observation that breath as well as blood spurted from the wound, which would indicate a perforated lung. Alexander would have been very lucky to survive such a wound and recovery would have been a protracted process, yet our sources have him on his feet and mounting a horse within a couple of weeks.[18] This rapid a recovery is much more consistent with an alternative tradition that the arrow lodged in Alexander's breastbone or a rib "in front of the heart" and therefore did not perforate his lung (Plutarch, *Moralia* 327B, 341C-D, 345A and Plutarch, *Alexander* 63.6).

---

[18] Arrian, *Anabasis* 6.13 and Curtius 9.6.1-3.

8) Arrian locates the theft of Bucephalus among the Uxians against the weight of the evidence from other sources

Arrian, *Anabasis* 5.19.6 only mentions the theft of Alexander's steed, Bucephalus, in the context of a brief retrospective after the horse's death at the time of the Battle of the Hydaspes. However, to quote A B Bosworth[19]: "[Arrian] dates it erroneously to the Uxian campaign." All other surviving accounts (Curtius 6.5.18-21, Diodorus 17.76.5-8, Plutarch, *Alexander* 44.3) place the theft among the Mardians near the southern shores of the Caspian Sea. Bosworth subsequently allowed the possibility that Arrian was correct on the grounds that all the other surviving sources might have obtained their information from Cleitarchus.[20] He further observed that there was another tribe called Mardians, who occupied a region south of Persepolis, whereas the Uxians were based northwest of Persepolis. Since the two tribes were near neighbours, the Uxians might perhaps have been regarded as synonymous with the Persian Mardians and Cleitarchus might have confused the Persian Mardians with the Caspian Mardians. Of course, it is equally true that the confusion between the Persian Mardians and the Caspian Mardians might have been perpetrated by Arrian or his source (Ptolemy or Aristobulus) and the fact that he mentions the matter only briefly and out of context militates in favour of this being the case. Plutarch, Curtius and Diodorus all tell the tale in its historical context and were all well aware of many primary sources on Alexander and so were in a position to correct any error in the story. Furthermore, N. G. L. Hammond concludes that Plutarch did not use Cleitarchus for the tale of the theft due to differences in his account relative to Curtius and Diodorus.[21]

9) Arrian's account of Persepolis is so contracted as to seriously mislead and his omission of Thais is highly suspect.

Arrian, *Anabasis* 3.18.10-12 does not mention Persepolis by name at the time Alexander went there, but merely speaks of Alexander capturing the treasure of Persia before the garrison could plunder it and confusingly refers to Alexander capturing a treasure from Parsagada in the next sentence. He then mentions the burning of the palace, without saying exactly where the palace was, but notes that Parmenion opposed this decision. Arrian's account is especially misleading in that it glosses over the undoubted fact that Alexander only burnt the palace about three or four months after he arrived at Persepolis and Arrian also omits mention of the role of Thais in inciting the conflagration, which is a famous story from the Vulgate (Curtius 5.7.3-7, Diodorus 17.72, Plutarch, *Alexander* 38.2). In particular, Athenaeus 13.576E cites Cleitarchus directly on the matter of the incineration of Persepolis, saying that Thais subsequently married

---

[19] A. B. Bosworth, Commentary on Arrian's History of Alexander, Vol 1, OUP, 1980, p.353.

[20] A. B. Bosworth, Commentary on Arrian's History of Alexander, Vol 2, OUP, 1995, pp.314-315.

[21] N. G. L. Hammond, Sources for Alexander the Great: An Analysis of Plutarch's 'Life' and Arrian's Anabasis Alexandrou, Cambridge, 1993, p.78.

Ptolemy after Alexander's death and bore him two sons and a daughter. Since Cleitarchus seems to have been a resident of Alexandria when he wrote his *History Concerning Alexander* between 280-250BC, it is rather unlikely that he made this story up. It follows that Arrian again wrote economically and sanitisingly concerning the truth regarding the burning of Persepolis.

10)   Arrian (in following Ptolemy) has Alexander led to and from the oasis at Siwa by talking serpents and he places the foundation of Alexandria prior to Siwa and cites an implausible return route directly to Memphis.

Ptolemy's talking serpents (*Anabasis* 3.3.5) are an obvious absurdity. Hardly anyone argues otherwise. However, Arrian, *Anabasis* 3.4.5 notes that Aristobulus recorded that Alexander returned from Siwa via the same route by which he got there, but then asserts that Ptolemy had written that Alexander returned by a different route directly to Memphis. He does not say what that route was, but there are a couple of oases almost in the path of a return route directly eastwards across the desert, so that route is not entirely impracticable. Therefore a return route via these oases to Memphis has been defended by Arrian's advocates. However, it would have been very dangerous relative to a return to the Mediterranean coast. It would have risked getting lost again, as had happened on the way to Siwa, whereas a return to the coast had the merit that any vaguely northward bearing would eventually contact the Mediterranean.

More importantly, most sources (Curtius 4.8.1-2, Diodorus 17.52, Justin 11.11.13, Pseudo-Callisthenes 1.30-32) state that Alexander founded Alexandria on the way back from Siwa, in which case he *must* have returned along the coast. Nevertheless, Plutarch has been read as supporting Arrian by describing the foundation of Alexandria prior to the vist to Siwa, but this support is of little value in that Plutarch often departs from strict chronological order and does not actually state that the foundation preceded the oracle visit. Furthermore, (as I explain in more detail in addressing whether Alexander visited Upper Egypt below) the date of 25th Tybi (7th April in the Julian calendar) given by Pseudo-Callisthenes 1.32.10 for the foundation of Alexandria tends to support a foundation subsequent to the Siwa visit.

11)   Arrian gives Porus a preposterously widely spaced formation comprising too many elephants at the Battle of the Hydaspes

Arrian, *Anabasis* 5.15.4-5 claims that Porus deployed 200 elephants each spaced at least 100 feet from its neighbours at the Battle of the Hydaspes, whereas Curtius 8.13.6 and the *Metz Epitome* 54 mention only 85 elephants and Polyaenus 4.3.22 states that they were distributed at 50-foot intervals. The Cleitarchan elephant formation is therefore a very reasonable 1275m long, whereas Arrian's figures imply an Indian front line over 6km long! It does not even require any military expertise to realise that Arrian's figures are absurd. Arrian's source (probably Ptolemy for this material, since he is named as the source at the start of *Anabasis* 5.15) would seem to have indulged in rounding up and doubling of the numbers for the sake of impressing his readership.

12)   Arrian says that troops died of thirst in the Gedrosian desert, whereas Alexander had wells dug in advance and in actuality the troops starved to the point of lacking the energy to march on due to shortage of provisions

The Vulgate account of the Gedrosian disaster is quite clear, logical and persuasive. Firstly, Alexander had realised that water supplies would be a critical factor on some of the drier sections of his route, so he sent teams ahead to dig wells to supply the army. Secondly, it is implicit in the Vulgate account that Alexander had also realised that a shortage of provisions might be encountered: hence his plan was that the fleet should help to supply the army and potentially vice versa as the need arose. The main factor to upset this plan was that the fleet became trapped in port in India by persistently adverse winds until Alexander and the army had already completed the majority of the trek. Out of concern for his missing fleet, Alexander tried to keep the army's route in touch with the exceptionally barren coastline. This policy in combination with the absence of supplies from the fleet led the army to run short of provisions. Eventually, Alexander was forced to march inland in search of food, either to be obtained from the territory itself or by bringing his forces within range of re-supply from Alexander's eastern Satrapies. However, it took weeks of marching across >200km of virtual desert to reach a location (apparently the Gedrosian capital of Pura) such as to relieve the supply shortage. By that time many troops, non-combatants and baggage train attendants had literally succumbed to starvation. They fell by the wayside because they lacked the energy to keep up with the forced march, not due to dehydration. There is no evidence in the Vulgate of any real difficulty with water supplies. The territory is not even nowadays so dry that the policy of digging wells would not be satisfactory and it appears to have been wetter, if anything, in antiquity. Arrian seems to have indulged in a false supposition regarding his statement (*Anabasis* 6.24.4-6) that the troops died of thirst: he simply had not grasped the strategic situation or the vast size of the Gedrosian wastes, in which it was indeed feasible for troops literally to starve to death even when their need for water had been catered for.

The severity of the disaster has been overstated due to Plutarch's statement (*Alexander* 66.2-3) that only a quarter (~30,000 troops) of the army that had entered India came through Gedrosia. Plutarch points out that Alexander had gone into India with an army of 120,000 men, so he draws the naïve equation that the casualty rate on the march back was 75%. However, we know that the majority of Alexander's forces returned with Craterus via a longer and relatively safe inland route through Arachosia. Furthermore, there appears to have been almost no attrition among the senior men during the Gedrosian march, so the death rate among the rank and file was probably not so dramatic as some of the rather sensationalist rhetoric found in the Vulgate would imply.

13) Arrian says that Gaugamela took place 600 stades from Arbela, but that would put it on the western side of the Tigris – actually it appears to have been no more that 300 stades from Arbela

A full analysis of the site of the Battle of Arbela/Gaugamela is given below, but even a cursory look at the undisputed aspects of the geography (e.g. location of Arbela relative to the River Tigris) makes it obvious that Arrian's assertion that the battle took place 600 stades from Arbela is completely wrong. Both of the feasible alternatives for the battle site are about 300 stades from Arbela as the crow flies and no more than 400 stades as the roads may have wound.

14) Arrian fails to mention the Persian deployment of caltrops at Gaugamela as the reason for Alexander's move to the right as noted in Polyaenus 4.3.17 & Curtius 4.13.36

It is well attested that Alexander performed a very peculiar maneuver in the early stages of the Battle of Arbela/Gaugamela. He advanced his right wing, including his own position with the Companion Cavalry, at an oblique angle, so as greatly to extend his position to the right. Normally, this would have been to court disaster, due to the potential consequential thinning of his own centre rendering him extremely vulnerable to a frontal cavalry charge by the Persians. However, the explanation in the Vulgate sources makes complete sense of this curious situation. Curtius 4.13.36-37 tells us that Alexander had received intelligence from a Persian deserter (named Bion) that Darius had planted iron spikes to bring down charging cavalry (technically known as caltrops) over a large area of the battlefield confronting Alexander's right wing. Alexander moved rightwards towards unprepared ground in the first instance simply to evade these obstacles. He did not need to worry about the thinning of his centre in consequence, because they in turn were protected from a Persian cavalry charge by the same caltrop field. In fact, Darius had unintentionally made it more difficult for the Persians to use their superior numbers to outflank the Macedonians by his planting of the caltrop field.

Arrian's account of the battle is, however, completely devoid of any mention of the caltrops. He is clear that Alexander advanced to the right so as to get his right wing clear of the ground prepared by the Persians, but he notes only that the rougher ground was more difficult for Darius's chariots. He does not explain the more pressing reason for Alexander to have avoided the prepared ground. This has the effect of making Alexander's strategy seem arbitrary and rather serendipitous, for, as all the sources make clear, his troops had to confront the scythed chariots anyway. It leaves Arrian's unfortunate readers in a complete state of incomprehension regarding what was really going on.

15) Arrian places the final peace offer from Darius during the siege of Tyre, whereas it actually came just before Arbela

Arrian, *Anabasis* 2.25 records that a delegation from Darius offered Alexander all the territory to the west of the Euphrates during the siege of Tyre. But other sources (Curtius 4.11.1 and Diodorus 17.39.1) state that this offer was made only much later, just a matter of days before the Battle of Arbela/Gaugamela. Alexander could have used such a letter in the context of the siege of Tyre to compel the capitulation of the city, since it would have shown the Tyrians that resistance in the name of Darius was pointless. Furthermore, he could have secured his territories in the Levant whilst he visited Egypt by accepting and still have found some cause to resume the war a year or two later. For these reasons it is not strategically credible that Darius made such an offer during the siege or that Alexander refused it at that juncture, whilst Tyrian resistance was proving so determined.

In each of these instances it can clearly be seen that there is a great weight of evidence that refutes Arrian's correctness. In many further instances, the balance of probability would appear to favour the Vulgate over Arrian, although it is also the case that in a wide range of other areas there is no significant disagreement between the Official and Vulgate traditions.

The Three Peace Offers from Darius

It would seem that Cleitarchus recorded three peace offers between the battles of Issus and Arbela/Gaugamela. The first two took the form of letters, but the last was conveyed by an embassy. However, in the aftermath of Issus when the first letter was sent, Diodorus 17.39 appears to describe details from the *second* letter of Darius to Alexander, which Curtius 4.5.1-8 places after the siege of Tyre and which Diodorus omits at that point. Curtius 4.1.7-14 cites a ransom for the Persian Royal Family and a suggestion that Alexander return to Macedonia for the first letter. Since Justin 11.12.1-5 broadly confirms Curtius' version, it appears likely that Diodorus has become confused between the two separate letters. This is probably also what led him to suggest that Alexander presented a forged version of the first letter to his council – a story of which there is no hint elsewhere. This is further supported by Diodorus 17.39.3-4, where he gives an account of Darius' renewed preparations for war, which match details given by Curtius 4.6.1-2 just before the siege of Gaza together with Curtius 4.9.1-5 after Alexander's return from Egypt. I am inclined to acquit Cleitarchus of the confused account presented by Diodorus 17.39 on the combined evidence of Curtius and Justin, who were assuredly also following the Alexandrian on the matter of the letters.

Dating Issues Including the Fall of Tyre and Arbela

The duration of the siege of Tyre is stated to have been seven months by Diodorus 17.46.5 and Plutarch, *Alexander* 24.3. Similarly Curtius 4.4.19 notes that the town was taken in the seventh month after the start of its investment. Arrian, *Anabasis* 2.24.6 states that Tyre fell in the Attic month of Hecatombaeon, which began on the day of the first New Moon after the

Summer Solstice; Plutarch, *Alexander* 25.2 tells the story that Tyre fell on the last day of the month, which was originally designated the 30th, but that Alexander redesignated it as the 28th in support of a prophecy of Aristander. This suggests that this month was "hollow", meaning that it had only 29 days and the 29th day was therefore called the 30th, since it was the last. In 332BC the Summer Solstice fell on about 26th June and the next New Moon occurred on about 20th July, so the last day of Hecatombaeon would be about 17th August (all these dates being given according to the Julian Calendar: the fall of Tyre would be on 12th August in the Gregorian Calendar, because there was a five day offset between the two calendars in the late 4th century BC.)

Alexandria was founded on 7th April (25th Tybi) 331BC according to Pseudo-Callisthenes and Alexander had returned from Egypt and reached Thapsacus on the upper reaches of the Euphrates in Hecatombaeon (8th July – 7th August) in the same year according to Arrian, *Anabasis* 3.7.1.

The Battle of Arbela/Gaugamela can be precisely dated, because a Lunar Eclipse occurred on 20th September 331BC (Julian) with totality beginning at around 9pm local time. This was eleven days before the battle (Plutarch, *Alexander* 31.4). This is precisely consistent with the emendation proposed by Kinch (and adopted by me) to Curtius 4.9.14 to the effect that Alexander reached the Tigris fourteen days before the battle (see Reconstruction section 5.44 below).

We also have an exact lunar date for the battle in the Attic Calendar recorded by Plutarch, *Camillus* 19.3: he gives 26th Boedromion (in 331BC). Since the battle occurred eleven days after a Full Moon (Lunar eclipses necessarily occur at Full Moon, of course), it must also have occurred on the 26th day after a New Moon (there being nearly 15 days between the New and Full Moons). Hence Plutarch's date is also validated by the eclipse. Arrian's assertion that the battle occurred in the next Attic month (Pyanepsion) is smilarly shown to be false by the eclipse observation (at least insofar as it was given in a version of the Attic Calendar that was matched to Lunar phases – however, the Athenian Archon did operate a festival calendar, which he often nudged to and fro relative to the Lunar phases for political reasons: hence in his calendar the Battle of Arbela might have occurred in Pyanepsion.)

Plutarch, *Alexander* 37, states that Alexander was based at Persepolis for four months, which would be roughly February through May of 330BC. He also made a thirty-day roving expedition (southwards?) into the mountains during that period, which can be dated by Curtius 5.6.12 mentioning the evening setting of the Pleiades. This puts it roughly in the range of late March through April. The story of this mini-campaign is not explicitly recounted elsewhere than Curtius.

Arrian, *Anabasis* 3.22.2 states that Darius died in the Attic month of Hecatombaeon in 330BC, which was 28th June – 27th July in the Julian calendar.

As I have argued elsewhere,[22] Cleitarchus began his first five books on Alexander's accession and its respective anniversaries: hence books four and five began on the third and fourth anniversaries of his accession (27th Boedromion according to the Attic Lunar calendar). The third anniversary occurred on 25th September (Julian) 333BC and came between Alexander's recovery from illness and the Battle of Issus. Arrian, *Anabasis Alexandrou* 2.11.10, states that this battle was fought in the Attic month of Maimacterion, which corresponded to 28th October – 26th November in 333BC. The fourth anniversary took place on 13th October 332BC and came between the fall of Tyre and the siege of Gaza. The latter held out for two months according to Diodorus 17.48.7, so Alexander's entry into Egypt should be dated to mid-December of 332BC. Cleitarchus ended his fifth book and the first of the two parts into which he divided his entire History Concerning Alexander on the day of the Battle of Arbela, the 26th Boedromion, just because the next day was the fifth anniversary of Alexander's accession. The 27th of Boedromion in 336BC happened to coincide with the Autumnal Equinox, which was the occasion for the festival at which Philip II, Alexander's father, was assassinated.

The fixed points established by these dates form the framework for the chronology of this key period. Other events may be dated by interpolating them appropriately within this framework.

The Appointment of the King of Sidon

Diodorus 17.47 recounts the story of the appointment of "Ballonymus" (i.e. Abdalonymus, as given more correctly by Curtius 4.1.15-26 and Justin 11.10.8 and meaning "Servant of the gods" in Phoenician) following the siege of Tyre after noting that the rulership of Tyre was given to Abdalonymus after its fall (Diodorus 17.46.6). It has long been supposed that the differences between the correct story of the initial appointment of Abdalonymus at Sidon in Curtius and Justin and the version in Diodorus, which is relocated to Tyre, mean that Curtius and Justin were following a different source than Diodorus on this matter, whilst Diodorus was following Cleitarchus, who was therefore giving a completely garbled account of events. However, I infer instead that Diodorus was prompted to tell the story of Abdalonymus's installation as King of Sidon retrospectively by the *additional* award of the territory of Tyre to Abdalonymus. Indeed Curtius 4.1.26 confirms that Alexander did indeed add an adjoining territory to Abdalonymus's domains. I would suggest that Diodorus himself told the story correctly of Sidon, but that an early editor of an archetypal manuscript of Diodorus subsequently incorrectly corrected the name of the city (which occurs just twice in Diodorus 17.47) to Tyre, because Diodorus' earlier omission of the matter together with his failure to explain clearly why he was referring back to events at Sidon made it seem to that inexpert editor that all

---

[22] *Alexander the Great in Afghanistan*, A. M. Chugg, 2011, Section 8, pp. 157-185.

Abdalonymus's territory should properly be located at Tyre. This rectification of an incorrect emendation has the effect of reconciling Curtius-Justin with Diodorus through inferring a single point error, which inherently incorporates a logical explanation of how it could easily have come about. This is a much more straightforward explanation of the conundrum than to suppose that Curtius and Justin independently abandoned their usual source (Cleitarchus) on the matter of Abdalonymus and that Cleitarchus relocated the whole story to Tyre. My suggestion is also bolstered by the fact that Diodorus would otherwise appear to have made Straton (king of Sidon in Curtius 4.1.16) the king of Tyre during Alexander's siege, whereas Arrian, *Anabasis Alexandrou* 2.24.5 writes that the king of Tyre was called Azemilcus.

Did Alexander Visit Upper Egypt?

It is generally supposed that Alexander never got much further upstream on the Nile (i.e. further south) than Memphis. That is what is shown on virtually every modern map of his itinerary. This assumption is mainly based the silence of most sources on the matter coupled with the view that he had insufficient time to allow for the exploration of Upper Egypt. Nevertheless, in what seems to be the only actual surviving statement on the issue (excluding the fact that the *Alexander Romance* implausibly tells the story of a visit by the king to Queen Candace in Meroë), Curtius appears to report that Alexander did in fact penetrate further upstream immediately following his arrival in Egypt and prior to returning and undertaking his famous visit to the Temple of Ammon at Siwa:

Curtius 4.7.5: *A Memphi eodem flumine vectus ad interiora Aegypti penetrat conpositisque rebus ita, ut nihil ex patrio Aegyptiorum more mutaret...*

"From Memphis he sailed on up the same stream [the Nile], penetrating into the interior of Egypt and he settled its affairs without tampering with any Egyptian national custom."

Secondly, after the king's return from Siwa, Curtius is clear that Alexander wished to visit Ethiopia, but did not have the time.

Curtius 4.8.2-4: *...et... Memphim petit. Cupido haud iniusta quidem, ceterum intempestiva incesserat, non interiora modo Aegypti, sed etiam Aethiopiam invisere: Memnonis Tithonique celebrata regia cognoscendae vetustatis avidum trahebat paene extra terminos solis. Sed imminens bellum, cuius multo maior supererat moles, otiosae peregrinationi tempora exemerat. Itaque Aegypto praefecit Aeschylum Rhodium et Peucesten Macedonem quattuor milibus militum in praesidium regionis eius datis...*

"Alexander made for Memphis. He was afflicted by a desire that was not so much unjustified as inopportune to travel not just to Upper Egypt but to Ethiopia as well. Being eager to investigate the vestiges of antiquity, the renowned palace of Memnon and Tithonus was drawing him virtually beyond the limits of enlightenment. However the impending war, of which by far the most challenging phase was yet to come, curtailed his time for sightseeing. Hence he gave the government of Egypt to Aeschylus of Rhodes and Peucestes of Macedon, allotting them four thousand troops to garrison the region."

In Greek mythology, Memnon was the son of Tithonus and an Ethiopian king, who came to the aid of Troy during the Trojan War. It therefore appears that Curtius is implicitly confirming that Alexander had already visited Upper Egypt at this juncture, but was thwarted in an ambition *additionally* to visit a famous "palace" complex in Ethiopia.

Alexander appears to have arrived in Egypt in December of 332BC (as has been argued above). If Curtius is correct, then any visit to Upper Egypt must have been concluded prior to the beginning of the expedition to Siwa. Alexander is also stated by Curtius, Diodorus and Justin to have founded Alexandria in the course of his return journey from Siwa to Memphis. The Alexander Romance (a.k.a. Pseudo-Callisthenes) 1.32.10 concurs and is clear that the Alexandrians celebrated the anniversary of the foundation of their city on the 25th day of the Egyptian month of Tybi. In the Ptolemaic Period immediately after the foundation, it can be shown that 25th Tybi equated to 7th April in the Julian Calendar. However, some smoke has been generated around the issue by P. M. Fraser (Ptolemaic Alexandria, Vol 2, page 3, note 9) amongst others by noting that the Alexander Romance appears to have been compiled in Roman Egypt (most probably in Alexandria itself) and that 25th Tybi equated to 20th January (Julian) in the calendar used in the Roman period. Nevertheless, I side with C. Bradford Welles in finding it implausible that anyone would have changed a traditional date in order to keep an anniversary in the same place in the solar year (i.e. relative to the equinoxes) and even more implausible that the date was originally calculated in the Roman period, as though the anniversary of the city's foundation only became interesting to its citizens at that time! Furthermore, P. M. Fraser also notes the existence of another ancient codex, the "Horoscope of Alexandria", which furnishes a date of 16th April 331BC for the foundation of Alexandria. It is not unusual for the complexities of translating between various calendars to lead to an error of a week or so, but it is much harder to account for a discrepancy of several months.

The Vulgate (i.e. Cleitarchan) chronology would seem to place Alexander's departure from Egypt shortly after his return to Memphis, as it asserts that he had no opportunity for further exploration of the country. Furthermore, Arrian *Anabasis* 3.6.1 states that Alexander left Egypt "when Spring began to show itself". This places his departure no later than around early May of 331BC and that is relatively consistent with Arrian's statement (*Anabasis* 3.7.1) that Alexander reached Thapsacus in Hecatombaeon (8th July – 7th August 331BC) and with the Julian date of 1st October 331BC for the Battle of Arbela/Gaugamela, which is precisely fixed by an antecedant Lunar Eclipse.

There is in consequence a considerable expanse of time (at least two months) between December of 332BC and the departure of the Siwa expedition some time in March of 331BC, during which Alexander might indeed have travelled further up the Nile. If he did so, it would be reasonable to infer that he left the main army near Memphis and transported an expeditionary force upstream in a flotilla of boats. The Nile so far outstripped the roads as a means of transport to Upper Egypt that no other route merits serious consideration. By such means Alexander might easily have travelled upstream by several tens of miles per day and downstream at twice that pace.

Even in the so-called "Official Tradition" represented by Arrian's *Anabasis Alexandrou*, there is no substantive reason to exclude the possibility of a trip to Upper Egypt. The main reason for advocates of Arrian's infallibility to have doubted the occurrence of the reported trip upstream is that this stance better suits their case for a foundation of Alexandria prior to Siwa and a return route eastwards via the other oases (chattering serpents and all) Archaeological evidence is very limited, but the existence of the famous chapel dedicated to Alexander at Karnak might hint that he actually reached the spot in person, although there is no reason strictly to require his presence for its creation to have been instigated.

The Location of the Battle of Arbela or Gaugamela

The matter of the location of the Battle of Arbela (aka Gaugamela) is still disputed. Disproportionate reliance has been placed on Arrian, *Anabasis* 3.8.7 & 6.11.4-6, who states that the battle took place near a village named Gaugamela on the River Boumelus, where Darius camped, and that this was 600 stades (on the best authority and at least 500 stades according to all accounts) away from Arbela (modern Arbil in Iraq). However, a stade is about 180m, so 600 stades is 108km. Even allowing for some winding of the route, that implies a radius of ~100km from Arbela. As shown in Figure 2.1, this is most unlikely. In the light of all other information on the battle, Arrian's distance from Arbela would put its site beyond Nineveh and near the Tigris, very close to the point at which Alexander forded the river.

There are two main rival theories for the actual site, between which scholarship has as yet been unable to decide.[23] Aurel Stein back in 1938 argued for a site just east of Mosul in the expansive plains on the direct route from Mosul to Arbil.[24] But F. Schachermeyr (recently supported by Micheal Wood in a TV documentary on the battle) has argued for Tel Gemel north of Mount Maqloub (see Figure 2.1).[25] Schachermeyr wrote to local contacts to confirm the location

---

[23] E.g. P. A. Brunt's Loeb translation of Arrian's Anabasis Alexandrou, App IX, section 2.

[24] Aurel Stein, Limes Report, Geographical Journal vol 92, 1938, pp.62-66 & vol 95, 1940, pp. 428-438 and subsequently Geographical Journal, 1942, vol 100, 155 ff.

[25] F. Schachermeyr, Alexander der Grosse, Salzburg, 1949, p.511, note 153; cf. Streck, RE, VII, cols 861ff and E. W. Marsden, The Campaign of Gaugamela, Liverpool 1964, p.20 and Donald

of Tel Gemel, which, it seems, is named for a camel. Aurel Stein had told a story of how a Mr Taylor, Chief Engineer of the Iraq Petroleum Company in Kirkuk, had informed him that "Tel Gomel" was marked on a War Office Map at 1:125,000 scale, No. J38/T about 6 miles due north of the confluence of the Khazir with the Greater Zab. However, it appears that Schachermeyr's later information was correct on this point, which nevertheless constitutes something of a red herring, since the value of the evidence from such a vague name association across twenty-three centuries is slight.

The particular relevance of the camel is explained by Plutarch, *Alexander* 31.3, who asserts that Gaugamela means Camel's House and Strabo 16.1.3-4 elucidates further: "Now the city Ninus (Nineveh) was wiped out immediately after the overthrow of the Syrians. It was much greater than Babylon, and was situated in the plain of Aturia. Aturia borders on the region of Arbela, with the Lycus River (Greater Zab) lying between them. Now Arbela, which lies opposite to Babylonia, belongs to that country; and in the country on the far side of the Lycus River lie the plains of Aturia, which surround Ninus. In Aturia is a village Gaugamela, where Darius was conquered and lost his empire. Now this is a famous place, as is also its name, which, being interpreted, means "Camel's House". Darius, the son of Hystaspes, so named it, having given it as an estate for the maintenance of the camel, which helped most on the toilsome journey through the deserts of Scythia with the burdens containing sustenance and support for the king. However, the Macedonians, seeing that this was a cheap village, but that Arbela was a notable settlement (founded, as it is said, by Arbelus, the son of Athmoneus), announced that the battle and victory took place near Arbela and so transmitted their account to the historians. After Arbela and Mt. Nicatorium (a name applied to it by Alexander after his victory in the neighbourhood of Arbela), one comes to the Caprus River (Lesser Zab), which lies at the same distance from Arbela as the Lycus." The more important detail to be gleaned from this is that the village of Gaugamela lay in the plains of Aturia *surrounding* ancient Nineveh.

Diodorus 17.53.4 similarly states that Darius wished to fight in the plains around Nineveh (adjoining modern Mosul – see map) and Curtius (at 4.10.8) says that Alexander advanced after fording the Tigris "keeping the Tigris on his right and the mountains that are called the Gordyaeans on his left" and (at 4.9.9-10) that Darius advanced from Arbela, bridged the River Lycus (almost certainly the modern Greater Zab) then moved on 80 stades (~15km) to the River Boumelus, where he encamped. Since the modern River Khazir is about 15km from the Greater Zab on the modern road from Mosul to Arbil, this strongly supports Aurel Stein over Schachermeyr and Wood, since the two rivers are 30km apart near Tel Gemel. It is also hard to see how Tel Gemel could be described as situated in "a plain surrounding Nineveh", since there is a

W. Engels, Alexander the Great and the Logistics of the Macedonian Army, 1978, p.70 and A. B. Bosworth, Commentary on Arrian's History of Alexander, Vol 1, 1980, pp.293-295.

not insignificant intervening mountain range, including Mt Maqloub, where lies the Mar Mattai monastery. It is also difficult to understand how Alexander could be said to have kept the Tigris on his right, if he actually marched directly away from that river towards Tel Gemel. Neither does Tel Gemel even match Arrian's six-hundred stade range from Arbela: it is about 70km or 390 stades from Arbil. In short, Tel Gemel matches none at all of the ancient descriptions of the battle site.

But there is an extraordinarily flat plain, which Alexander would inevitably have encountered, if he actually kept the Tigris on his right, in the vicinity of the modern village of Karemlesh between Mosul and the River Khazir. This looks a perfect match for the ground chosen by Darius. Indeed, its extreme flatness may be partly explained by the fact that Darius is said (Curtius 4.9.10 & Arrian, *Anabasis* 3.8.7) to have had every hillock on his chosen battlefield levelled. This site is very much among the plains immediately surrounding Nineveh and the separation of the rivers on the road to Arbela is very close to 15km here. There is also a tall ridge on the northern edge of the site that might be the Mt Nicatorium mentioned by Strabo and another ridge just to the left of Alexander's line of march as he passed the site of Nineveh might be the hill that Alexander took over from Mazaeus in the days preceding the battle and where he established his fortified basecamp (Curtius 4.12.15 & 4.12.18-19 & 4.12.24). It is even possible to see just why Mazaeus abandoned this hill: Alexander's line of march through the plain below it threatened to cut him off from the main body of the Persian army. Additionally, this explains why Alexander "fretted whether he should launch his attacks from the crest of the ridge against the Persian right wing" as noted by Curtius 4.13.16, for his elevated encampment lay very much towards the right of the Persian lines. Finally, it makes clear why, during the battle itself, it was Mazaeus on the Persian right wing who sent one thousand cavalrymen around Alexander's left flank to attack Alexander's encampment (Curtius 4.15.5).

Alexander was only marching for about five of the fourteen days after he crossed the Tigris (forded c. 18th or 19th September 331BC prior to a lunar eclipse on 20th September with the battle fought eleven days later on 1st October).[26] Hence if he crossed at the most likely ford at Abu Wijam, as also proposed by Aurel Stein,[27] the battlefield should be about 60km south and west of that ford, which is highly consistent with a site a little beyond Nineveh.

The geographical and topographical considerations therefore overwhelmingly favour Karemlesh over Tel Gemel. But neither candidate (nor any credible candidate) is close to being consistent with Arrian's 600 stades, which simply

---

[26] See Plutarch, *Alexander* 31.4 for the eleven days and the eclipse, which took place on 20th September 331BC (Julian) and Curtius 4.9.15-21 & 4.10.2 for fording the Tigris and the subsequent eclipse.

[27] Aurel Stein, Geographical Journal, vol 100, 1942, p.157.

seems wrong. And the argument from the modern place name of Tel Gemel does not weigh significantly in the matter, not least because Karemlesh also claims to have had a camel-derived place name in the past. Its Wikipedia entry under "Karamlish" states: 'Karamlish at the time [of the Battle of Gaugamela] was called Ko-Komle, which meant in Aramaic "The Camels' Square."'[28] The implication is that the Greeks rendered Ko-Komle as Gaugamela. However, the authority for this may be no more than the evidence of Plutarch and Strabo mentioned above taken together with the modern association with the site of Alexander's battle. In fact, Arrian, *Anabasis* 3.8.7 would seem to locate the original Gaugamela at Darius' camp at the point where the traditional route from Nineveh to Arbela forded the Khazir/Boumelus, which is about 12km east of Karemlesh. It would certainly appear unlikely that Darius would have encamped such a huge host very far from a major watersource.

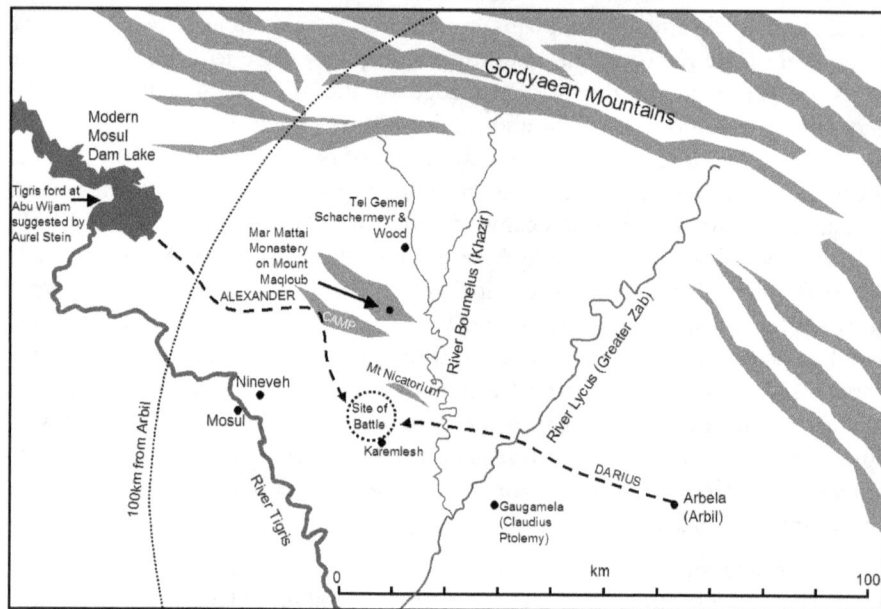

Figure 2.1. The site of the Battle of Arbela/Gaugamela

The great *Geographia* of Claudius Ptolemy provides the clinching evidence. This gives latitudes and longitudes for both Arbela (80E, 37.25N) and Gaugamela (79.5E, 37.25N) under its list of towns for Assyria in Chapter 1 of Book 6. Claudius Ptolemy placed Gaugamela half a degree of longitude due west of Arbela. For identifiable locations between Rome and Samarkand it can be shown that 1 degree of longitude in the *Geographia* is about 0.75 modern degrees of longitude. A modern degree of longitude translates to a distance of about 90km at the latitude of Arbela, so Ptolemy placed Gaugamela about 35km due

[28] http://en.wikipedia.org/wiki/Karamlish

west of Arbela. This is very close to the confluence of the Khazir (Boumelus) with the Greater Zab (Lycus). Clearly it is overwhelmingly likely that Gaugamela lay on one or other of these rivers just north of their confluence. Equally transparently, this dramatically confirms the rest of the evidence in supporting a battlefield just west of the Khazir and south of Mt Maqloub in the vicinity of modern Karemlesh. Conversely, since Tel Gemel lies as far north as it is west of Arbela, it is most unlikely to be situated anywhere near the ancient town of Gaugamela.

The Sack and Burning of Persepolis

It is important to distinguish between two separate events: firstly the sack of the lower town of Persepolis when Alexander first arrived at the city and secondly the incineration of the palace area some months later and not long before the king's departure from the vicinity. Indeed Curtius has Alexander undertake a month long campaign in the mountains surrounding the city between the two events.

There were obvious motivations for the initial sack. Alexander had clearly been incensed by the treatment of the mutilated Greeks from the workshops of Persepolis, who had met him on the road just prior to his arrival. Furthermore, armies in the ancient world expected to be afforded opportunities to sack enemy cities, when they had triumphed in the battlefield. Alexander had held back his Macedonians at Babylon and Susa, because they had surrendered, but Persepolis was the very heart and soul of the Persian kingdom and it had fought on to the end. Alexander would therefore have been under enormous moral pressure to allow a sack: it was simply the done thing in the particular set of circumstances. Denying his army its traditional right to indulge in rape and pillage in such a situation risked the disgruntlement of the troops, which in turn risked the future of the expedition. Nevertheless, the king ordered the preservation of the magnificent palace complex, partly because the immense treasures contained within it were properly now the property of the Macedonian crown and partly because he planned to winter there and so had need of comfortable accommodation.

The incineration of the palace is a more complicated matter. Arrian makes it a cold-blooded decision (*Anabasis* 3.18.11-12), whilst the Cleitarchan Vulgate explains that it was done on the spur of the moment in the context of a drunken comus and was inspired by Thais the Athenian hetaera. However, both traditions agree that Alexander excused it as symbolic revenge "for the injuries done to the Greeks", presumably including the mutilations, but especially focussing upon the incineration by the Persians of Greek shrines, notably those on the Athenian Acropolis, a hundred and fifty years beforehand.

It is of course entirely possible that both the Official and the Vulgate accounts are simultaneously true. There is no reason to think that Alexander had abandoned his antipathy towards the principal seat of the Persian kings during his stay there and the fact that Persepolis was razed just as Winter was ending and the mountain passes were opening up allowing the Macedonians to resume the pursuit of Darius may not have been a coincidence. Either Thais may have known that she was pushing at an open door in urging the conflagration or the entire comus may have been stage-managed as a piece of political theatre. Alexander might well have deemed it poetic justice that his enemy's capital should be desroyed at the bidding of an Athenian courtesan, whether it came about through planning or upon a whim. Thais herself said as much according to Diodorus 17.72.2 by vaunting the irony of women's hands being seen to destroy the greatest architectural masterpiece of the Persians.

It is yet more ironical, however, that Alexander speedily regretted the act (Curtius 5.7.11), but the greatest irony of all was that the blaze actually engendered the preservation of the stone skeleton of Achaemenid Persepolis until our own day, since the destruction was so complete that no attempt was ever made to reconstruct the site or to re-use its masonry.

Did Darius Agree To Surrender in July 330BC?

Alexander appears to have been familiar with the works of Xenophon. Arrian, *Anabasis* 2.7.8-9 records that he cited matters from Xenophon's *Anabasis* in addressing his troops and there are many instances where his behaviour seems to have been inspired by the example of Cyrus in Xenophon's *Cyropaidia*. A particular instance would be Cyrus' reuniting of Pantheia, the Lady of Susa, with her husband, Abradatas, in return for the latter's submission to his rule (*Cyropaidia* 6.1.45-49). Alexander appears to have adopted this as a model for his own policy towards Darius and his captured wife, Stateira, and other family members after Issus. At any rate in Alexander's first letter to Darius, as quoted by Arrian, *Anabasis* 2.14.8, he states: "You must then regard me as Lord of all Asia and come to me... Ask for your mother, wife and children and what you will, when you have come, and you will receive them. You shall have whatever you persuade me to give." Cyrus won the fealty of Abradatas, who became Cyrus' loyal lieutenant. Similarly, according to Diodorus 17.54.6, Alexander offered Darius the opportunity to retain his kingship over the Persian Empire, provided that he acknowledged Alexander's overlordship.

Such was the background to the circumstances in the Summer of 330BC when Alexander was in hot pursuit of Darius between Ecbatana and the Caspian Sea. At this point Curtius 5.8.12-13 has Darius remark in a speech to his council: "Unless perchance it should prove more fulfilling to dance attendance upon the decisions of the victor and emulate the example of Mazaeus and Mithrenes by being insecurely assigned the rule of a single province, always supposing Alexander now favours fawning upon his fame rather than indulging his anger?" Mazaeus had recently surrendered Babylon and retained its governance and Mithrenes had surrendered Sardis and had been given the Satrapy of Armenia in

331BC. Hence Darius appears to be alluding to the earlier offers that he might retain the rule of Persia and even its empire, if he accepted Alexander as his overlord. Darius therefore seems to have believed that such terms were still available in 330BC, though he still maintained here before his courtiers that he would not accept them.

Arrian, *Anabasis* 3.20.3 states that Alexander halted for five days at about this time, abruptly and mysteriously suspending his hot pursuit of Darius. The only likely reason for this is that he thought he had reached an arrangement with Darius, for he was normally quite relentless in his conduct of military operations. Therefore the possibility arises that Darius did ultimately decide to accept Alexander's terms and to become a sort of glorified Satrap of Persia within Alexander's all-encompassing dominions.

Curtius 6.3.13 has Alexander confide to his men: "…when his sovereign was even in want of succour from foreigners, Bessus set him in fetters like a common captive, though we the victors would assuredly have spared him. And then in the end he slaughtered Darius in order that we should not be able to save him." This is partly based on the fact that Darius was known to have been considering seeking help from foreigners at the time that Bessus deposed him. Ostensibly the foreigners were Patron's Greek mercenaries, but possibly Darius's hopes extended also to the Macedonians. These words certainly tend to confirm that Alexander saw himself as the potential saviour of Darius rather than his persecutor at the end and that Alexander believed that Bessus understood and appreciated the political implications of this odd role reversal.

If Darius made a surrender plan known to his subordinates or if they otherwise discovered that Darius was treating with Alexander, then this may have provided the immediate motive for Bessus dethroning and arresting Darius. It is particularly significant that Bessus chose to kill Darius, forever staining his reputation with the crime of regicide, instead of simply leaving his sovereign to be dealt with by Alexander. Clearly, Bessus did not believe that Alexander would kill Darius for him. The compulsion for him to murder his king must have derived from a real fear that Darius would otherwise have become a puppet ruler of Persia under Alexander, which would undoubtedly have undermined Bessus's potential support as the new Great King.

Alexander's Route

Between the Battle of Issus and the death of Darius a number of questionmarks hang over Alexander's route. This subsection briefly reviews the main points at issue.

The first major difficulty arises regarding Alexander's route for his return from Ammon (Siwa), which has already been discussed in the context of Arrian's errors. I conclude that Arrian's curt statement that Alexander travelled directly east across the desert to Memphis is not very credible. In particular, it is inconsistent with the best evidence on the timing of the foundation of Alexandria. The accounts in both the Vulgate and the Alexander Romance traditions show that Alexander returned via the Mediterranean coast by retracing the route he indisputably took to get to Siwa. On this point the evidence of the Romance (Pseudo-Callisthenes) carries more weight than usual, because its author was Egyptian and most probably lived in Alexandria itself.

The next point concerns how far north up the Mediterranean coast Alexander marched on his return from Egypt before striking inland. Arrian, *Anabasis* 3.6.4 notes that Alexander marched inland to Thapsacus immediately after having devoted a paragraph to Alexander's return to Tyre. There is no reason to infer that Alexander struck inland from Tyre itself, but that is nevertheless what many have done due to a supposed lack of other evidence on the route at this point. However, Engels has observed that it would have made much more sense for Alexander to have marched up the coast as far as possible, roughly to the vicinity of Seleucia, the port of Antioch, in order to take maximum advantage of support from the fleet in supplying his army.[29] Furthermore, Jacoby Fragment 3 of Cleitarchus from Stobaeus *Florilegium*, IV 20, 73 is connected with the town of Byblos on the Levantine coast north of Tyre and is stated to be from the fifth book of Cleitarchus corresponding to the fifth year of Alexander's reign. Since the king's first visit to Tyre was in the fourth year of his reign, this fragment constitutes significant evidence that Alexander returned to Byblos on his journey back north. Hence Alexander did not strike inland from Tyre (as almost all modern maps of his route would have us believe). Instead he continued up the coast until he was as close as possible to the upper reaches of the Euphrates and only then did he strike inland to reach that river.

Alexander is reported by Arrian, *Anabasis* 3.7.1-2 to have crossed the Euphrates at Thapsacus. This city is known to have lain on the upper reaches of the Euphrates, but there are several alternative candidates. However, Ptolemy's *Geographia*, Chapter 18 of Book 5, places Thapsacus on the Euphrates just east of the modern town of Ar Raqqah and the ancient town of Nicephorion. Furthermore, Pliny, Natural History 5.21 states that Thapsacus later became known as Amphipolis. In their 1855 translation of this text, John Bostock and Henry Thomas Riley note that Amphipolis' "ruins are to be seen at the ford of El Hamman, near the modern Rakkah". The Dictionary of Greek and Roman Geography (1854, ed. William Smith, LLD) notes that: "About 36 miles below Balls (the Alalis of Ptolemy), following the course of the river, are the ruins of Sura; and about 6 miles lower is the ford of El-Hammam, which Col. Chesney identifies with the Zeugma of Thapsacus, where, according to local tradition, the army of Alexander crossed the Euphrates (Expedition for Survey, &c. vol. i. p. 416)." Hence the best information seems to point to a site close to modern Ar Raqqah.

---

[29] Donald W Engels, Alexander the Great and the Logistics of the Macedonian Army, University of California, 1978, p.65 & Map 8.

There is also some uncertainty regarding which ford over the Tigris was used by Alexander, but the most likely on the basis of its position relative to the battlefield at Gaugamela seems to be that at Abu Wijam, as also proposed by Aurel Stein.[30]

In discussing the location of the Battle of Arbela/Gaugamela I have concluded that Alexander's route ran past modern Mosul and ancient Nineveh and continued through the plain to the south of Mt Maqloub, where the battle took place. The alternative theory that Alexander marched round the north of Mt Maqloub has been promoted by Schachermeyr, because he discovered that the modern Tel Gemel lay to the north of Mt Maqloub. The irony is that Aurel Stein had promoted Tel Gemel as a place name that could be (rather loosely) associated with the battle site, because he had received garbled information that it lay south of Mt Maqloub, his own preferred location for the engagement. In fact the place name connection is so remote as to be unworthy of any weight in the matter. All the useful evidence, mainly from Curtius, Diodorus and Strabo, but also supported by Claudius Ptolemy's *Geographia* (as discussed above), suggests a location for the battle to the south of Mt Maqloub.

On quitting Susa, Alexander headed southeast with Persepolis as his objective. He crossed the river that our sources call the Pasitigris, but which seems also anciently to have been named the Eulaeus (e.g. in Ptolemy's *Geographia*). This is the modern River Karun. Ariobarzanes blockaded the route into Persis at the gorge that was called the Susian Gates in the Vulgate (Curtius 5.3.17, Diodorus 17.68.1, Polyaenus 4.3.27) or the Persian Gates in Arrian, *Anabasis* 3.18.2 and Strabo 15.3.6 (729). This seems to be the modern Tang-i Khas.[31]

In May 330BC Alexander resumed his pursuit of Darius, marching on Ecbatana by way of Parsagada and (probably) modern Isfahan. Darius having fled northwards towards Hyrcania, Alexander followed on his heels. Darius had just crossed the pass called the Caspian Gates (the modern Tang-i Sar Darrah on the southern flank of the Elburz Mountains) moving eastwards into Parthia, when he was arrested at the village of Thara (Justin 11.15.1 - possibly modern Lasjerd) by Nabarzanes and Bessus and placed in fetters in a covered wagon. The Persians then continued eastwards, heading for Bactria. But Alexander was threatening to overtake them, which prompted them to stab Darius, whom they left for dead somewhere near modern Samnan. One of Alexander's men named Polystratus found Darius still alive, but he had expired by the time Alexander himself reached the scene. Alexander continued on to Hecatompylus, probably the modern Sahr-i Qumis near Qusheh.

---

[30] Aurel Stein, Geographical Journal, vol 100, 1942, p.157.

[31] Aurel Stein, Old Routes of Western Iran, London, 1940, p.25.

3. Book 4: 25ᵗʰ September 333BC - 13ᵗʰ October 332BC

The Battle of Issus; An Interview with the Queens; The Treasures at Damascus; The First Letter from Darius; A New King for Sidon; The Siege of Tyre

KEY
<u>**Underlined bold text for attributed Fragments of Cleitarchus**</u>
Bold text where there is overwhelming evidence
Bold italic text where there exists direct-firm evidence
Normal text where direct-weak evidence applies
Italic text where the evidence is conjectural
Grey text for connecting passages, if Cleitarchus' version is indeterminate

4.1 *This book recounts the events concerning Alexander in the fourth year of his reign.*

4.2 Darius, having received news of Alexander's sickness, hastened to reach the Euphrates with all the swiftness that so laden a host could achieve. He built a bridge across the river, but still just five days later had got his army over in order to occupy Cilicia the sooner. Meanwhile Alexander, *having* recovered from his illness, *arrived in Anchiale, which was built by Sardanapalus. Here he pitched his tent in the course of moving up country against the Persians. Not far away lay the tomb of Sardanapalus upon which stood a statue in stone with the fingers of its right hand converged as though they were being snapped. Upon it was inscribed in Syrian characters: "In a single day Sardanapalus the son of Anacyndaraxes constructed Tarsus and Anchiale. Other things not being worth this much, let you eat, drink and be merry." He meant it seems that other things are not worth a snap of the fingers.* <u>**Sardanapalus died eventually from senility after having been deposed from his Syrian sovereignty.**</u>[32]

4.3 Now Alexander reached the city of Soli. Having brought it under his authority, he exacted a bond of two hundred talents from its citizenry and stationed a garrison of his soldiers in its citadel. Then with games and a furlough he repaid the prayers that had been offered to make him well, making plain how sincere he was in his disdain for the foreigners, since the games were celebrated

---

[32] Jacoby Fragment 2 of Cleitarchus from Book 4 of his History Concerning Alexander preserved by Athenaeus 12.39 (530A): Syrian means Assyrian (a Cleitarchan idiosyncrasy); Cleitarchus may well have sourced this snippet of Persian history from the *Persica* written by his father Deinon.

in Aesculapius's and Athena's honours.[33] The joyous news was brought, whilst Alexander was viewing competitions, that at Halicarnassus his men had outfought the forces of the Persians. Additionally, the Myndii and the Caunii and the greater part of their regions had been brought within his dominions.

4.4 Hence having staged a pageant through the games he moved camp, bridged the River Pyramus and reached the city of Mallus, whence, after another overnight encampment, he arrived at the stronghold of Castabalum. There the king met **Parmenion**, who **had been sent ahead to reconnoitre the route through the** *Syrian* **Gates, the** **pass that they must traverse** in order to reach a town called Issus. **Having** *driven off the Persians and* **taken possession of the narrowest part of the pass, he had left a skeleton garrison in place.** Then Parmenion had seized Issus, which had also been abandoned by the barbarians. Having fanned out from there, he had expelled those who had held the high hills in the hinterland and had posted garrisons everywhere so as to secure their track. Thereafter, as was said beforehand, as both harbinger and perpetrator of these deeds he came right back.

4.5 From there **Alexander moved his army to Issus,** *which he held by intimidating its populace.* There he took counsel as to whether they should carry on any further or else wait where they were for the scheduled arrival of fresh troops from Macedonia? Parmenion considered that there was no better locale for them to give battle, for in that place the frontline forces of each king would be equal, since the narrows could not accommodate a vast array of people. Alexander's side should avoid wide plains and open country, where they could be surrounded and crushed by an outflanking strategy. Parmenion feared that their own fatigue, rather than their enemies' bravery, would deny them the victory, for fresh Persians would confront them continually, were they able to deploy their ranks more extensively. The logic of such sensible advice was readily appreciated, so it was amidst the mountain passes that their adversary was awaited.

4.6 There was a Persian called Sisines in Alexander's army. The Satrap of Egypt had once sent him to Philip and, being courted with gifts and every courtesy, he had elected exile in preference to his patrimony. Thereafter he followed Alexander into Asia, being considered amongst the most loyal of his allies. And it happened that a Cretan soldier handed him a letter, sealed with a signet ring, the device of which he did not recognise. It had been sent by Darius's chiliarch, Nabarzanes, exhorting Sisines to effect something in keeping with his ancestry and his loyalties, for this, wrote Nabarzanes, would bring him into great honour with their king. As his intentions were innocent, Sisines often endeavoured to bring the letter before Alexander, but, finding the king to be overburdened by his duties and his preparations for war, he repeatedly procrastinated in favour of

---

[33] The god of healing and the goddess of wisdom: Alexander was vaunting his recovery from illness as being due to the intercession of these deities on his behalf.

a better opportunity, thereby arousing suspicion that he was plotting treachery. For in fact the letter, prior to its delivery, had come into Alexander's possession. And he had read it and re-sealed it using a ring with an unknown impression and had bidden that it be given to Sisines to assess the loyalty of the barbarian. But since over several days Sisines failed to approach the king, it seemed he had suppressed the letter in the cause of heinous scheming. Hence he was slain in the column by the Cretans whilst marching, undoubtedly at Alexander's bidding.

4.7 The Greek troops whom Thimodes had received from Pharnabazus had already reached Darius, constituting his primary and practically his solitary hope. They earnestly urged him to retrace his route and to return to the wide-open plains of Mesopotamia. Else, if he deplored that plan, that he should at least divide his copious forces, so that his realm's entire fighting strength should not be struck down by a single stroke of fortune. This advice was not so unpalatable to the king as to his paladins, who declared that the Greeks, being of unreliable and purchasable loyalty, were intent upon treachery and that they sought to fragment his army for the sake of no other strategy than that they might go off by some back way in order to betray to Alexander everything to which they had been party. Nothing, they said, would be more prudent than to surround them with his entire army and wipe them out with flights of javelins and archery as a warning that there would be no escape from punishment for perfidy. But Darius, being ethical and merciful, said that he would certainly not sanction such a sin as to order the butchery of his own soldiers, who had followed him trustingly. For who would ever afterwards entrust their safety to him among the foreign communities, if his hands were stained with the blood of so many of his own mercenaries? Nobody should lose his life as the price for having offered idiotic advice, for none would join in consultations, if it were perilous to make recommendations. Most particularly, they themselves were convened to counsel him daily and expressed many an opinion, but the man was not deemed to be of better loyalty, who spoke with more discretion.

4.8 Accordingly, although Darius offered the Greeks his personal thanks for their thoughtfulness, he bade that they be informed, nevertheless, that if he were to retrace his course, he would without doubt be surrendering his realm to the enemy force. The conduct of warfare relies upon reputability and he who retreats may be deemed to flee. And actually, there was scarcely any sense in protracting the hostilities, since in a desolate region, ravaged in turn by his own host and by his enemies, there were insufficient supplies for such a vast array, especially when winter was just getting underway. Nor was it possible to divide his army, if he were to comply with the custom of his ancestors, who had always engaged all of their warriors in the decisive battles of their wars. And, by Heracles! this erstwhile fearsome sovereign, who had been buoyed up by a false sense of confidence due to the absence of his opponents, had renounced rashness in favour of reticence on becoming aware of the imminence of Darius's presence and had ensconced himself amidst the mountain corridors in the manner of a skulking beast, which lurks in its forest lair on hearing the racket from rovers. And now he was even feigning infirmity to deceive his soldiery. But Darius would no longer be allowing him to refuse a decisive battle. In that hollow in which those cowards were cowering, he would crush them one and all... But this bravado was more for show rather than being justifiable.

4.9 Nevertheless, Darius *decided to disencumber his forces, so he* diverted his non-combatants and his baggage train including his monies and valuables to Damascus in Syria *with a token military escort.* However, the wife *(who was also his sister)* and the mother of Darius accompanied the main column as was the custom of their country's court. His *two* maiden daughters and infant son also remained with their father and **he advanced rapidly *into Cilicia* to engage with Alexander, *knowing that the latter was in possession of the passes in the mountains and reckoning that he would not dare to do battle in the plains. Disrespecting the sparseness of the Macedonians, but much impressed by the enormity of the army of the Persians, the local inhabitants forsook Alexander in favour of Darius. So with unstinting willingness they furnished the Persians with food and supplies, foreseeing their victory in their minds' eyes.***

4.10 It chanced that Alexander reached the pass that affords access into Syria on the same night that Darius arrived at the place that is called the Amanic Gates.[34] The Persians did not doubt that the Macedonians were on the run, having abandoned Issus, which they had previously taken, for indeed some of their wounded and sick were seized, having been unable to keep up with the column. At the instigation of his paladins, who were rabid in their barbaric savagery, all these captives had their hands hacked off and the stumps cauterised. They were then led around in order that they be familiarised with his army, and when they had seen all there was to see, he bade them report to their king concerning everything that they had been witnessing. Then Darius moved his camp *from Issus* to base himself upon the River Pinarus[35] in order to stay at the backs of those he supposed to have run away. But the men whose hands he had severed made their way to the Macedonian encampment, saying that Darius was dogging their steps and was following them as fast as he was able. This was barely believable, so Alexander sent scouts back along the littoral to reconnoitre whether Darius himself was advancing in his rear or whether some general was trying to give the impression that the arrival of the entire Persian army was near.

---

[34] Alexander was heading southwards with the Mediterranean coast on his right, but Darius had moved northwards past him further inland and came through the Amanican Gates to appear in Alexander's rear (it seems rather unexpectedly). Alexander was compelled to perform a volte-face and to retrace his steps northwards to meet Darius in the narrow coastal plain near the River Pinarus a little way south of Issus.

[35] The Latin of Curtius 3.8.16 (*motis ergo castris superat Pinarum amnem*) has usually been translated to the effect that Darius moved his camp and crossed the River Pinarus, but Callisthenes (Polybius 12.17-22) wrote that Darius encamped on the banks of the River Pinarus, so Curtius likely meant that Darius moved his camp to lie literally on top of the Pinarus.

4.11 But, whilst the scouts were retracing their tracks, a huge host was glimpsed in the distance. Thereafter all over the flats fires began to flare and a blaze appeared to be burning everywhere without intermittence, since the sprawling horde of men had dispersed especially spaciously on account of their beasts of burden. Therefore, rejoicing that the contest would take place there, in that most ideally narrow of courses, as he had begged in his every prayer, Alexander commanded his forces to lay out their camp just where they were. However, as commonly occurs when the occasion of a decisive battle nears, **the king's confidence gave way to fears.** *The numerical superiority of the enemy was cause for anxiety and* he was afraid of Fortune herself, whose favour had furthered his affairs so prosperously and, not unreasonably considering what she had done for him, he was concerned about her inconstancy. Just a single night now lay between him and the outcome of such a critical fight. Conversely, he reckoned the rewards outweighed the jeopardy and, although it was dubious whether he would win a victory, it was at any rate certain that, should he die, it would be heroically and with great glory. *Certainly, to delay the confrontation would be to increase their insecurity, for it would foster despondency among his military.*

4.12 Therefore he told his soldiers to refresh themselves and thereafter at the third watch to be armed and ready. Alexander himself ascended to the crest of a lofty ridge and, lit by the enveloping light of multiple torches, he sacrificed to the guardian gods of the vicinity in accordance with the custom of his country. The third blast of the trumpet was heard by the troops as had been ordered and they were now well prepared for both marching and for battle. They were told to advance at the double, such that by dawn they had reached the narrow strip of land where they had determined that they should make their stand. Those **scouts sent forward on a foray reported that Darius lay thirty stades away, his forces drawn up for battle and making for a menacing spectacle. Thereupon Alexander** halted his formations, donned his armour and **decreed his dispositions.**

4.13 Panicked peasants brought the news to Darius of the arrival of his foes. He could hardly believe that those fugitives that he had been pursuing were actually advancing upon him. Therefore no little stress obsessed the minds of all, for they were fitted out for marching rather than for combat, so they raced to snatch up their arms for the spat. But the very haste of those that scurried about and their invocation of their colleagues to take up their arms instilled still greater trepidation. Others went up onto the mountain ridge in order to get a good view of the formation of the enemy forces, whilst many more bridled their horses. No single chain of command controlled this disorderly army, amongst which diverse disruptions had stirred everyone into a frenzy. Originally, Darius had ordained that the mountain ridge should be occupied by a detachment in order to engage his enemy's rear as well as his front. Also along the shoreline that afforded his right flank protection he planned to throw forward further troops so as to harry his foe from every direction. Additionally, twenty thousand soldiers he had sent forward with a battalion of archers were ordered to ford the

Pinarus River, which coursed between the rival arrays of soldiery, and told to block the advance of the Macedonian military. If they could not hold their ground, they were to withdraw into the mountains and covertly to go right around the endmost of the enemy. But Fortune upset these worthy intentions, proving more influential than all calculations. For out of fear some did not dare to execute their mission, whereas others vainly pursued its execution, since when some parts show indecision, the whole is thrown into confusion.

4.14 Darius deployed his forces in the following fashion. Nabarzanes covered the right wing with his cavalry bolstered by about twenty thousand slingers and archers. On the same wing, Thimodes led the Greek mercenary infantry, comprising thirty thousand soldiers, unquestionably the backbone of Darius's army and the equal of the Macedonian phalangite fighters. On the left wing twenty thousand barbarian infantry were commanded by the Thessalian Aristomedes and the king deployed his most pugnacious peoples in support of these. Darius himself meant to fight on that side of his army accompanied by three thousand elite cavalry, his usual bodyguards, and forty thousand infantry. Then the Hyrcanian and Median cavalry came after these and adjoining them, extending both to their right and their left, were the cavalry of other nationalities. Six thousand slingers and javelin-flingers preceded these formations, whilst they were stood at their specified stations. He had arrayed his forces to fill up every accessible spot in that corridor, and the wings reached to the ridges on one side and on the other plastered the shore. The wife and mother of the king and the rest of the retinue of women were received into the core of the corps.

4.15 *Alexander conceived this to be a heaven-sent opportunity to cripple the power of the Persians in a single victory,* **so he arrayed his infantry and cavalry appropriately.** He placed his phalanx to the fore, for no others amongst the Macedonians were mightier in war. Nicanor, the son of Parmenion, had custody of the right wing with Coenus, Perdiccas, Meleager, Ptolemaeus[36] and Amyntas standing by him, each leading his own battalion. Craterus and Parmenion himself were on the left wing, which stretched to the sea, but Craterus was bidden to obey Parmenion. *Cavalry were stationed on either wing: the right flank was covered by the Macedonians in combination on their left with the Thessalians* and the left wing was held by the Peloponnesians. Ahead of this battlefront Alexander deployed a company of slingers intermingled with archers. Thracians and Cretans also sallied forward, since they too were only lightly armoured. But against those sent forth by Darius to make the mountain ridge their base he flung the Agrianians, just lately arrived from Thrace. Furthermore, he instructed Parmenion to expand his lines insofar as was feasible towards the sea in order to form his fighting front further away from the mountains, which were occupied by the foreign forces of his enemy. But, having dared neither to make a stand against the oncoming

---

[36] Ptolemaeus the son of Seleucus: he died in the ensuing battle.

Macedonians nor to get in behind them as they passed them by, these particular barbarians, being especially intimidated by the sight of the slingers, had opted to fly. This eventuality secured the flank of Alexander's formation, which he had feared might be assailed from a greater elevation. *At first* the Macedonian phalanx advanced in a depth of thirty-two ranks, for the narrow corridor did not permit a more extensive cordon. But then the mountain gorges gradually began to broaden and afford more space, so that, not only could the infantry assume their normal number of ranks, but *the cavalry*, who had *occupied the whole front*, could also wheel into place around the flanks.[37]

4.16 At this point the two armies came in sight of one another, though still beyond the range of spears, whereupon *the* foremost **Persians raised up rough and ragged cheers, which spread through all their half a million warriors. These were reciprocated by the Macedonians with more force than the strength of their numbers by virtue of the reverberations from the peaks and desolate mountain pastures.** For crags and highlands situated roundabout always echo and amplify any audible shout. **Alexander *forged ahead of his foremost standards and* held up his hand frequently to halt his array, *so that they should not through impetuosity be winded when they entered the fray*** *and to accustom their vision to toleration of the sight of their seething opposition.* ***And* as he rode along his ranks he addressed his soldiers in various terms as suited their respective characters. The Macedonians, winners of so many wars in Europe,** *who not so much at his but rather their own instigation* **had engaged upon the subjection of Asia** *and the uttermost Orient,* **he reminded of the traditional bravery of their nation. They** *were the deliverers of all the world's territories, who* **would someday surpass the boundaries reached by Dionysus and Heracles.** *They would not only impose their yoke upon the Persians, but also upon all nations. Bactria and India would be provinces of the Macedonians. What they regarded with wonder currently was the least of what there was to see, but everything would be revealed to them by victory. Profitless endeavours amidst the pinnacles of Illyria or the crags of Thrace were not their destiny, but rather the riches of the entire East prospectively. And there would scarcely be any work for their swords, for a shove of their shields would shift those panic-stricken wavering hordes. In addition to this, Alexander hailed his father Philip, who had defeated the Athenians, and he put his men in mind of the subjugation of the Boeotians and the tearing down of their most renowned town. He recalled their battlefront at the Granicus at one juncture and the many cities that they had either stormed or received in surrender at another, reflecting that everything*

---

[37] The account of the Battle of Issus by Alexander's court historian, Callisthenes of Olynthus, survives via Polybius 12.17-22; he explained that Alexander drew up his phalanx initially 32-deep as he came northwards back through the pass, but that he was able to reduce this to 16-deep then 8-deep as the coastal plain widened such that he was able to broaden his front; it seems likely that Cleitarchus drew upon this account.

behind their backs had been overthrown and trampled in their tracks. *He also told them that the impending battle would be both the termination of their toil and the culmination of their glory.*

Figure 4.1. Alexander addresses his officers before Issus (André Castaigne, 1898)

4.17 When he came upon Greek troops, Alexander asked them to recall that it was the peoples of these countries that had formerly made war upon Greece, firstly through the arrogance of the first Darius and then that of Xerxes, who had required of them both land and water, so that neither drink from their springs nor their regular provender were left to those that had to surrender. By these enemies their temples had been ransacked and incinerated, their cities had been stormed and the stipulations of both human and divine law had been violated. He *even* bade the Illyrians and Thracians, those used to living by banditry, to peer carefully at the ranks of their enemy that were gleaming with gold and purple finery, not outfitted with arms but rather with booty. *Let them march forward like men and strip the gilding from those passive women, exchanging the rough relief of their mountains and bared sods, stiff with perpetual frost, for the fecund tracts and purlieus of the Persian squads.*[38]

4.18 *Nor was Darius inactive in the motivation of his army, for he assumed the duties of his commanders in circulating past everybody, rousing individuals personally, reminding them of the Persians' immemorial illustriousness and the perpetual empire that the immortal gods had given them to possess.*

4.19 Now the armies came within mutual range of arrows *and on both sides the buglers blew the signal for them to come to blows.* Thereupon the Persians launched their cavalry in a dashing charge against the left wing of their adversary, for Darius opted to decide the contest between the horse, thinking that the phalanx was the flower of the Macedonian force. And already he was seeking to surround Alexander's right wing as well, but when the Macedonian saw this he bade two squadrons of his cavalry to go and hold onto the spur of the fell. The rest he had ride rapidly into the thick of the action, except that he detached the Thessalian horse from this confrontation, ordering their commander to circle back secretly behind his lines to join Parmenion, there to do diligently whatever could be done. And thereafter *the king defended himself valiantly, surrounded on all sides by* the Persians. *But being crowded together and virtually entangled these* were unable firmly to fling their javelins, yet they loosed them upon Alexander simultaneously so clustered that they collided as they converged, such that but a few struck weakly and ineffectually upon their adversary, whilst most dropped to earth harmlessly.

4.20 Therefore they promptly drew their swords, being obliged to engage in hand-to-hand combat, and the blood really began to gush and spurt after that. For the two forces were so closely locked together that their arms were clashing against one another and they were poking the points of their swords into the faces of each other. Not even the timid and the cowardly could give up the

---

[38] There is also a suspicion of innuendo in the Latin of Curtius 3.10.10, where rough relief (*aspera iuga*) could also mean doxies and bared sods (*nudasque calles*) is similar to naked servant-boys.

fight, but standing face to face they fought like dualists might, standing their ground until perchance victory made room for their advance. Therefore they paced forward eventually only when they had struck down an enemy. But, though they had been exhausted, they were engaged by a fresh adversary. And neither could the wounded depart the field as is otherwise customary, since their own side pressed upon them from behind and ahead lay the enemy.

Figure 4.2. Alexander's charge at Issus on the Alexander Sarcophagus from Sidon.

4.21 Alexander peered around in all directions in his anxiety to spot Darius, *who, being raised up by his chariot, was both a prime target for his enemy's offensive and an idol to furnish his own side with an incentive.* Upon sighting the Persian king, Alexander charged him with his cavalry trailing, *for he served himself as a soldier just as much as a commander,* coveting the chief accolade of slaying the Persian ruler and winning the victory by his personal endeavour. *By now the battle had engaged the entirety of both sides' cavalry and many fell casualty as the fray raged indecisively, due to the evenly matched capabilities of the adversaries. The scales swung this way and that as the lines swayed to and fro* locked in mortal combat. *Damage was done by every spear cast and thrust of the sword, since an easy target was presented by the constricted horde. Many were overcome by their injuries whilst confronting their enemies, but they kept on fighting until their expiry, so that their life left them sooner than their bravery. And the commander of each company fought resolutely at its head, inspiring corresponding courage in the ranks that he led. Injuries were inflicted in many varieties in the context of many kinds of heated hostilities as they held out for their respective victories.*

4.22 Oxathres, the brother of Darius, discerning that Alexander was pressing towards his sibling, *was concerned lest there should be no stopping him, since he conceived that he would share in the fate of his king.* Hence he interposed himself and the cream of his cavalry before the royal chariot directly, *considering that this exhibition of his brotherly fidelity would cause him to be exalted by the people of his country, who already admired his combative ability. Standing out sharply from the rest due to his panoply and the vigour of his body and distinguished by a rare courage and loyalty,* he *certainly* shone in that fight, skillfully felling some *that pressed forward recklessly and putting others to flight.* But surrounding their king the Macedonian horsemen *roused one another through mutual exhortation and in company with their sovereign they* smashed through the cavalry lines of the opposition, *each determined to dispatch Darius ahead of the competition without any thought of self-preservation. Then the carnage truly reached ruinous proportions.* All around the chariot of Darius his most illustrious lords lay in legions, *where, before the gaze of their king, they had died most gloriously, all face down as they had fallen in the fighting having received some frontal injury.* Many of the most prominent Persian commanders perished in this struggle: among these Antixyes, Rheomithres and Sabaces, the Governor of Egypt, *leaders of vast armies,* were especially notable. *Around them a less familiar crowd of infantry and cavalry were piled in a huddle.* Of the Macedonians *too not so very* many *but yet some of the most valiant* were laid low and Alexander himself suffered a slight slashing blow to his right thigh *from a blade, when he was mobbed by the foe.*

Figure 4.3. Alexander threatens Darius at Issus (Alexander Mosaic, Pompeii)

4.23 By this time the horses harnessed to the chariot of Darius had been struck by spears *and had become frenzied by the accumulations of corpses from the battle. Hence, being stampeded by their pain and their fears,* they had begun to thrash the yoke, rocking the king riding in the vehicle and conveying him almost into the midst of the enemy. Darius *personally wrestled with the reins, demeaning his customary dignity, then leapt out, dreading being delivered still living into the power of his adversary. He* mounted upon a spare for the team of four that was held by his retinue *for such an emergency.*[39] As he made the switch under

[39] It is obvious from the very close parallels in the rest of their texts here that Diodorus 17.34.6-7 is following the same source as Curtius 3.11.11-12, but unnecessary difficulties have been created by rendering *tethrippon heteron* as "another chariot". Although *tethrippos* is used to mean a four-horse chariot (Latin: *quadriga*), it literally means the team of four horses themselves (i.e. *tetra-hippos*), so

constant attack in the mêlée, he panicked *and threw away his insignia shamefully, so that they should not betray him as he* <u>turned to flee</u>.[40] *Beholding their king in this condition, those around him followed his decision and then each neighbouring company successively resorted to desertion, so that the entirety of the Persian cavalry was soon retreating rapidly. Thus indeed the rest were scared into scattering and such as were afforded a route for escaping raced away casting aside the arms that they had assumed but lately to protect their persons: in such a degree does panic produce a revulsion for precautions.*

4.24 The cavalry sent out by Parmenion were pressing hard upon the escaping enemy and luckily all of them on that wing had been persuaded to flee. But towards the Macedonian right the Persians were harrying the Thessalian horsemen vehemently and one squadron had been trampled by their charge already, whereupon the Thessalians suddenly wheeled their steeds about, abandoning their flight and hurling themselves back into the fight, felling with abundant butchery barbarians who were straggling through overconfidence in their victory. Both the Persian mounts and their riders were weighed down with leaf armour to the knee, so, though they maintained maximum speed, they manoeuvred only with difficulty. Thus, naturally, by weaving about on their steeds the Thessalians engaged them with impunity. When this gainful engagement was reported to Alexander, who had not yet ventured to press the pursuit of his adversary, being now the victor universally, he began to harry the heels of the fleeing enemy. Not more than a thousand cavalry followed the king as he rode down this huge horde of his opponents, but who whilst winning or in flight holds a headcount of his contingents? Hence so very few Macedonians drove the Persians like cattle and their escape was protracted by the same panic that pushed them into flight from the battle. *As their paths passed through narrow defiles and across rough country they jostled and trampled one another and many perished without a blow from the enemy. For men were crammed together in a press, some without their armour, others retaining full battle dress. Some still with their swords bared slew others who were thereby skewered. But most of the cavalry spewed out into the open country, vigorously urging on their steeds and reaching the refuge of the allied cities. At this point the Macedonian phalanx and the Persian infantry clashed but briefly, for the collapse of the cavalry had presaged a complete and universal victory. All the Persians resorted to retreat quite rapidly and, as so many myriads sought safety via narrow routes, corpses*

---

tethrippon heteron (literally "another four-horse") can instead mean a spare horse for the four-horse team. This allows agreement with Curtius that Darius escaped on a spare horse rather than in a second chariot. Arrian 2.11.4 also has Darius transfer to a horse, but later in his flight. The Alexander Mosaic vividly depicts this scene, including especially the terror of the chariot team and the spare horse being brought before Darius.

[40] That Cleitarchus (inevitably) recorded the defeat of Darius at Issus is confirmed by Cicero, *Ad f.* 2.10.3, which is Jacoby Fragment 8 of Cleitarchus.

---

soon covered the country. Yet the Greeks who had stood with Darius with Amyntas as their commander, previously one of Alexander's officers but at that time a defector, being separated from the rest got out without any semblance of a rout.

Figure 4.4. The flight of Darius at Issus (André Castaigne, 1898)

4.25 *With the onset of night* **the remains of the army of the Persians easily managed to disperse in diverse directions.** Some took the direct route to

Persia, whilst others detoured amidst the crags and secluded mountain gorges. A few retreated to the camp of Darius, but now **the victors gave up the pursuit and** also **reached the royal tents looking for loot and found them crammed with every kind of opulence.** The troops made off with an **enormous mass of silver, gold and gorgeous garments, rather the apparatus of decadence than equipment for defence. And** they plundered still more extensively, **not just from the royal treasures, but also comprehensively from the king's relatives, friends and commanders.** The roads were strewn with more beggarly belongings, which their greed had scorned relative to richer pickings.

4.26 *Then they got to the ladies:* **not only the womenfolk of the royal family, but also those of the king's relatives and friends that had accompanied the army, conveyed in gilded waggons in conformance with an ancestral custom of the Persians. And each of them had with her a surfeit of splendiferous furnishings and feminine finery, befitting her fabulous wealth and luxury. The fate of these female captives was completely lamentable. Formerly, they had been loth to be driven even in a sumptuous vehicle reflecting their refinement and no part of their persons had lacked raiment. Now each erupted from her tent clad only in a single garment, a sort of shirt that she rent, wailing and invoking the deities in prostrating herself at her conqueror's knees. Her hands shook as she shed her jewellery and her hair flew as she fled through the rugged territory. Subsequently, these escapees were wont to coalesce, when each sought the aid of those equally in distress. Some of their captors hauled these unfortunate females by their hair, whilst others tore off their finery leaving them quite bare and applied slaps of their hands or thwacks of their spearshafts to drive them here and there.** *And their adornments were prised from them the more forcefully when they prized them the more dearly. Neither were their persons even spared the thrusts of Macedonian lusts, such that the camp resounded with every sort of scream and screech according to the fate of each.* **Thus the victors debauched the most precious and esteemed chattels of the Persians, treating them as Fortune's benefactions.** *The scene was lacking in no form of outrage, since the cruelty and licentiousness of the victors was visited upon persons of every rank and age.* Although **the most moderate of the Macedonians viewed these vicissitudes of Fortune with forbearance and felt pity for those that had been so violently rent from their former existence,** nevertheless, **with the confiscation of the comforts conferred by their exalted station, these women were corralled by the men of a hostile and foreign nation and herded into a hopeless and humiliating subjugation.**

4.27 Then indeed one could discern Fortune's fickle face, since those that adorned Darius's pavilion, lending lush luxury and plush opulence to the place, kept its contents in a comfortable condition now for Alexander, just as for their former master. For these alone the troops left unravished, since it was established by precedent that they should receive the conqueror in the conquered king's tent. But *in particular* the captured mother, wife and children of Darius had captivated the attention and the compassion of everyone. *The mother, not merely due to her majesty but also her maturity, merited veneration and* the wife *on account of her beauty, unmarred by adversity, deserved adoration. She* had enfolded in her embrace a son, who had not yet reached six years of age, *born into the prospect of his father's huge yet lately relinquished heritage. However,* two teenage maidens, her granddaughters, were clasped to the old lady's breast, *being, not merely for their own sake but for hers also, overwhelmingly distressed. His family were unaware of Darius's fate, whether he had survived or had perished in a disaster so great, but they saw their own tent looted by armed combatants, who behaved improperly out of ignorance.* The queens were surrounded by a vast crowd of Asian noblewomen with mangled hair and rent garments, oblivious of their former magnificence. These, falling to the ground implored their assistance, invoking them by royal and rulership titles that no longer had any relevance. The queens were incapable of providing any succour, *but, unmindful of their personal disaster, were demanding to know which wing Darius had fought upon and what exactly was the struggle's outcome? They insisted: "We are not yet captives, if our lord the king still lives!" But* Darius, with many a change of mount, had extended his flight across stades beyond count.

4.28 *Hence the* Royal Pages *now secured the tent of Darius and prepared a bath and Alexander's dinner. Then they awaited his return from the pursuit and by lighting torches they created a great glimmer, so that he should discover Darius's entire paraphernalia made ready for him as a harbinger of his conquest of the whole of Asia.*

4.29 In the course of that battle there were *neutralised or* slain more than one hundred thousand Persian infantry and not less than ten thousand cavalry *of whom forty thousand were taken into captivity.*[41] But on Alexander's side some four thousand five hundred men suffered injury and just three hundred foot were lost together with one hundred and fifty cavalry, so slight was the cost of so vast a victory.

4.30 *On determining the decisiveness of his defeat Darius dedicated himself to his deliverance, mounting steed after steed to speed his disappearance, desperate to evade Alexander's custody by reaching the Upper Satrapies and a degree of safety.* Alexander *pursued him avidly with the Companion Cavalry and the best of the rest of his horsemen,*

---

[41] The Persian losses and casualties are agreed by Curtius 3.11.27, Diodorus 17.36.5, Plutarch 20.5, Arrian 2.11.8 and Justin 11.9.10.

only too keen to get his quarry into his possession, though he had a headstart of four or five stades. *So* he chased Darius in his flight *for two hundred stades* until both hope and the light began to fade, whereupon he turned back fatigued from tracking the renegade and returned to the camp *at about midnight* with nothing to show but Darius's chariot and his bow as trophies of the fight.[42] *Having washed off his weariness by bathing,* he bade that his closest Friends be invited to join him for dining, for a mere graze received upon his thigh was not going to deny him his revelling. But **the diners were dismayed by a sudden doleful din issuing from the neighbouring pavilion** and the detachment that was on watch at the king's tent armed themselves, fearing lest it mark the instigation of a more considerable commotion. **The cause of this unexpected fuss was that the mother and the wife of Darius together with their noblewomen were bewailing the supposed death of their king with much moaning and groaning. For one of the eunuchs** amongst these captives, who had chanced to stand outside their tent, had recognised Darius's mantle, which, as already noted, he had cast off the better to thwart his betrayal. It had been in the hands of him who had brought it back upon its discovery. But reckoning that it had been wrenched from the king's corpse, the eunuch **delivered a false report of Darius's expiry,** *claiming that Alexander had returned from the chase after having stripped his body.*

4.31 On becoming aware of the women's error Alexander is said to have shed a tear for the downfall of Darius and the devotion of his kindred. *And initially he bade Mithrenes, who had surrendered Sardis and was fluent in the Persian language, to go give them solace. But then, fearing lest a visit from a turncoat should cause the captives to recapitulate their consternation and disconsolation,* he sent Leonnatus, one of his leading lords, bidding him mention their mistake in making a living man the object of their mourning and lamentation. *Leonnatus entered their pavilion with a handful of guardsmen and bade it be announced that he had been sent by his sovereign. But, when they espied the soldiers' arms, those that were in the foyer, reckoning that their mistresses were done for, scurried inside shrieking that they had lived their last day, killers of captives having arrived before their door. Hence, since they neither dared to let them in nor could keep them at bay, they silently awaited the victor's verdict and made no foray.*

4.32 *Having waited a while for someone to invite him in, Leonnatus left his escort in the foyer when nobody dared to meet him and went on in anyway. This act in itself upset the women, since he seemed not so much to have been admitted as to have forced his way in. Therefore the queenmother, Sisygambis, and the consort prostrated themselves at his feet and began to plead that, before they themselves were liquidated, they should be allowed to bury the body of Darius as the customs of his*

---

[42] See Plutarch, *Alexander* 20.5-6 for Darius's headstart and Alexander's trophies.

country dictated. Having performed the last rites for their king, they would cease to shirk their own killing. Leonnatus revealed that Darius still lived and that they themselves would not only enjoy immunity but would retain all the trappings of their original queenly dignity. *In the morning Alexander himself would come round. Then the mother of Darius at last allowed herself to be raised up from the ground. And in the light of Leonnatus's welcome revelation, the women ceased their lamentation and lauded Alexander as deserving of veneration.*

4.33 *At dawn* **the next day,** after having carefully conducted the burial of all the bodies he could discover of the Macedonians, Alexander bade that the same respect also be accorded to the corpses of the most distinguished Persians and he mandated the mother of Darius to bury those she wished according to the customs of their country. She confined herself to ordering the inhumation of a few of her close kin and those in a fashion befitting their current situation, judging that the magnificence of the funeral celebrations with which the Persians perform the last rites would be distasteful when the victors were receiving cheap cremations. Thereupon, having dealt properly with the remains of the dead, **Alexander** sent a herald ahead to the captives announcing his own approach and, curtailing the encroachment of his swarming coterie, he **entered their tent with solely Hephaistion in his company.** This man was by far the dearest to the king of all his associates having been brought up alongside him and having shared in all of his secrets. He also enjoyed the unique privilege of being allowed to admonish Alexander, but he exercised this freedom in such a manner that it appeared rather to have been authorised by his sovereign than appropriated by Hephaistion. And, *although he was the same age,* he outstripped his ruler in *handsomeness and* physical stature *and the dress of each was similar.* Hence the queens supposed him to be the king and accordingly commenced their customary reverencing of him. Whereupon some of the eunuchs that had been taken prisoner gesticulated to show which was Alexander, so that Sisygambis fell at his feet *excusing her ignorance due to never before having seen the king. But, taking her hand to raise her,* this was the response of the ruler: "Mother, you did not err, for he too is Alexander." *By using a title to address her that was most familiar, he meant to proffer the promise of preferential treatment in the future to those who had been distraught a little earlier.*

Figure 4.5. Alexander and Hephaistion visit the Persian Royal Family (Charles Le Brun)

4.34 *Indeed, had he continued up to the end of his days to behave so chivalrously, I consider that he would have been more triumphant than he actually appeared to be, when he was emulating Dionysus's pageantry in processing victoriously from the Hellespont to the outer Ocean successively through every country. Then he would have suppressed his arrogance and fury, faults he never overcame fully. Then he would have refrained from slaying his friends at his suppers and would have dreaded to execute without trial distinguished officers, his close companions in the conquest of so many nations. But Fortune had not yet overinflated his ego. For he that bore her breath so temperately and moderately at its onset proved unable to cope when she really began to blow. But at that time at any rate he behaved in such ways that he surpassed in both propriety and clemency all the kings of former days.* He treated the remarkably lovely royal virgins as just as inviolate as if they had sprung from the same parents as he. And **the wife** as well, whom no other lady at that time excelled in beauty, **he was so far from subjecting to lechery that he took special care to prevent anyone from debauching her body whilst he held her in his custody. He commanded that all her accoutrements be returned to each lady, including her servants and her jewellery *and he added many another lackey so as virtually to double the entirety. He promised to each of the daughters a dowry that exceeded that due from Darius in its bounty and he undertook to raise the boy with the dignity due to a son of his own, retaining his royalty.***

Figure 4.6. The Persian Queens greet Alexander and Hephaistion (André Castaigne, 1898)

4.35 Sisygambis responded tearfully: "O Sire, you deserve that we should pray for you as we prayed for Darius, our own sovereign, formerly and I see this as befitting a king who has surpassed him, not merely in prosperity, but also in equity. Indeed you call me 'mother' and 'queen', but personally I avow myself to be your humble servant. I both retain the exalted status of my former existence and am able to cope with the constraints of the present. It is for you to decide to what extent your authority over us is to be characterised by clemency rather than by cruelty." *As many of the women were shedding a tear,* **Alexander bade them all be of good cheer and called upon the young boy to come near.** *Then the son of Darius wrapped his arms around the king's neck in an embrace, fearless of the unfamiliar face, when Alexander lifted the child up to his shoulder.* **Being touched by the six year old's composure, the king kissed him and caught the glance of Hephaistion: "How I wish that Darius had inherited something of the same disposition!"** *And with that they quit the pavilion.*

4.36 Alexander consecrated three altars on a bank of the River Pinarus to Zeus, Heracles and Athena, then he headed for Syria. Parmenion was sent ahead *with the Thessalian cavalry* to Damascus, where lay the treasure of Darius. However he learnt that he had been preceded by a satrap of the Persian king and was concerned lest the contempt of his opponents were invited by the scantiness of his following, so he sought to fetch reinforcements. But by chance the scouts that had been sent forward by Parmenion came across a man from the Mardian nation, who, on being led before the commander, handed him a letter sent by the governor of Damascus to Alexander. He added that he was in no doubt that the governor would surrender all the royal chattels as well as the treasure. After ordering that they should guard the Mardian, Parmenion opened the letter, in which it was written that Alexander should promptly send one of his commanders with a few men in order to possess himself of that which Darius had deposited at Damascus. Accordingly, in order to return the Mardian to the defector he despatched an escort of wardens, but the man entered Damascus before daybreak having slipped from the grasp of these custodians.

4.37 This behaviour disturbed Parmenion, who feared treachery. Hence he did not venture whilst lacking guidance to pursue an unfamiliar itinerary. Nevertheless, trusting in the good fortune of his king, he ordered that some peasants should be seized to serve as guides for their journey. These being quickly acquired, he reached the city in three days, where the governor had already been fearing for their faith in his fidelity. Therefore he feigned but feeble faith in the fortress's fortifications in ordering that his monarch's funds, which the Persians term 'gaza', together with his most precious possessions should be carried forth as if he meant to flee, whilst actually intending to present it as a prize for the enemy. Many thousands of men and women followed him as he left the city, a throng that stirred the pity of everybody, save him to whose trust they had been committed. For so as to profit more from his perfidy, he was prepared to cast before their adversary a prize preferable to any amount of money: namely the nobles and the wives and children of Darius's aristocracy, and the envoys from the Greek cities as well, whom Darius had left in the hands of the defector as though in his most secure citadel.

4.38 'Gangabae' is the Persian term for bearers who carry burdens upon their shoulders. When they could not bear the rigours of the journey, since a storm had brought a sudden fall of snow and the ground was rigid with frigidity, these bearers decked themselves in robes adorned with purple and gold embroidery that they had been carrying in addition to the money. And none ventured to forbid them, for Darius's difficulties gave free rein even to the humblest of men. Hence they presented Parmenion with the appearance of a military column of significant importance. Therefore with due diligence as if for a proper engagement he curtly exhorted his forces to set spur to their steeds and swiftly to charge upon the enemy. But those laden with baggage let it fall and took to their heels as terror seized them one and all. The armed guards escorting them were likewise stricken by consternation and they threw away their arms in resorting to recognisable routes for evasion. The governor, by acting as though he too were terror-stricken, ensured that complete panic set in. All the royal riches were strewn across the entire plain: the monies meant for the pay of vast levies; the regalia of numerous noblemen and the adornments of so many illustrious ladies; golden vessels and golden bridles; pavilions appointed with regal magnificence as well as many a conveyance, abandoned by its occupants, but still filled with immense opulence; presenting even looters with a pitiful appearance, if such sentiments could hold greed in abeyance. For from an array of riches reaching beyond belief and built up by so many years of toil some items were now seen to be rent by briars whilst others were trodden into the soil, as the hands of the pillagers were inadequate to the scale of their spoil.

4.39 And then they came upon those who had been first to flee. Numerous women were dragging their tiny offspring along *in the emergency*. Among them were the three virgin daughters of Ochus, who prior to Darius had held the sovereignty. A revolution had formerly reduced them from the royalty of their father's estate, but on this occasion Fortune exacerbated their fate even more cruelly. There were also in the same huddle the wife of the aforementioned Ochus and the daughter of Oxathres, brother to Darius, plus the wife of Artabazus, his foremost noble, and his son, who was named Ilioneos.[43] In addition, they captured the wife together with the son of Pharnabazus, who had been designated commander of the entire coastline by Darius, as well as the three daughters of Mentor and the widow and son of Memnon, that most illustrious leader. Scarcely any noble house evaded this vast disaster.

4.40 But Alexander, reckoning self-restraint to be kinglier conduct than the ravishing of his enemies' women, neither violated these ladies nor any others before marriage with the exception of Barsine, the widow of Memnon. Since she had received a Greek education and was of a personable disposition and because Artabazus, her father, was the son of a king's daughter,[44] Alexander decided at the instigation of Parmenion, *as is stated by Aristobulus in his history*, to associate with a lady of such great beauty and distinguished ancestry. *The king eventually came to love his prisoner and later had a son whom he named Heracles by her*.

4.41 Also taken at this time were those Spartans and Athenians, who had violated their oath of alliance with Alexander by following the Persians. By far the most distinguished among the Athenians both by their birth and by their renown were Aristogeiton, Dropides and Iphicrates. Likewise men of distinction at home among their fellow Spartans were Pasippus and Onomastorides together with Onomas and Callicratides. The sum of struck coinage captured was two thousand six hundred talents[45] and the weight of wrought silver amounted to five hundred talents. Furthermore, thirty thousand men together with seven thousand beasts of burden bearing goods upon their backs were taken. But divine vengeance rapidly wreaked due punishment upon the betrayer of such a tremendous treasure. For one of his henchmen slew the traitor and bore his head before his king, I suppose even in adversity deeming Darius worthy of reverencing. And this was an opportune solace for having been betrayed, since he was both avenged upon a renegade and he perceived that not everybody felt that his royal authority had begun to fade.

---

[43] Probably named after Troy (Ilion), reflecting the Phrygian satrapy of Artabazus.

[44] His father was Pharnabazus, who had married Apame, the daughter of Artaxerxes II, some time between 392-387BC.

[45] A talent was 6000 drachmae (normally) of silver – a weight of about 25 kilogams.

4.42 Though but lately the monarch of such an enormous army, which he had led into battle whilst raised up in his chariot as if celebrating a victory rather than contesting a tussle, Darius was now in flight through vast and virtually desolate regions, places he had previously all but filled with his immense formations. Just a few men accompanied the king, for not all had escaped in the same direction and those with him found their steeds failing, since they could not match their monarch's regular mount rotation. He first reached Onchae, where four thousand Greeks still greeted him as sovereign; *then Darius raced on towards Babylon via the Euphrates*, since it seemed to him that he would control only that which he managed rapidly to seize. And *upon reaching Babylon, Darius rallied the survivors from the Battle of Issus. His defiance was still fierce, despite the wretched reverse, but he wrote to Alexander offering a fabulous fee for the return of his wife and family.*[46]

4.43 Meanwhile Alexander now gave the governorship of the part of Syria called 'Hollow'[47] to Parmenion, by whom the treasures had been recovered at Damascus, bidding him to look after both the booty itself and the captives with careful attention. The Syrians, not yet having been sufficiently intimidated by their calamities in the conflict, rejected the new regime, but they were quickly subjugated and obediently did as they were directed. Then too the island of Aradus capitulated. Straton, who was then ruling this island, also controlled the coastline and many areas stretching far inland. After accepting his fealty Alexander moved his camp to Marathus, a *nearby coastal* city.[48] There *the letter from Darius reached the king*, who was greatly offended by its arrogant wording. It annoyed him especially that *Darius* had described himself as His Majesty but had not seen fit to favour Alexander with the same dignity. Furthermore, he *had specified* rather than petitioned *that, upon accepting enough money to purchase Macedon in its entirety, Alexander should return his mother, wife and children* immediately. Then, if he wished, Alexander might fairly seek to fight for the supremacy. If, finally, he could consider counsel that was more cautionary, he would be satisfied with his own country: he would withdraw from the bounds of another's sovereignty and

---

[46] Diodorus 17.39 goes on to describe details from the second letter of Darius to Alexander, which Curtius 4.5.1-8 places after the siege of Tyre and which Diodorus then omits. Curtius 4.1.7-14 cites the ransom and a return of Alexander to Macedonia for the first letter. Since Justin 11.12.1-5 broadly confirms Curtius's version, it appears that Diodorus has become confused between the two separate letters. This is probably also what led him to suggest that Alexander presented a forged version of the first letter to his council – a story of which there is no hint elsewhere. This is further supported by Diodorus 17.39.3-4 giving an account of Darius's renewed preparations for war, which matches details given by Curtius 4.6.1-2 just before the siege of Gaza and Curtius 4.9.1-5 after Alexander's return from Egypt. I am inclined to acquit Cleitarchus of the confusion arising in Diodorus 17.39 on the combined evidence of Curtius and Justin, who were assuredly also following the Alexandrian on the matter of the letters.

[47] Coele Syria, comprising the broad valley between the ranges of Mount Lebanon (Libanus and Antilibanus).

[48] Marathus faced the island of Aradus.

---

would be his ally in all amity. Darius stood ready both to swear to such terms and to accept Alexander's pledge in reciprocity.

4.44 Alexander's riposte was written much in this fashion: "Salutations to Darius from His Majesty King Alexander. That *former* Darius, whose name you have assumed, visited complete disaster upon the Greeks holding the Hellespontine shore and upon the Greek colonies of Ionia furthermore. Thereafter he traversed the seas with vast armies, so as to wage war upon Macedonia and the Greek cities. Then afterwards we were again assaulted by Xerxes from the same race, who brought a monstrous horde of barbarians for us to face. Though vanquished in a naval engagement, he nevertheless left Mardonius on Greek soil, so that even whilst absent he might fire our fields and despoil each associated settlement. And regarding Philip, my father, as is well known by everybody, he was slain by people whom your people had bribed with the prospect of a phenomenal fee. Your warfare is without chivalry, for, though you do not want for weaponry, you seek to purchase the life of every adversary, as when you wished recently to hire an assassin to do away with me for a thousand talents, despite your sovereignty over such an enormous army.[49] Thus I am the defender in this war, rather than the aggressor. And the gods back the better cause withal. I have put the better part of Asia in my power and I have bested you yourself in battle. Insofar as you have not even fought fairly in our warfare, I am under no obligation to offer you any salvation. Nevertheless, if you come to me in supplication, I promise that your mother, wife and children shall be returned to you without ransom. For I know both how to conquer and how to conciliate those that I have overcome. Yet if you fear to place yourself at my mercy, I will pledge my word that you may come before me in perfect safety. Finally, whenever in future you write to me, remember not only to do so as to a king, but also as to your own sovereign." He made Thersippus his emissary for this letter's delivery.

4.45 Alexander marched down into Phoenicia and received the surrender of its people,[50] starting with Byblos, a fortified citadel. From there **he reached Sidon**, a city celebrated for the fame of its founders and for its antiquity. **There Straton held the monarchy with the backing of Darius's authority. But because he had tendered his fealty under pressure from the populace rather than voluntarily, he was deemed unsuitable to continue in the sovereignty and Hephaistion was delegated to determine who among the Sidonians was most worthy of supremacy.**[51] **Just then Hephaistion was**

---

[49] The allusion is to the accusation by Parmenion that Darius had promised Philip the Doctor a thousand talents to arrange Alexander's death, cf. Curtius 3.6.4.

[50] Curtius 4.1.15 & Diodorus 17.40.2.

[51] Diodorus 17.47 recounts this story after the siege of Tyre after noting that the rulership of Tyre was given to Abdalonymus after its fall. I infer that Diodorus was prompted to tell the story retrospectively by the award of the territory of Tyre and that Diodorus himself told the story correctly of Sidon, but that an editor subsequently incorrectly corrected the name of the city to

the guest of two **young men, who were eminent among their countrymen, so initially he thought of them.** But when they were offered the chance to **reign, they declined on account of the custom of their country that, unless they were of the royal strain, no one was admitted to that exalted dignity. Hephaistion** admired the magnanimity with which they spurned that which others sought with swords and for which they burned, so he **responded:** "My congratulations to you on having been the first to fathom how much more magnificent it is to refuse rulership than to accept it. But **please therefore propose somebody of royal genealogy,** who will remember that he owes to you his sovereignty."

4.46 They perceived that many, fixated by so great an opportunity, were flattering the particular friends of Alexander in coveting the monarchy. However, **they noted that none was more satisfactory than a certain Abdalonymus, who definitely had a distant connection with the royal tree, but was** *employed in* **cultivating a market garden** near the edge of the city, **making a meagre living on account of his poverty.** As is often the case, **the cause of his penury was his** *innate niceness and* **honesty** and intent as he was on his day-to-day activities he had hardly heard of the clash of arms that had reverberated throughout all Asia's territories. *When Hephaistion agreed to his enthronement,* **the aforementioned dignitaries abruptly entered the garden with the official royal raiment, whilst,** as it happened, **Abdalonymus was watering** *and weeding* **the allotment.**[52] **Thereupon, after they had saluted him as their sovereign, one of them announced: "You need to exchange the ragged garments you are wearing for the regalia that you see me holding.** Cleanse your person of its perpetual caking of mud and dust. **Adopt the demeanour of a monarch** and bring your characteristic moderation to the office, for which it is fitting and just. And when you sit upon the throne, directing the lives and the deaths of the citizens of your country, be careful not to forget the poverty, in which – no, because of which, by Heracles – **you are receiving the sovereignty."** To **Abdalonymus** it all seemed like a reverie. Occasionally, he queried as to whether those that were sporting with him so outrageously had taken leave of their sanity? But the dirt was washed off him whilst he wavered in dubiety and he **was wrapped in the robe** *emblazoned with gold and purple* as the emissaries swore their fidelity. *Then he was conducted through the marketplace in the same people's company, whilst they proclaimed his sovereignty,* so that he arrived at the palace as a king in actuality.

4.47 Readily thereafter, as is its tendency, rumour raced through the entire city. **Many showed enthusiasm** *and marvelled at Fortune's variability,* but

---

Tyre, because the earlier omission of the matter made it seem that all Abdalonymus's territory should be at Tyre.

[52] Curtius has Abdalonymus drawing out weeds, but Diodorus, Justin and Plutarch in his *Moralia* all agree that he was drawing water, so perhaps Curtius misunderstood his source.

others exhibited animosity. The wealthiest citizens complained to Alexander's friends concerning the new king's penury and servility. Alexander ordered that he should appear before him immediately, and after looking at him lengthily, he declared: "The nature of your origins is not belied by your outward appearance, but it is nice that you have borne privation with resilience." And Abdalonymus responded: "I hope that I shall be able to suffer sovereignty with the same equanimity. These hands of mine supplied what I sought. I owned nothing, but lacked for naught." From Abdalonymus's conversation **Alexander** gained an impression of a noble disposition. Consequently, he **bade that** not only **the regal appurtenances of Straton**, but also many items from the Persian treasure **be given into his possession.** In addition a region bordering upon the city was placed under his dominion **and the king invested him as a royal companion. Thus his career provides an object lesson in the forcefulness of Fortune's intercession.**

4.48 So now all Syria was under Macedonian control and **Alexander marched on through Phoenicia, where, with the sole exception of Tyre, the cities submitted voluntarily.** Alexander encamped on the mainland from which this city was separated by a narrow channel of the sea. Tyre outstrips all the other cities of Syria and Phoenicia in both size and renown and it seemed simpler to enter into an alliance with Alexander rather than submit to his rule in this town. Therefore **her envoys presented the king with the gift of a golden crown** and out of hospitality they sent him as well a profusion of provisions from their citadel. **Alexander** bade that these presents be received as signalling amity and he **addressed the envoys** kindly, **saying that he would appreciate the opportunity to sacrifice to Heracles**, whom the Tyrians reverenced particularly.[53] He noted: "The Macedonian monarchy believes that this deity was the ancestor of our dynasty and additionally an oracle has alerted me that I should perform such a sacrifice actually." **The envoys replied that there was a temple of Heracles outside their main city in their settlement at Old Tyre,** *where he could perform the rite propitiously* and in a temple of greater antiquity. Alexander *had a tendency to lose his temper, so he* did not conceal his anger, but retorted: *"In essence you are placing your faith in your locality. As inhabitants of an island, you scorn this land army. But I shall shortly show that you are joined to this landmass integrally and* I would have you know that I shall either be permitted to make an entry or I shall storm my way into your city."

4.49 On being sent back with this response, the envoys commenced cautioning their countrymen that a king whom Syria and Phoenicia had admitted ought also to be allowed entry by them. **But the Tyrians confronted the threat of a siege with alacrity.** *They wished to ingratiate themselves with Darius by maintaining an untarnished loyalty and they supposed that he would*

---

[53] This was Melkart, the tutelary god of Tyre, whom the Greeks identified with Heracles by virtue of syncretism.

---

reward with great generosity those that accorded him such fidelity. They would divert Alexander into a tedious and arduous campaign, buying Darius time to prepare to fight back again. For the Tyrians had sufficient confidence in the defensibility of their island emplacement *and its fighting complement* as to decide that they would withstand an investment.

4.50 For **four stades separate the mainland from the city** across a choppy strait, which is particularly exposed to the African breeze that repeatedly rolls breakers inshore off the high seas. And nothing presented a hindrance more than this wind to the operations by means of which the connection of the island to the shore was being planned by the Macedonians. It is hard to lay down a mole even in calm and tranquil marine conditions, but in practice from its onset through the thrashing delivered by its dashing sea the African wind demolishes any agglomerations. No mole can be made so firm that the swell does not erode its foundations, either by seeping through the structure's concretions or else cascading over the crest of the construction in rougher wind conditions. In addition to this difficulty, there was another of like severity. The walls and towers of the city were surrounded by particularly deep stretches of the sea. They could not fire artillery, except from ships well out to sea. And approaching to set up scaling ladders was denied to infantry, since the ramparts dropped sheerly beneath the briny. In fact **Alexander** lacked a navy, but he **saw that even if he could have sailed against the city**, drifting and unsteady, **he could have been kept off by the artillery on the parapets** *and by the fleet of the enemy.*

4.51 Meanwhile a thing inspired confidence in the Tyrians that sounds trivial. In accordance with their country's customs commissaries had come from the Carthaginians to celebrate an annual holy festival. For Carthage had been founded by the Tyrians, so the concern of the colonists for their ancestral abode was perpetual. Consequently, they commenced encouraging the Tyrians to brave the siege with tenacity, since reinforcements from Carthage would soon reach their city. For *at that time,* the seas were infested with Punic fleets quite extensively, so **the Tyrians had high hopes for support from their Carthaginian colony.** *Their resolve was bolstered by Dido's story, for she had founded Carthage then carried on with the conquest of a third of the world's territory. They thought it would smack of ignominy, if their ladies should be deemed to have shown more bravery in the colonisation of a new country than they themselves displayed in defence of their liberty.*[54] Accordingly, **they** opted for war and **deployed artillery upon their parapets and turrets.** They issued weaponry to men in possession of their fighting faculties **and assigned artisans, in whom the city abounded, to their arms factories.** The whole city resounded with the din of preparations for hostilities.

---

[54] This mention of Dido's foundation of Carthage taken from Justin 11.10.13 may superficially seem Roman in character, but modern scholarship traces the story of Dido back to Timaeus of Tauromenium, who appears to have been one of Cleitarchus's sources.

Grappling irons too, which are called 'harpagones', they readied to fling upon the operations of their enemies, together with 'crows' and other contrivances for the defence of cities. They contrived all kinds of contraptions, so that inventive weapons were mounted around the entire circuit of their fortifications, especially on the side facing the Macedonian operations.

4.52 However, when iron was introduced into the furnaces as required for forging and bellows fanned the fires to blazing, it is said that beneath the flames rivulets of blood began to appear, which the Tyrians took as a sign that the Macedonians had much to fear. **Among the Macedonians** likewise, **when some soldiers happened to be breaking up loaves of bread, they reported that it shed drops of blood before their eyes.** *The king being perturbed, the most insightful of the seers, Aristander, pronounced that had the crust of the loaves bled, it would have augured Macedonian disaster, but since the blood seeped internally, it foretold, on the contrary, the destined fall of the besieged city.* Both because his naval fleets were *as yet* distant and on account of the impediment that appeared to be posed to the rest of his agenda by a protracted investment, Alexander sent heralds to urge peace upon the Tyrians. But in violation of international conventions they were killed and cast into the deep by the city's denizens. *Being* consequently incensed by the undeserved deaths of his emissaries already and *determined that the Macedonian army should not tolerate the insolence of a solitary undistinguished community,* Alexander resolved to besiege the city *with dauntless daring and unremitting energy.*

4.53 However, they had to pave their way by laying down a mole to connect the mainland to the city. Hence the morale of the troops was immensely undermined when they appreciated the profundity of the stretch of sea, which could hardly be filled even with the intercession of deities. What boulders big enough could be found? Where would they obtain tall enough trees? In order to muster the material for such a massive mound, it would be necessary to strip bare entire territories. Additionally, the strait was strewn with surf and the more constrictedly it swirled between the island and the promontory, the fiercer grew its ferocity. But Alexander, who was no novice at manipulating the minds of military guys, declared that as he slept a vision of Heracles holding out his right hand had seemed to materialize. With Heracles opening his path and acting as his guide, he made to enter the city and dreamt himself inside. Besides this he also made mention of the Tyrian execution of his heralds in violation of international convention. And in addition he noted that this was the sole city to have had the temerity to interrupt the progression of their victory. Then to each commander the task of reproaching his men was delegated and the project got underway, when everyone had been sufficiently motivated.

4.54 At the outset Alexander demolished Old Tyre *on the mainland,* **so that a** **great stock of rock was at hand and he engaged many myriads[55] of men** **upon the labour of shifting stones to make a mole two plethra[56] wide from** **one side to the other.** From Mount Libanus he transported timber for raft and tower construction. *From the neighbouring cities he enlisted the* *endeavours of the entire population, thus realising a rapid progression of* *the operation, since his workers were legion.* And the structure had not yet risen above the swells, but had already reached a reasonable height above the bed of the sea, when **the Tyrians sailed up** *in cockleshells* **to assail the** **Macedonians with mockery.** *They marvelled that these warriors of* *dauntless reputation were bearing packs upon their backs like a bunch of* *beasts of burden and* **they wondered whether Alexander would win his** **contest with Poseidon?** But their taunts simply served to accentuate the soldiers' enthusiasm. Already the mole was gradually emerging above the surface of the sea and simultaneously it grew broader and crept towards the city.

4.55 At this point, though its accretion had barely been perceptible previously, **the Tyrians** *were perturbed on perceiving the mole's enormity and* **began** **to sail around the structure,** *still surrounded by sea,* **in many craft of** **shallow draught and additionally to shower missiles upon those at work** **in its lee** *with archers and slingers backed by ballista and catapult* *artillery. Therefore* **many Macedonians were injured or killed with** **impunity,** *since the skiffs could either be engaged or withdrawn quite* *readily. Missiles of every variety rained down upon throngs of the* *unarmoured, such that no assailant missed his quarry, since their targets* *were unprotected and unprepared. For it was not just from the front that* *missiles would appear, but additionally from the rear, since the builders* *were spread across a pier not so very wide and none could manage to* *dodge a spear cast from either side.*

4.56 *Alexander responded rapidly to recover from the risk of a harrowing* *rout. He manned all his vessels and personally led them out, heading* *with all haste for the Tyrian harbours to block the retreat of the* *Phoenician aggressors. They reacted nervously, rowing back to Tyre as* *fast as they might, lest he seize their city, whilst it was depleted of those* *able to fight. Both fleets beat their oars to a rapid tempo, focussing* *furious effort upon the row, and, although the Macedonians were* *encroaching at speed, the Tyrians reached the harbourmouth with a* *slight lead, so they pushed on in to elude destruction, only losing the tail* *of their formation, so that Alexander was thwarted in this action.*

4.57 *The king pressed on with the mole construction, but the* *Macedonians were diverted from the building operations into the*

---

[55] A *myriad* is literally 10,000 in Greek and is the word used by Diodorus 17.40.5.

[56] A *plethron* is one hundred feet.

---

protection of their own persons. Furthermore, the further from the shore that the mole was projected, the more the deeps swallowed up whatever was injected. Hence the king bade that awnings of hide and canvas be erected, such that his workmen were more adequately protected and he deployed a dense screen of ships upon the sea, so that his men might labour in more safety. Additionally, on the crest of the mound he erected two towers, from which projectiles could be cast upon approaching craft in vast showers. In response the Tyrians directed their vessels to a section of the coast beyond their opponent's view and butchered those who were fetching rubble by landing a fighting crew. On Mount Libanus too the Arabian peasantry fell upon the Macedonians when they found them disorderly. They slew about thirty and took rather fewer into captivity.

Figure 4.7. A raid upon the mole at Tyre (Roberts, mid-19th century)

4.58 These matters caused Alexander to split his army and, so as not to seem laggardly by besieging a single city, he left Perdiccas and Craterus in charge of that activity and himself headed for Arabia with a task force equipped lightly for mobility. Meanwhile the Tyrians used sand and stones to weigh down the stern of a vessel of exceptional size such that its prow was prominently forced to rise. They bedaubed it with bitumen and sulphur and got it underway by means of oars. Then with massive momentum it mounted the causeway, when its sails too had caught the wind's full force. And upon torching its prow, its rowers leapt into skiffs just behind, which had trailed the ship's course with this mission in mind. But the blaze engulfing the galleon instigated a spreading conflagration, which, before any possibility of prevention, enveloped the towers and other gear that had been placed at the head of the pier. Then those that had leapt into the little boats flung torches and tinder to feed the flames around every structure. At this juncture not only had fire engulfed the tower gantries but even the platforms at their extremities, whereupon those located in the towers were either incinerated or, casting off their panoplies, they plunged into the seas. However, choosing rather to capture than slay the swimmers, the Tyrians wielded staves and stones to mangle their fists, until they had been incapacitated and could be taken aboard without posing any risks.

4.59 Nor was it fire in isolation that wrecked Alexander's operation, but **it happened that** on that same day **a vigorous north-westerly gale dashed the whole depth of the sea against the mole.** *The structure split open at its seams under the recurrent concussion, so that the waters surged through, rupturing the core of the construction. Consequently, the stacks of stone that held up the heaped earth were demolished rapidly, so that* **a large part of the causeway collapsed into the depths of the sea.** When Alexander returned from Arabia presently, there were scarcely any traces of the massive mound still remaining to be found.

4.60 In these circumstances, as occurs commonly when things go badly, each of them said that the others were blameworthy; although each might more reasonably have rued the savagery of the sea. *Despairing of salvaging a structure stricken by Nature's ire, Alexander considered abandoning the siege of Tyre, but* **driven by relentless ambition the king renewed his engineering operation.** He arranged for the front of the mole rather than its flank to face into the wind on this occasion, affording the rest of the works some protection, since they were as it were shielded behind this salient of the construction. He also extended the width of the causeway in order that towers erected in a central reservation should be out of range of ammunition.

4.61 Furthermore, **Alexander sent men up the mountain to fell huge trees and to haul them back to base with their branches still in place. These he flung into the deep seas around the mound and piled up stones to pin them down. Then he resumed planting more trees upon such rockeries, before heaping earth upon the bases formed by these. So, by successively interspersing rocks and whole trees, it was as though he had knitted together the entire mole with stone and wood, such that the violence of the waves could now be withstood.**

4.62 Nor were the Tyrians tardy in trying any trick that could be contrived to stop the mole making headway. Distinguished service was done by those that dived beneath the sea beyond visual range of the enemy and slipped unseen to reach the causeway. They placed hooks around protruding boughs to drag upon a tree and, when one came free, it carried much material with it into the depths of the sea. Thus relieved of their ballast, tree trunks and logs were extricated without complications, until the entire structure supported upon them copied the collapse of its foundations.

4.63 The king was dispirited, so whether he would withdraw from the siege or press on was as yet uncertain, whereupon a fleet arrived from Cyprus and on the same occasion Cleander came with Greek troops new to the Asian invasion. The ships, numbering one hundred and ninety vessels, were divided into two wings by Alexander: the left was left in the charge of Pnytagoras, sovereign of Cyprus, with Craterus as joint-commander, whilst on the right a quinquereme served as the flagship of Alexander. Despite themselves possessing a significant navy, **the Tyrians were not prepared to risk engaging in a battle at sea. They deployed a total of three vessels just beyond their harbour's battlements and the king himself rammed and sank these opponents,** *before returning to his encampments.*

4.64 The next day, sailing his fleet right up to the fortifications, Alexander shattered the walls at all locations mainly by means of battering ram concussions. The breaches were rapidly repaired with rocks by **the Tyrians**, who also **initiated the construction of inner fortifications** *five cubits inside the outer* for their **preservation should the outer fail in further aggressions.** *This inner wall was ten cubits from face to face and they used earth and rubble to fill the intervening space.* But everywhere they were goaded by the threat of disaster. For, *a very short time after,* the mole had been *rebuilt by Alexander and by relentless labour he had* advanced *it* to within a spear cast of the ramparts of his enemy. *Then he moved up his artillery to the end of the promontory and caused his catapults to pelt the masonry, whilst his ballistas beset the men upon the parapet. And additionally, fusilades from his archers and slingers injured many who came in a hurry to man the walls of their city. While this assault was underway from the causeway,* the king *sailed his whole fleet around the city on a survey, meaning to display his intent shortly to* beset the Tyrians simultaneously by land and by sea.

4.65 The Macedonians lashed pairs of quadriremes[57] together *so that their prows were in contiguity, but their sterns were as far apart as could be. This gap at the rear was bridged with sail-yards and stout poles tied together tautly. Upon these they laid decking to support the military together with* their siege engines and artillery. *Thus configured* they rowed these quadriremes up to the city, where their projectiles were discharged upon the enemy *in safety, since their towering prows protected the soldiery. Hence Alexander toppled a plethron's breadth[58] of the fortifications and into this breach burst the Macedonians, but they were showered with missiles by the Tyrians, who managed to put them to flight and afterwards repaired the breach under the cover of night.*

---

[57] Galleys with 2 banks of oars on each side with 2 rowers per oar (Diodorus 17.43.4 has triremes, but Curtius 4.3.14 has the more detailed account with the larger and more unusual type of galley specified more than once). Quinqueremes probably had 3 banks of oars with 2+2+1=5 rowers.

[58] A plethron is 100 feet.

4.66 With their siege engines and artillery readied for a fight, Alexander instructed his fleet to surround the walls of Tyre in the middle of the night. The ships were already moving in on the city everywhere and the Tyrians were paralysed with despair, when thick cloud speedily spread in obscuring the sky and whatever light had filtered forth from the heavens began to die. Then the sea gradually grew increasingly choppy, until the gathering gale whipped up swells that caused collisions between the vessels. At that point the lashings that linked the quadriremes began to be rent asunder and the decking disintegrated, dragging the troops down under into the deep with a tremendous thunder. It was indeed hopeless to try to handle the coupled ships in such turbulence. The troops obstructed the labours of the sailors; the rowers disrupted the routine of the soldiers and competence deferred to ignorance, as so often happens in such an instance. For the helmsmen, used usually to giving direction, did then as they were bidden for fear of extinction. Finally, by thrashing the oars more vigorously, it was as if the sailors wrenched their ships from the clutches of the sea and beached them upon the shore with many having suffered some injury.

Figure 4.8. Alexander directs an assault upon Tyre (Antonio Tempesta, 1608)

4.67 It happened that those same days saw the arrival of thirty Carthaginian emissaries, not so much a help to the besieged as a solace for their miseries. For they announced that Carthage was encumbered by a conflict around the home city, fought rather for survival than for supremacy. At that time the Syracusans were ravaging the African regions and had pitched their camp not far from the city walls of the Carthaginians. Despite the dashing of their high hopes due to this situation, **the Tyrians** were not crestfallen, but **voted to transport their women, children and elderly men to Carthage** in the envoys' care, *being all the braver in facing whatever they might have to bear through keeping those most dear to them from having to share in the communal jeopardy confronted by their city. And they did succeed in sending some of their spouses and offspring to safety, whilst themselves readying their own eighty triremes to engage with their enemy.*

4.68 A Tyrian citizen swore at a public assembly that he had had a dream in which Apollo,[59] *a deity they worshipped especially attentively,* had **threatened to desert their city.** *Additionally, in his vision the mole the Macedonians had laid across the sea had been transformed into a tract of forestry. It was believed by many that the man had concocted his story to gain Alexander's approbation, so there was a move to stone him among the younger sections of the population, but the archons arranged his extrication and he sought refuge in the Temple of Heracles, where he won sanctuary from the people's wrath through his pleas. Yet* despite that this visionary was a person of scant authority, being inclined to believe the worst in their anxiety, the Tyrians fettered the statue of Apollo with a golden halter, *which they chained to Heracles's altar. For they had consecrated their city to the majesty of* this *deity, so* they considered *that he* would confine Apollo to their locality. The Carthaginians had appropriated this statue from the Syracusan territory[60] and had set it up in their ancestral country. Indeed, after capturing other cities they had adorned Tyre rather than Carthage with much of the booty.

4.69 *Some of the Tyrians actually advocated the revival of a rite that had been discontinued for many years: the sacrifice of a freeborn boy to Cronos. It appears that without the opposition of the archons, in accordance with whose counsel everything was done, humanity would have been vanquished by superstition. This form of* Cronos veneration, *a sacrilege rather than a sacrement,* has been bequeathed to the Carthaginians by their founders, the Phoenicians. Whenever they are pressing for success in some emergency, they vow the forfeiture of one of their offspring as a burnt offering to the deity, provided that the outcome favours their policy. A bronze statue of Cronos stands in their city with hands cupped over a brazier ready to receive the boy for roasting. As the flame of the rite begins toasting his body, his limbs contract and his

---

[59] Probably Baal or the Sun God.

[60] Curtius 4.3.22 says that the statue came from Syracuse, but Diodorus 13.108.3-4 would imply that it was actually captured in the suburbs of Gela on the southern shore of Sicily, so it would be better to infer that Cleitarchus wrote that it was taken from the Syracusan sphere of influence.

mouth seems to grin like a person laughing merrily, until he is devoured completely by the fire and his cinders sift down into the pyre.[61]

4.70 *At this juncture, the causeway reached the ramparts and connected the city to the mainland, so that the fighting along the walls became hand-to-hand. The Tyrians witnessed at close range the peril posed by the Macedonian army and readily conceived the calamity that would be consequent upon the capture of their city. Therefore they fought so unrestrainedly as to despise all jeopardy. When the Macedonians moved up towers as tall as the walls, lowering gangways to attack the battlements,* the Tyrians relied upon the cunning of their engineers and deployed many unprecedented counter-measures in their defence. *Using barbs to teethe their armaments, they forged large tridents and cast them at close range to strike their assailants. These lodged in the shields of their tower-top opponents. Next they hauled upon cords attached to the tridents. Each victim was faced with the option of either dropping his protection and exposing his person to perforation by a shower of projectiles or plummeting from his tall tower and perishing through pitifully clinging to his sole safeguard against these missiles. Other Tyrians ensnared their prey by casting fishing nets over them as they were fighting their way across a gangway. With the Macedonians enmeshed and vulnerable, the Tyrians could tug them and topple them, plunging them into a fatal fall.*

4.71 The Tyrians tethered stout poles in order to scupper such ships as came beneath their walls, for they shot these from ballistas, so that when the tethers tautened they would abruptly dive into the vessels. They also slung from these same poles both scythes and sickles to lacerate either their adversaries or their vessels. Additionally, **the Tyrians** *contrived other ingenious expedients in order to neuter Macedonian manliness. With these they* subjected the most daring of their opponents to inescapable and pitiable distress. They fabricated shields out of bronze *and steel* and filled them with sand *and mire. Then they brought them to the boil by* roasting them constantly over a fierce fire. When the sand was searingly hot, they used an appliance to upturn the pot, spewing the stuff from their battlements over those that were attacking with most valiance. *And no scourge was more feared than this, for* the searing sand sifted beneath their breastplates and cuirasses and the intense heat scorched their skin, *for the grains could not be shaken out once they had made their way in.* They shrieked out prayers like those under torture, but none could relieve them from their awful dolour. *Being deprived of their senses by the excruciating agony, they cast aside their arms and tore off their armour in their insanity.*

---

[61] Jacoby Fragment 9 of Cleitarchus from Schol. Plato Resp. 337A (Photius: Σαρδόνιος γέλως) clearly derived from here in accordance with Curtius 4.3.23.

Defenceless and completely vulnerable to injury, these soldiers died readily *without an opportunity to menace the enemy.*

4.72 *The Phoenicians effused fire, flung javelins and cast stones simultaneously, weakening the will of their assailants by the intensity of their artillery. They lowered long poles, each fitted with a blade like a sickle, and cut the cords carrying the rams, rendering them unserviceable. With their fire-throwers they flung great gobs of glowing metal into throngs of their foes, and these could not fail to find targets where so many stood packed so close.* Besides *all* this they hurled iron claws and crows[62] from their catapults, snagging those stood behind a tower's parapets and tugging them over their rims to make their exits. *With many men manning their battlements, the Tyrians kept all their engines busy in their defence and inflicted numerous casualties among their opponents. Thus they caused complete consternation and the butchery of their barrage was barely consistent with contention, but the Macedonians did not lose their resolution. As those to the fore fell and bled, those further back moved up in their stead and were undeterred by the fearful fate of some or other comrade.*

4.73 *Alexander mounted boulder-flinging catapults at strategic locations, inducing reverberations where they struck the fortifications. From his siege towers, ballistas kept blasting bolts at the parapets taking a terrible toll of their Tyrian targets. Therefore the defenders fashioned marble wheels[63] with a lattice of windows so as safely to view the scenery, for they ranged them before the battlements and rotated them by means of machinery.[64] In this way they deflected or destroyed missiles from the Macedonian artillery. Additionally, the Tyrians stuffed seaweed into stitched up hides or skins sewn together, rigging these to break the blows*

---

[62] Types of grappling iron.

[63] Diodorus makes two separate mentions of these wheels at 17.43.1 and 17.45.3 respectively. This is one of several reasons to suppose that Diodorus is not telling the events of Tyre in strict chronological order or in the order given by Cleitarchus. Additionally, Diodorus tells all the omens and portents of the siege together at 17.41.5-8, whereas Curtius relates them separately at various points during the siege. It is much more likely that Diodorus should have gathered them together for his epitome than that Curtius scattered them about. Finally, it turns out to be feasible to merge the accounts of Curtius and Diodorus sensibly on the basis of the order of events given by Curtius, but the opposite strategy would appear to lead to a messy outcome. It seems that Diodorus read the whole account of the siege by Cleitarchus, and then penned his summary from memory, whereas Curtius gives something closer to a sentence-by-sentence translation. Nevertheless, Diodorus's account of Tyre is unusually full, revealing that Curtius omitted significant sections of their common source and sometimes severely epitomised matters that Diodorus relates in more depth. In conclusion, Diodorus paid particular attention to events at Tyre, considering them historically important, whereas Curtius cut material that he found repetitive or stylistically sub-standard or which perhaps contradicted other accounts of the siege.

[64] This interpretation seems the best sense to be found in the rather obscure descriptions of these devices in Diodorus 17.43.1 and 17.45.3.

---

of the boulders by the sponginess within the leather. In short the Tyrians tirelessly practised every technique for their protection and displayed great talents in their tactics for self-preservation. They showed valiance in confronting their opponents, forsaking the shelter of their towers and battlements and making forays onto the gangways to meet Macedonian bravery with matching gallantry. Grappling hand to hand, they duelled with every adversary in making a stalwart stand in defence of their city.

4.74 *Some Tyrian warriors wielded axes for the lopping of any enemy limb that was exposed for the chopping. A Macedonian commander, called Admetus, was outstandingly sturdy and conspicuously courageous. He stood firm defiantly in the face of furious Tyrian attacks, dying instantly and heroically when his skull was split by the stroke of an axe.*

4.75 *Alexander realised that the assaults by the Macedonians had been checked by the resistance of the Tyrians. With the coming of nightfall he withdrew his troops with a trumpet call.* At this point the king, out of utter frustration, gave raising the siege and invading Egypt some serious consideration. *For having overrun the rest of Asia with great rapidity, he found himself idling in the vicinity of a single city and therefore foregoing many a glorious opportunity.* But he was as much embarrassed by the prospect of withdrawal as by remaining and he saw that his reputation, through which he overthrew more than through campaigning, would be much diminished, if he left Tyre to testify that he could be vanquished. Consequently, although just one of his Friends, Amyntas the son of Andromenes, called for the siege to be continued, he commanded that the assault should be renewed.

4.76 Therefore, in order that nothing be left untried, he moved up more ships with his elite soldiers inside. Whereupon **it happened that out of the waves they witnessed arise the back of a sea-monster of remarkable size. It thrashed its immense bulk up onto the mole that the Macedonians had engineered, rifting the surf asunder as its whole body reared. There it loitered for a while harmlessly, where both sides could see it clearly, before it plunged back down into the sea from the crest of the causeway** and, *alternately surging up out of the swell and disappearing beneath the spray,* it dived down into the depths finally *not far away from the ramparts of the city.* Both sides drew superstitious comfort from the portent that they believed this event to represent. The Macedonians deemed Poseidon to have pointed the way for their works' enlargement, whereas the Tyrians supposed that the same deity had dragged the beast onto the mole to avenge the assault upon the sea, indicating that the structure would collapse imminently. *Through the attention that they paid to their own interests each camp was swayed to believe that the god would come to its aid.* But in celebrating the sign, the Tyrians turned to feasting and overindulgence in wine. And at sunrise, still the worse for its powers, they embarked upon ships wreathed with garlands and flowers; such was their eagerness to foresee the celebration of their actual victory rather than merely its augury.

4.77 It happened that Alexander had issued an order for his fleet to assault the seaward sector, having left thirty of his lesser vessels near the shore. The Tyrians captured two of the latter and sorely terrorised the remainder, until Alexander heard the clamour and sailed his navy to the source of the uproar. The first Macedonian ship to arrive at the scene was a quinquereme that was fleeter than the rest of the fleet. Two Tyrian galleys that it came between charged it abeam and the first of these it turned to meet. But it was rammed by the beak of the other, which it held fast reciprocally. Then, being still free to manoeuvre, the first galley tried to charge decisively from the opposite side. But arriving with remarkable timing a trireme from Alexander's navy rammed the galley, which would else have struck the quinquireme imminently, with such force that the Tyrian helmsman was flung from its stern into the sea. Soon many more Macedonian vessels were arriving and the king was also fast approaching. Whereupon by backing water the Tyrians managed with difficulty to tear their entangled ship free and all their vessels made for port simultaneously. The king pursued them aggressively and, though the harbour denied him entry, since he was fended off from its walls by the Tyrian artillery, he nevertheless either captured or sank nearly all the ships of the enemy.[65]

4.78 The troops were permitted two days of inactivity. Then **Alexander** *addressed the Macedonians exhorting them to match his own gallantry.* **He commanded that his army advance its navy and its siege engines simultaneously and he began a general assault by land and by sea in order to cow the enemy by its sheer ubiquity. This onslaught was pressed with furious ferocity.** *And he outfitted his vessels with gear for siege warfare, since he noticed that the wall near the naval base[66] was weaker than elsewhere, so he lashed triremes together to bear his best engines in order to launch an attack just there.*

4.79 *Now Alexander performed a feat of daring that was barely believable even by those that witnessed this bit of the battle.* With great bravery and even greater jeopardy, *for his royal raiment and glinting arms made him a magnet for Tyrian weaponry,* the king mounted his loftiest wooden siege gantry and swung a gangway across to reach the wall of the city. And it was a wondrous sight to see, when he made a solitary sortie to gain a footing on the battlements, neither fearing Fortune's jealousy nor the

---

[65] Arrian, *Anabasis* 2.21.9, states that thirteen Tyrian vessels participated in this raid: three quinquiremes, three quadriremes and seven triremes. Their initial targets were anchored Cypriot vessels.

[66] Apparently on the southern side of the city facing Egypt – see Arrian, *Anabasis* 2.22.7.

---

threat from the Tyrian defence. With his valour vaunted before the magnificent military that had vanquished the Persian army, he called upon the Macedonians to follow as he fought his way forward, felling those Tyrians that came near with a thrust of his spear or a slash of his sword. And he pushed others off the parapet with his shield's rim, putting paid to his adversaries' valiant vim.

Figure 4.9. The fall of Tyre (1696)

4.80 At the same time in another zone the hammering of many rams had loosened the joints of the stone, so that a long stretch of the fortifications had begun to fall and the Macedonians were making an entry through this broad breach in the wall. Simultaneously, the fleet forced its way into the harbour, whilst the forces accompanying Alexander surged across the gangway and occupied towers abandoned by the enemy in the mêlée. Thus the city was taken *and a portion of the inhabitants, crushed by so many setbacks at once, turned to their temples for deliverance. But* most Tyrians were persistent in their resistance, *barricading their alleyways with impediments and* yelling mutual encouragements. Some of them hurled themselves at their adversaries expecting to die, but not without retribution. Others bolted the doors of their homes and forestalled their enemies by a death of their own volition. A great many got up onto the rooftops and pelted the advancing opposition with stones and whatever was at hand for ammunition. Alexander ordered that the roofs should be set ablaze and that all should be slain save those that had fled into the sanctuaries. Although he had heralds proclaim these decrees, no Tyrian under arms deigned to seek asylum with his deities. Boys and maidens had packed the temples, but the menfolk all stood in their houses' vestibules, facing up to the fury of their foes in wretched rabbles.

4.81 Nevertheless, the Sidonians, who were among the Macedonian occupiers, were the salvation of many. Although they had accompanied the victors in gaining entry to the city, they recalled their Tyrian consanguinity - for they considered that Agenor had founded both communities – so they covertly provided their protection to Tyrian refugees, abstracting them to Sidon by hiding them in their ships which they used as ferries. Fifteen thousand were rescued from the sack through such furtive activities. But **all save a few of the men under arms were slain in the spoliations and the scale of the bloodshed may be inferred from the fact that** *over seven thousand warriors were cut down within the fortifications.*[67] **Subsequently, the king's fury furnished the victors with a tragic spectacle: two thousand Tyrian fighters left alive by the killing frenzy were crucified along a large length of the littoral.**[68] *Alexander sold the women and children into slavery, for, although most of the non-combatants had been removed to Carthage* and *Sidon successfully, more than thirteen thousand were found to remain and entered captivity.* The king did no harm to the Carthaginian emissaries, but issued them with a declaration of hostilities, though these were left in abeyance on account of current exigencies.

4.82 *So* **Tyre** *had suffered the siege courageously rather than judiciously and* **met with complete calamity in the seventh month**[69] **after she began her contumacy.** *Alexander removed the gold fetters from Apollo's statue and bade that he be called 'Apollo Philalexandros' too.*[70] *He performed*

---

[67] Curtius 4.4.14 has *VI milia* (6000), whilst Diodorus 17.46.3 gives "more than 7000" (Arrian, *Anabasis* 2.24.4 states 8000).

[68] The large-scale executions at Tyre were evidently prompted by the execution of Alexander's emissaries and Macedonian prisoners of war (Arrian, *Anabasis Alexandrou* 2.24.3) in contravention of the normal rules of warfare by the Tyrians during the siege plus the fact that the Macedonians considered that the Tyrians' use of red-hot sand had been excessively cruel.

[69] Diodorus 17.46.5; Curtius 4.4.19; Plutarch, *Alexander* 24.3; Arrian, *Anabasis* 2.24.6 states that Tyre fell in the Attic month of *Hecatombaeon*, which began on the first New Moon after the Summer Solstice; Plutarch, *Alexander* 25.2 tells the story that Tyre fell on the last day of the month, which was originally designated the 30th, but that Alexander redesignated it as 28th in support of a prophecy of Aristander – which suggests that this month was "hollow", meaning that it had only 29 days and the 29th day was therefore called the 30th, since it was the last. In 332BC the Summer Solstice fell on about 26th June and the next New Moon occurred on about 20th July, so the last day of *Hecatombaeon* would be about 17th August (all these dates being given according to the Julian Calendar.)

[70] *Philalexandros* is "lover of Alexander".

---

elaborate sacrifices to Heracles, rewarded those of his men who had served heroically in the hostilities and held a lavish funeral for his casualties. Lastly, he installed Abdalonymus as king of Tyre in a further extension of his territories.

Figure 4.10. A view of Tyre still connected to the mainland by Alexander's mole (1889)

4.83 These were the concerns of Alexander *in the fourth year of his reign.*

4. Book 5: 14th October 332BC – 1st October 331BC

Second Peace Offer from Darius; The Siege of Gaza; Occupation of Egypt; Expedition to Siwa; Foundation of Alexandria; The March back to Byblos; The Preparations of Darius; Alexander's Advance into Mesopotamia; Crossing the Tigris; Death of Stateira; Third Peace Offer from Darius; The Battle of Arbela.

5.1 *This book recounts the events concerning Alexander in the fifth year of his reign, but it begins by outlining events that transpired elsewhere in the aftermath of the battle at Issus.*

5.2 The widespread war that was being waged by the mightiest monarchs of Europe and Asia in the hope of having hold of the whole world had also engaged the arms of Greece and Crete. **Agis, the king of Sparta, mustered and hired eight thousand Greek mercenaries who had escaped from** Cilicia and returned to their homes following **the battle at Issus** in order to foment a war against Antipater, the viceroy of Macedonia*, so as to try to transform affairs in favour of Darius. He had both funds and ferries from the Persian king, so* **he set sail for Crete,** *where he captured most of the municipalities* **and made them support the Persian side.** The Cretans vacillated in their loyalties according to the country of their invaders, whether of Spartan or Macedonian nationality.

5.3 That Amyntas, who had fled from Macedonia and deserted to Darius, *fought for the Persians in Cilicia. He* **got away from the field of battle at Issus with a following of four thousand Greeks and reached Tripolis** *in Phoenicia ahead of Alexander.* **There he selected** *sufficient* **ships** *from the Persian fleet* **to transport his troops,** *incinerating the remainder.* **Sailing them over to Cyprus, he recruited more soldiers and ships and** decided to **set out for Egypt,** since he perceived that a person might possess as if it were really his right whatever he had seized in the existing circumstances. He was currently in conflict with both kings and always ready to sway with the swing of things. So, having impressed upon his troops the opportunities afforded by such tall undertakings, he informed them that **Sabaces, the governor of Egypt, had fallen in the hostilities at Issus.** Hence the Persian garrison was both leaderless and powerless, whereas the Egyptians, persistently oppressed by their occupiers, would regard Amyntas' men as allies rather than as enemies. They were driven by necessity to pursue every possibility, for, Fortune having forsaken their first opportunity, any future seemed preferable to their situation currently. Therefore his troops clamoured collectively for him to lead them wherever he saw fit. **Hence,** reckoning whilst their hopes were high to exploit such spirit, **he sailed into the Pelusian mouth** *of the Nile,* **deceitfully declaring that Darius had designated him as the substitute for Sabaces.**

5.4 Having thereby taken possession of Pelusium, Amyntas sailed his soldiers upriver to Memphis. At the news of this, the Egyptians, an irresolute people better at initiating than effectuating anything, all scurried forth from their various villages and towns intending to annihilate the Persian garrisons. These, although alarmed, nevertheless failed to forsake their hope of holding on to Egypt. But **in approaching Memphis Amyntas outfought the Persians in the fighting, forcing them to fall back into the city. And** *having encamped,* **the victors began looting estates in the country,** *carrying off everything as booty as though they were amongst the enemy. Thereupon the Persian commander,* **Mazaces, though he saw that the unsuccessful tussle had unsettled his soldiers psychologically, nevertheless pointed out that** Amyntas's men were dispersed widely and had become incautious through overconfidence in their victory. Thus *jointly with the Egyptians* the Persians were impelled *confidently* to charge forth from the city *to recover what they had held previously. That strategy proved just as successful in its culmination as it was wise in its conception.* **Amyntas's men were slain one and all along with their leader.** Such was the forfeit ceded to both sovereigns by this commander, who showed no more loyalty in serving the king to whom he had defected than in his desertion of Alexander.

5.5 Similar fates befell other Persian officers. A group of Darius's commanders, who had survived the Battle of Issus, accompanied by all the contingents that had followed them in their flight, and also reinforced by young men from Cappadocia and Paphlagonia, **sought to bolster Persian interests** by recapturing Lydia. Alexander's general, Antigonus, was in control of Lydia and, despite having given up much of his garrison to Alexander, he nevertheless belittled the barbarians in leading his battalions out to do battle with them. There as **elsewhere** the fortunes of their foes fared unfavourably, for the Persians were put to flight in each of three fights at successive sites. In parallel, a Macedonian fleet gathered from Greece captured or capsized the ships of Aristomenes, whom Darius had sent into the war in order to recover the Hellespontine shore. Thereafter, Pharnabazus, admiral of the Persian fleet, exacted money from the Milesians and installed a garrison in the chief town of Chios, setting sail for Siphnos via Andros with a hundred vessels. From these too he extorted funds and garrisoned their islands. *But the fights between all these were slighter matters than the one contest upon which all the others hung, to which Fortune's fixed gaze clung.*

5.6 *One day around that time a letter from Darius was delivered, but now written as to a ruler. He proposed that Alexander should join himself in matrimony to his daughter, whose name was Stateira, and that her dowry should be the region ranging between the Hellespont and the Halys River in its entirety.*[71] Darius would be satisfied with the lands looking east from that riverside. If perchance Alexander should hesitate to accept this offer, *let him ponder that* Fortune never lingers long in the same vicinity and *that* men

---

[71] The Halys is the modern Kizil Irmak; Arrian, *Anabasis* 2.25.1 mentions the Euphrates in its stead; cf. Justin 11.12.3-4 & Diodorus 17.39.1 (mentioning the Halys river boundary.)

inasmuch as they experience success are always proportionately the more exposed to jealousy. He feared lest, like the birds that are levitated into the heavens by their innate lightness, Alexander were to be carried away by a callow and hollow vanity. Nothing was harder at his age than to cope with such prodigious prosperity. Darius retained a multiplicity of resources and could not always be caught in confined courses. Alexander had to get across the Euphrates and the Tigris and then both the Araxes and the Choaspes, the massive moats of Darius's dominions. He would have to pass through *empty* plains, where he could be shamed by the sparsity of his battalions. How long would it take him to penetrate Media, Hyrcania, Bactria and India adjoining the Ocean, not to mention the Sogdian and Arachosian nations and the rest of the races extending to the Tanais River[72] and the Caucasus Mountains? He would use up his youth merely in traversing such expanses, even if his passage were uncontended. Furthermore, he should curtail his calls for Darius to come before him, since his arrival would see Alexander's life ended.

5.7 *Alexander responded to those that had brought the letter that Darius was dangling what did not belong to him and wished to apportion what he had entirely relinquished.* Lydia, Ionia, Aeolia and the Hellespontine coastline were being offered him as a dowry, the very prizes of his own victory! ***Terms are dictated by the victor and conceded by the loser.*** If Darius alone did not know which role they respectively occupied, then let Ares, *the god of war*, firstly decide. Let him also be aware that Alexander, when setting out overseas, had not targeted the takeover of Lydia nor Cilicia, since they would be trivial trophies for such wholesale hostilities, but rather of Persepolis, seat of the Persian sovereigns, and thereafter of Bactra, Ecbatana and the easternmost territories. Alexander was capable of following wheresoever Darius might flee, so let him cease to threaten with rivers one whom he knew to have crossed the sea. *Instead let Darius come before him in person to make his plea.*

5.8 But although the kings had at least been in correspondence with one another, the Rhodians were *meanwhile* ceding their city and their harbours to Alexander, who had consigned Cilicia to Socrates and had bidden Philotas to govern the region around Tyre. The section of Syria that is called hollow was set in the hands of Andromachus by Parmenion, so that the latter could participate in what remained of the invasion. And having bidden Hephaistion to sail the fleet along the Phoenician shores, ***the king got to to Gaza*** with all his corps.

5.9 *In roughly that same period the cyclical* Isthmian Games *were held[73] and were attended by a crowd drawn from all over Greece.* In council

---

[72] Alexander's expedition mistook the modern Syr Darya for the Tanais (actually the Don), but the more correct ancient name was the Jaxartes.

[73] The Isthmian Games were held biennially at Corinth in the Spring preceding the Summer of the Olympics and two years thereafter; since Alexander reached Gaza in the Autumn of 332BC, an Olympic year, the games referred to here must have been celebrated in the Spring of that year.

there the delegates of the League of Corinth voted on behalf of the Greeks, people of a pragmatic disposition, **that fifteen envoys should carry a crown of gold to the king** *in recognition of his deeds promoting their welfare and liberty* **and that they should tender the congratulations of the Greeks on his Cilician victory.**[74] These selfsame Greeks but a little bit beforehand had been attentive to unreliable reports with the intention of following wheresoever Fortune might waft their wavering thoughts.

5.10 All the while, not only was Alexander himself besieging cities that rejected the yoke of his dominion, but his marshals too, being excellent leaders, had launched many an invasion: Calas into Paphlagonia; Antigonus into Lycaonia. Balacrus, having bested Hydarnes, the Satrap of Darius, re-took Miletus and Amphoterus and Hegelochus with a fleet of one hundred and sixty vessels brought the islands between the Greek mainland[75] and Asia under the authority of Alexander. Having taken Tenedos too, they stood ready to occupy Chios at the urging of its denizens. But Pharnabazus, as the deputy of Darius, detained those who desired to defect to the Macedonians and delivered the city back into the hands of Apollonides and Athenogoras, gentlemen of the pro-Persian faction, with a token detachment of soldiers. Alexander's commanders maintained their siege of the city, reckoning not so much on their own efforts, but on the disaffection of those invested. Nor were they mistaken in this view, since a wrangle arising between Apollonides and the officers of the garrison furnished an opportunity to force an entry to the city. And when a regiment of Macedonians surged in through a shattered gateway, the citizens who had previously plotted to betray the city joined forces with Amphoterus and Hegelochus. The men of the Persian garrison were slain and Pharnabazus together with Apollonides and Athenogoras were handed over in chains along with twelve triremes with their rowers and commandos and, besides these, thirty crewless vessels, fifty pirate sloops and three thousand Greeks, whom the Persians had hired as mercenary troops. These last were distributed to strengthen the Macedonian contingents, the pirates were subjected to capital punishments and the captured oarsmen were incorporated amongst the Macedonian ships' complements.

5.11 It chanced that ***Aristonicus, the despot of Methymna,***[76] being ignorant of everything that had occurred **at *Chios, approached the*** barrier at the ***harbour*** mouth ***with*** a flotilla of ***pirate vessels*** in the first watch of the night. When the guards demanded to know his identity, he retorted that it was Aristonicus come to visit Pharnabazus. They replied that Pharnabazus was resting right now and that it was not feasible to visit him at the moment. However, they assured him that the hospitality of the port was available to his

---

[74] I.e. the Battle of Issus.

[75] *Achaia* in the manuscripts, this being an Homeric name for mainland Greece.

[76] On the island of Lesbos.

ally and associate and that he would have access to Pharnabazus during the following day. Aristonicus did not hesitate to lead the way through the entrance trailed by ten pirate sloops, and, whilst they were docking their ships at the harbour quay, the watch put back the barrier and alerted those on nearby sentry duty. Since none of the pirates dared to put up a fight, **all were clapped in irons and** subsequently **turned over to the Macedonians,** Hegelochus and Amphoterus.

5.12 From there the Macedonians sailed to Mitylene. This port had recently been seized by Chares of Athens, who held it with a garrison of two thousand Persians. But since he was unable to endure a siege, he surrendered the place in exchange for being allowed to scurry away unscathed, making for Imbros. The Macedonians spared those who surrendered.

5.13 Despairing of the peace that he had supposed he could procure through letters and delegations, Darius assiduously devoted himself once more to the restoration of his manpower and his capacity to wage war. Therefore he commanded the leaders of his forces to gather in Babylonia, and also bade Bessus, Satrap of Bactria, to muster as massive an army as he could and to deliver it up to him. These Bactrians are the most opportunistic amongst those peoples and of an uncouth character and deeply disdainful of Persian luxury. Situated not so far from the Scythians, a most rapacious race used to living predaciously, they always wear their weaponry. But Bessus discomforted Darius, who doubted his loyalty, for he barely tolerated a subordinate role with any equanimity. And since he aspired to sovereignty, treason was to be feared as his only opportunity.

5.14 Meanwhile Alexander was diligently seeking to determine which domain was Darius's destination, but it could not be revealed, due to the Persian practice of keeping the secrets of their kings most carefully concealed. Neither intimidation nor temptation can elicit the communication of any confidential information. The ancient tradition of the kings sanctioned silence on pain of extermination. A loose tongue is more severely chastised than any other transgression and their Magi maintain that no major matter may be managed by those that find it hard to keep their silence, which Nature has ordained to be most effortless for mankind. On this account being ignorant of all the arrangements being made by his enemy, **Alexander marched upon Gaza and besieged the city.**

5.15 The governor of Gaza was Betis,[77] who exhibited extraordinary loyalty to his king in defending vast fortifications with a skeleton garrison. Alexander, having surveyed the site, bade that mines be begun since the light, friable soil suited a subterranean operation. For deep drifts of sand are driven across the land by the nearby sea, such that neither rock nor stone is prone to hinder

---

[77] Batis in Arrian, *Anabasis* 2.25.4, who states that he was a eunuch (and is echoed on this point in the Itinerarium Alexandri XVIIII [Volkmann's text]).

excavation. Therefore he began tunnelling in an area that could not be seen by the garrison and to divert their attention from these operations he bade that siege towers be advanced towards the fortifications. Yet the same soil was unsuitable for trundling towers, since the sand subsided beneath the wheels, repressing their progress and fracturing the platforms in the turrets. Many men were wounded with impunity, since the same efforts when withdrawing the towers as when they were advanced enhanced their vulnerability.

5.16 So the signal was issued for withdrawal and the next day Alexander commanded his men to ring the perimeter of the wall. And at the rising of the sun prior to advancing his army he besought the backing of the gods by sacrificing according to the custom of his country. It chanced that a raven unexpectedly released a clod that it was carrying in its talons, which fell so as to disintegrate upon hitting the head of the king. The bird itself perched upon a nearby tower that had become smeared with bitumen and sulphur, to which its wings adhered. Being thus frustrated in its attempts to fly free, those at hand took it into captivity. A review of the incident by an augur seemed timely, as Alexander was not unaffected by a superstitious mentality. Consequently, Aristander, whom he held in the utmost credulity, foretold that the overthrow of the city was actually portended by this augury, but that there was a risk that Alexander would receive some injury. Hence he cautioned the king not to initiate an assault on that particular day. Though vexed that this single city stood in the way of him entering Egypt risk free, Alexander nevertheless signalled a withdrawal in deference to his visionary.

5.17 This boosted the boldness of the besieged, who burst out from a gate to set upon their retreating enemy, reckoning that the irresolution of their opponents would be their own opportunity. But they threw themselves into the fighting with more fervour than firmness, for, when they saw the Macedonian banners perform a volte-face, they promptly checked their progress. Thereupon the clamour of those engaged reached *the king*, whereupon, heedless of his predicted peril, but donning a corselet, which he rarely wore, upon being harangued by his friends, he *fetched up at the fore of the fighting*. Upon spotting him, a certain Arab, *one of Darius's warriors, dared a deed larger than his luck. He* stuck his sword behind his shield and*, as though he were a turncoat, prostrated himself at the king's knees.* Alexander bade the supplicant arise and be inducted amongst his own levies. *But, suddenly seizing his sword* with his right hand, *the barbarian struck at the king*'s neck. *Yet Alexander, dodging the blow* with a slight twist of his torso, *slashed with his sword to sever* the vainly lunging limb of *his foe*. Thereby discharging the danger predicted for that day, he supposed it to have gone away.

5.18 But, as is proverbial, fate is inescapable, for whilst all too enthusiastically engaged in frontline combat, the king was struck by a bolt that drove through his corselet. As it was embedded in his shoulder, his physician Philip drew it forth, whereupon a gush of blood began to flow to everyone's consternation, since the corselet made it hard to know the depth of the projectile's penetration. Not even showing a shift in his complexion, Alexander bade that the bleeding be staunched and that the injury be dressed. He stood his ground before the standards for a long while, either disguising his pain or keeping it suppressed, until the blood that had been held back by the bandage a bit before began to seep persistently and the wound, which had not hurt whilst still numbed, swelled with the congealing of the gore. In consequence he commenced losing consciousness and began to buckle at the knees, whereupon he was seized by those around him and carried back to camp. And Betis returned to the city, believing that the king had been killed and exulting in his victory.

5.19 Yet even ere his injury had healed Alexander ordered that a mound be raised up to equal the elevation of the fortifications and bade that the walls be undermined by multiple tunnels. The populace erected new fortifications upon the original battlements, but even these could not match the tallness of the towers mounted atop the mound of the Macedonians. Hence missiles beset the interior of the town too. The ultimate downfall of the city was the undermining of a wall by a tunnel, since the enemy made an entry through its rubble. The king himself led the troops of the spearhead and, whilst he was rushing in rather recklessly, he was struck by a stone in the leg below the knee. Despite his first wound not yet having fully scarred, he nevertheless leant upon his spear and fought on in the vanguard, additionally fired by fury in that he had twice received an injury in the siege of that city.

5.20 Having made an outstanding fighting stand and being weakened by many wounds, Betis was abandoned by his band, but nonetheless fought on unflaggingly, though his armour was slick with his own blood and that of his enemies equally. But when missiles flew from all around *he was overwhelmed and bound by Leonnatus and Philotas.*[78] *These* **men led Betis** *alive* **before the king** and, although he was usually an admirer of valour even in an enemy, Alexander was carried away by the arrogant exuberance of youth in declaring: "You shall not die as you have wished, but rather be aware that you shall suffer whatever can be contrived against a prisoner." But Betis stared back at the king, his expression not merely undaunted but actually obstinate in saying not a single word in response to Alexander's threat. Then the king observed: "See how obdurate is his silence. He has not bent his knee nor uttered any plea for mercy. But I shall triumph over his tranquility and if not otherwise I shall certainly punctuate it with sighs." Then Alexander's anger turned to violence, for already at that time his recent achievements were imbuing him with foreign manners. Indeed, whilst Betis yet breathed, **thongs were thrust through his ankles. These were bound to the king's chariot and he was dragged around the circuit of the city by its team** with the king glorying in imitating Achilles,

---

[78] There appears to be a short lacuna in the manuscript text of Curtius at this point, which may tentatively be reconstructed from its context and a somewhat parallel account from Hegesias FGrH 142 F5.

from whom he traced his ancestry, whilst imposing punishment upon his enemy.

Figure 5.1. The siege of Gaza by André Castaigne (1898)

5.21 *Thus Alexander took Gaza violently after a two-month siege of the city.* There perished around ten thousand of the Arabs and Persians. Nor was it a bloodless conquest for the Macedonians. Certainly that siege is celebrated, but not so much for the fame of the city as for Alexander's exposure to a double jeopardy. **After settling the affairs of Gaza, the king himself hastened on into Egypt** *with his whole army,* **sending Amyntas to Macedonia with ten triremes to seek fit youths as fresh recruits**, since even successes entailed attrition of his troops and Alexander set less store on soldiers from the vanquished nations than on those from his own shore.

5.22 *Long since* **antagonistic to the power of the Persians, whom they considered to have ruled them haughtily** *and extortionately, perpetrating sacrilege against many a temple,* **the Egyptians were enthused by the prospect of Alexander's arrival.** For indeed they had even received Amyntas gladly, though he was a renegade arriving with dubious authority. Therefore a vast host of them had mustered at Pelusium, which seemed Alexander's likely point of entry. In fact on the seventh day after marching his army away from Gaza, the king reached that region of Egypt that is now known as Alexander's Camp. Thence he ordered his infantry contingents to make for Pelusium, while he himself with a disencumbered task force of selected troops sailed up the Nile. Neither did the Persians oppose his advance, being additionally panicked by the *native* revolt. And when he was already not far from Memphis, Mazaces, the viceroy of Darius, announced his abdication and crossed the river[79] to hand over eight hundred talents and all the royal accoutrements to Alexander. Thus **all of Egypt's cities came into the king's power without hostilities, since the natives welcomed Alexander on account of Persian impieties.** From Memphis he sailed on up the same stream, penetrating into the interior of Egypt **and he settled its affairs without tampering with any Egyptian national custom. Then Alexander elected to visit the oracle of Zeus-Ammon.**

5.23 Even for a small band travelling lightly the journey that they undertook was barely endurable. The land and the sky are utterly dry, for there the barren sands lie, which, being scorched by the sun's glow, set the surface simmering and sear the soles of the feet, giving rise to unbearable heat. The struggle is not only against the temperature and the aridity, but also with most obstructive sands that are piled high and give way beneath the tread so that feet forge forwards with difficulty. Actually the Egyptians pressed these problems excessively, but a burning desire obsessed the king's mind that he should consult Zeus, whom he, dissatisfied with pre-eminence among mortals, either believed or wished it to be believed was the founder of his dynasty. Therefore in the company of those he had elected to take with him he travelled downriver to the Mareotic marsh. **Halfway along the coast, the king was met by envoys from Cyrene bearing** *a crown and other* **gorgeous gifts,** *including three*

---

[79] Memphis stood on the west bank of the Nile, whilst Alexander was evidently approaching along the eastern bank.

hundred warhorses and five of their finest four-horse chariots. Their purpose was to petition for peace and to invite him to visit their cities. He received these emissaries and their gifts cordially and concluded a pact with them of alliance and amity. Then he continued to pursue his planned journey.

5.24 After taking on water, *on the first day and even the second the effort seemed endurable, since the wilderness where they were was not yet so desolate and sterile, though the land was already barren and infertile. But when* fields of tall dunes arose, *they vainly peered around for solid ground just as if they were cast upon a vast sea.* After four days *not a trace of a tree or any shrubbery met their gaze.* The water *as well, which camels had carried in skins,* ran out *and there was none to be found in the simmering sand and arid ground. Additionally, the sun imbued everything with scorching heat and their mouths were dry and parched, when* suddenly, *whether by the gift of the gods or mere fortuity,* the sky was filled with clouds *and the sun was veiled, a huge help to those harried by the heat, despite their water supply having failed. But actually, when* the storms *also* showered down chutes of rain from a cloudburst, *each man caught it in whichever way he could. Some, having been enfeebled by thirst, even began to gobble it with their gaping mouths. Consequently, their drought was ended unexpectedly, when they filled their skins from a pooling in a dip in the ground that they found providentially.*

5.25 Four more days were spent traipsing through desert wastes. *But when they were not very far from the seat of the oracle,* the sand dunes rendered their route untraceable. At that point they encountered a flock of cawing crows to their right and the guide told the king that they were following the way to the temple in their flight. *They flew forward fitfully ahead of the standards and when progress was slow, the crows would alight, then again take flight, as though they strove to show the way to the site.* The king took this for an omen and, thinking the god to be glad of his arrival, he hurried onwards towards the oracle. *And first of all he came upon the so-called Bitter Lake, then going on another hundred stades he skirted what are known as Ammon's cities and after a journey of a day* he at last approached the enclosure of the god's sanctuary.

5.26 *Extraordinary as it is to relate, though* the precinct is situated amidst desert dunes and waterless wastes devoid of every amenity, *it is so completely enveloped by thick forestry that the sunlight is all but filtered out by its dense canopy.* The wood is fifty stades in length and breadth and many freshwater springs well up haphazardly, irrigating its many types of tree, especially such as fruit generously. Its climate too, being most like to the warmth of spring, is wondrously temperate, cycling through all seasons of the year in the same wholesome state, *though surrounded by a searing hot landscape. It is said that the sacred enclosure was established by Danaos the Egyptian.* Towards the east the near neighbours of the vicinity are Ethiopian. *Southwards the place faces those Arabians who are known as Trogodytes, whose region runs on right to the Red Sea.* Other Ethiopians, *who are called Simui,* occupy the land that lies to the west. There are Nasamones to the north, *a Syrtican nation living off loot from the shipping, since they infest the shores and seize storm-tossed vessels that run aground in and about shoals that they have staked out.*

5.27 The inhabitants of the groves, who are called Ammonii, inhabit huts *in scattered groups.* The centre of the oasis is set aside as their citadel, the walls of which encircle it in three loops. The innermost circuit encloses the ancient palace of their kings. The next accommodates their wives', children's and concubines' dwellings *and the watchstations of that bailey.* There too lies the oracle of the god *and his sacred spring, the waters of which sanctify offerings dedicated to the deity. The outermost ring encompasses the barracks of the royal guards as well as the posts for standing sentry.*

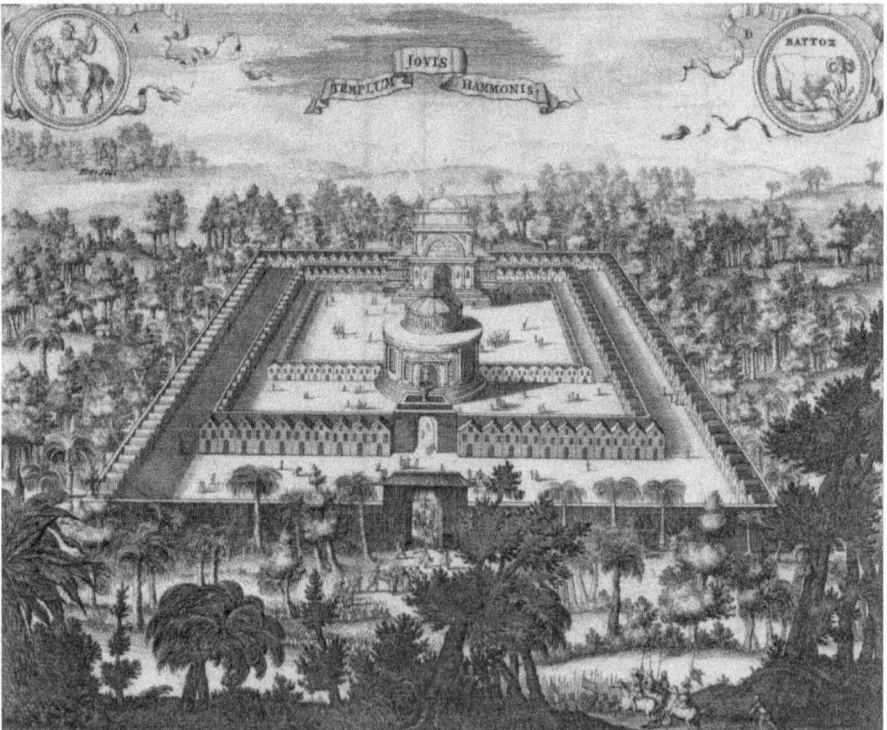

Figure 5.2. Imaginative reconstruction of the Temple of Ammon at Siwa (1685)

5.28 Outside the citadel but near at hand another shrine of Ammon lies in the shade of a grove of great trees, amidst which emerges a spring that is called the Source of the Sun *due to its activities. The temperature of its water varies counterintuitively through a daily cycle.* At dawn it streams forth lukewarm, but as the day progresses it cools in proportion to the passage of time, until at noon, *when the heat is at its hottest,* it comes out coldest. Then again at a like rate it warms towards the twilight and seethes out in its hottest state at around midnight. Thereafter it resumes its cooling trend until its waters end up tepid once more by first light.

5.29 That which is reverenced as the deity *does not have the same form with which carvers commonly characterise divinity. It* is embedded amidst an agglomeration of gems and emeralds *and most closely resembles a navel. It has a weird way of answering those that consult the oracle.* It is borne about on a golden boat by *eighty* priests *with multiple silver cups hung from either side of the vessel. With the god on their shoulders they veer involuntarily under divine guidance.* A multitude of maidens and matrons follow and according to the custom of their country they descant discordant chants, *by which they believe Zeus is propitiated, such that his oracular response is validated.*

5.30 *On the particular occasion of the king's arrival,* when Alexander was admitted into the temple and had regarded the god for an interval, the eldest of the priests, who was their prophet, approached the king, saying, "Hail to the Son. And let you receive as from the god too this title." And Alexander himself replied, "I receive it gladly, Father. Henceforth I shall be called Diogenes,"[80] *for he had forgotten his mortality.* Then he enquired as to whether fate had destined him to rule the world in its entirety? The prophet went within the shrine and the bearers shouldered the deity, which teetered so as to speak symbolically. And the prophet, *practised in fluent flattery,* declared that the king's command of every land would most certainly come to be. Then Alexander spoke again: "O divinity, reveal this final thing to me: have I made all the murderers of my father pay the penalty or did any go free?" "Silence!" the prophet exclaimed, "No mortal may undermine the source of your paternity. Yet for the felling of Philip all the perpetrators have been punished properly." And he added, "The sublimity of your deeds shall be the proof of your descent from the deity and even as you have previously known nothing but victory, so you shall be invincible[81] *until you assume your own divinity and then* throughout eternity."

5.31 *After the sacrificial offerings,* rejoicing in the oracular pronouncements, Alexander honoured *both the priests and* the god with precious presents. *Then the king consented that his companions consult the oracle as well. They asked nothing more significant than whether the*

---

[80] Diogenes was an epithet of several Homeric heroes, which may be translated as "Son of Zeus".

[81] I.e. *Aniketos,* the title also endorsed by the Pythia at Delphi in the Cleitarchan tradition.

god ratified their reverence of their ruler with divine honours and the prophet pronounced that with this too Zeus would be satisfied.

Figure 5.3. Alexander is greeted as the Son of Zeus by the eldest priest (1696)

5.32 *On the basis of a sound and balanced estimation of its fidelity the responses of the oracle could be perceived as specious. But Fortune makes those in whom she has compelled confidence in her alone more gluttonous for glory than capable of coping with it. On that account Alexander not only allowed himself to be dubbed Diogenes, but even bade it and, although he meant to magnify the fame of his deeds with such a title, he actually marred it. And the Macedonians, though accustomed to the command of a king, nevertheless enjoyed a semblance of greater liberty than other monarchist men, so they contested his claim to immortality more stubbornly than was sensible either for themselves or for their sovereign. But let this be kept for its due occasion, for now I shall proceed with the rest of my narration.*

5.33 **Alexander returned from Ammon so as to get to the Mareotic Lake, situated not far from the island of Pharos. He had initially intended to found a new city *upon the island itself. But, on surveying the topography of the vicinity, it was apparent that this location lacked the capacity to accommodate a substantial settlement, so he selected the site now occupied by Alexandria, which took its name from its founder.* He left men *from among his Friends* behind whom he bade build his city between the marshes and the sea.** *Hence he envisaged a circuit of eighty stades as its destiny and he bade that the leadership of Egypt be accorded to this Macedonian colony. Here too Hegelochus anchored in order to bring the pirate, Aristonicus of Methymna, before the king. After Alexander had asked this man what he meant by harassing shipping, he answered with uncowed conceit: "The same as you mean by seizing the whole world; but because I do it with a single ship, I am labelled a bandit, whilst you are called a king, considering that you use a great fleet."*[82]

5.34 Then Alexander made for Memphis. He was afflicted by a desire that was not so much unjustified as inopportune to travel not just to Upper Egypt but to Ethiopia as well. Being eager to investigate the vestiges of antiquity, the renowned palace of Memnon and Tithonus was drawing him virtually beyond the limits of enlightenment. However the impending war, of which by far the most challenging phase was yet to come, curtailed his time for sightseeing. Hence he gave the government of Egypt to Aeschylus of Rhodes and Peucestes of Macedon, allotting them four thousand troops to garrison the region and he called upon Polemon to defend the barriers across the Nile estuaries, assigning him thirty triremes to this end. Apollonius was placed in command of the Libyan lands adjoining Egypt and Cleomenes was to exact taxes from those Libyan tracts and from Egypt itself.

5.35 By bidding the inhabitants of the neighbouring cities to resettle in Alexandria, the king filled his new foundation with a populous populace. It is widely reported that when Alexander delineated the circuit of the future walls, as is the Macedonian tradition, *though* with barley meal *due to a lack of lime*, birds flocked to the location, making this meal their invitation to dine. And when

---

[82] That Hegelochus brought Aristonicus to Alexandria is suggested by Arrian, *Anabasis* 3.2.3-5.

many considered this a sombre sign, the seers dissented, saying that the city would acquire a large population through immigration and would supply sustenance to many a nation.

Figure 5.4. Alexander founds Alexandria by André Castaigne (1898)

5.36 Whilst Alexander was cruising downriver, Hector, a son of Parmenion, in the fairest flowering of his youth, was wishing to catch up with the king, to whom few were dearer. He therefore embarked upon boat of slight capacity, which was crowded with more than it could carry. And so it sank, immersing the entire company. Hector long contested with the current with his wet clothing and tightly fastened sandals impeding his swimming and he managed though semiconscious to reach the riverbank. But he was in a state of complete exhaustion and as he fought to resume his respiration, which panic and the peril had repressed, he gave up the ghost and died, since none came to his aid, the rest having got out on the opposite side. The king was gripped by great grief at his loss and on recovering his corpse gave him a magnificent funeral and send off.

5.37 This mourning was magnified by news of the death of Andromachus, to whom he had given the government of Syria. The Samaritans had roasted him alive. In order to avenge his incineration, **Alexander advanced into Syria** with the greatest expedition and the perpetrators of the atrocity were given up to him upon his manifestation. Thereafter he installed Memnon in Andromachus' position and those that had dealt death to his governor incurred execution. Certain despots, including Aristonicus and Ersilaus of Methymna, he put in the hands of their own populations, who tortured them to death on account of their transgressions.

5.38 Alexander next hearkened to the emissaries of the Athenians, the Rhodians and the Chians. The Athenians commended him on his victory and entreated that his Greek prisoners should be repatriated, whereas the Rhodians and the Chians lodged complaints against their garrisons. All of their petitions appeared correct and resolutions were put into effect. To recompense the citizens of Mitylene too, considering that they had stood by him outstandingly, he both defrayed the funds that they had laid out on the war and annexed to them a tremendous tract of adjoining territory. To the Cypriot sovereigns besides, who had not only defected from Darius, but had also sent Alexander a fleet whilst he invested Tyre, went honours commensurate with their helpfulness.

5.39 Since both Persian and Spartan soldiery was ravaging much of the island's territory, Amphoterus, admiral of the fleet, was afterwards sent to liberate Crete, being bidden as his first priority to rid the sea of flotillas engaged in piracy. For it was plagued by plundering corsairs, whilst both kings were engaged by the war. These things being set in train, the king dedicated a golden bowl and thirty goblets to Heracles of Tyre[83] and, intent upon confronting Darius, he ordered a march to the River Euphrates to be announced. *They went by way of Byblos, where* **Theias Byblios, who transcended all humanity in his handsomeness, was enamoured of his own daughter, called Myrra,**[84] *the result of their relationship being the birth of Adonis.*

5.40 Now Darius, on discovering the detour adopted by his foe from Egypt into Libya, pondered whether he should head for his realm's remoter reaches or linger in the vicinity of Mesopotamia. Undoubtedly, he would in person be able to incite the outlying peoples to participate in the war more successfully, as through his satraps he was rallying them only with difficulty. But when word spread abroad on good authority that Alexander with his entire army would pursue him unto whichever territory to which he might flee, being well aware of the vigour of his adversary, Darius decreed that all the contingents counted upon from distant nations should muster at Babylon. The Bactrians, Scythians and indeed the Indians having already gathered, forces from the remaining peoples were assembled in the same period.

5.41 Having swelled his ranks from every quarter, Darius directed an army *half again as large as he had led in Cilicia,* **but with many men wanting for weaponry. These he furnished** *with careful consideration,* **making swords and lances** *much longer than in the Cilician action, for he thought Alexander had derived advantage from their extension.* He manufactured mail for his cavalrymen and their mounts with overlapping leaves of steel. To those that before had had just a javelin, a sword and shield were

---

[83] The Greeks recognised the Tyrian god Melkart as a local version of Heracles.

[84] Jacoby Fragment 3 of Cleitarchus from Stobaeus *Florilegium*, IV 20, 73; it is an implication of the attribution of this fragment to the fifth book that Alexander marched up the coast past Byblos and that the guess that the army marched inland from Tyre is mistaken.

given. Herds of horses were handed over to the foot to be broken in, so that the cavalry might be more numerous than previously. **He followed this *up* with** *what he believed would be a means of intimidating his foe in the form of* two hundred scythed chariots, each drawn by four horses in a row,[85] *such war vehicles being peculiar to those peoples.* Steel-tipped spears poked forward from their poles and triple scythes three spans long were affixed to either end of the yokes projecting beyond the beasts, cutting edges to the fore.[86] Upon the wheels numerous blades were arrayed in opposing orientations. At the hubs another pair of scythes jutted straight out with their blades facing forwards. Still others were set in the rims, some slicing upwards and others slashing downwards. *Thus whatever should get in the way of the charging horses stood to be cut to pieces.*

5.42 *Darius adorned his entire army with emblazoned armour and commissioned courageous commanders. When his forces had been outfitted in this fashion,* the king marched forth from Babylon with a throng *half a million strong, at least a fifth of them on horseback.*[87] He kept the celebrated Tigris on his right and used the Euphrates to screen the left flank of his track, *proceeding through fertile farmland fecund enough to furnish fodder for the beasts and food sufficient for so many men. They filled the fields of Mesopotamia.* Then, after traversing the Tigris, when he heard that his opponent was not far distant, he sent forward Satropates, the captain of his **cavalry**, with a thousand select horsemen. Six thousand again **were assigned to** his marshal, **Mazaeus, to block the fording of the river by his enemy. His orders were additionally to devastate and incinerate the territory to which Alexander was about to make an entry.** For Darius reckoned that his adversary could be incapacitated by *consequential* insufficiency, since he had nothing except what he seized by pillaging, whereas arrangements were in place to deliver supplies to Darius himself either overland or by river.

5.43 *It was* **Darius***'s design that battle should be joined near Nineveh, since the plains thereabouts suited his intentions in affording him ample space to manoeuvre his army's vast formations. Hence he* encamped by **Arbela,** an obscure village that was to achieve distinction through his own

---

[85] Curtius 4.9.4 is explicit that they were *quadrigae* (four horse chariots).

[86] A model of a 4th century BC Persian chariot was found amidst the Oxus treasure: it has four horses with two poles projecting from either side of the carriage and linked by a single yoke passing over the base of the neck of each beast.

[87] There is some disagreement in the sources on Darius's numbers. This may partly be explained by the assumption that the host that left Babylon (reported by Diodorus 17.39.4 & 17.53.3) was substantially larger than the 245,000 men (reported by Curtius 4.12.12), which Darius actually deployed in the field of battle. The fact that Justin 11.12.5 has exactly half the numbers in Diodorus may indicate that the latter has read "a million" for "half a million". The number mounted may originally have been given as a proportion of the total, which would have facilitated the corruption of Cleitarchus's figures in the surviving sources.

ruination. *Here he drilled his forces every day, so that they became responsive and proficient through practice and continual training. His key concern was that confusion could come about in battle due to the diversity of tongues among the contingents he was fielding.* Caching most of his baggage and provisions at Arbela, he bridged the Lycus[88] and spent five days getting his army across just as in traversing the Euphrates *two years* previously.[89] Thence he advanced around eighty stades, encamping beside another tributary, known as the Boumelus[90] *locally*. This territory was advantageous for the deployment of his forces, comprising featureless plains ideal for horses. Not even shrubs or stunted bushes obstructed the ground and it afforded a clear prospect into the far distance all around. And wherever anything protruded above the surrounding field, he bade that it be flattened and that every eminence be levelled.

5.44 Those *scouts* who gauged Darius' strength, insofar as it could be estimated remotely, could scarcely convince Alexander of their fidelity, given that so many thousands had *previously* been slain, when they reported that the force now fielded was larger again. However, as a despiser of every danger and especially the threat from being outnumbered, the king encamped beside the Euphrates on the eleventh day *after striking inland from the coast*. Having thrown bridges across the river, he commanded his cavalry to cross initially and his phalanx subsequently. Meanwhile Mazaeus arrived to oppose his crossing with six thousand horsemen, but did not dare to engage the Macedonian. After a few days had been afforded to his forces rather to raise their morale than to rest them, he began rapidly to advance against his enemy, fearing lest Darius should flee to remote regions of his realm, such that the pursuit would pass into a vast country entirely empty of occupation and devoid of rations. Therefore on the four*teen*th day before *the battle at* Arbela he got to the Tigris.

5.45 *Darius had deemed that Mazaeus might hold the ford and defend the rivercourse against the Macedonian offensive. But the general judged the torrent to be impassable due to its depth and the swiftness of its current, so his defence of it was inattentive. Instead he engaged in the despoiling of the countryside and, when it was wasted far and wide, considered that the enemy could not be supplied. But Alexander advanced to the ford on the advice of a local guide. When he arrived the entire territory across the river was smoking from recent incineration, since Mazaeus was setting fire to whatever he came across* as though he were the enemy in the region. Initially, since the veil of the fumes had dimmed the daylight, Alexander halted for fear of ambush, but then when the scouts he sent forward declared all was clear, he advanced a few of his horse to attempt to

---

[88] The Greater Zab?

[89] On his way to Issus: Curtius 3.7.1.

[90] The Khazir?

ford the watercourse. While they were close to the banks the water reached no higher than their steeds' flanks, but at its mid-stream apex, they were in it up to their necks. Neither does any other river in Eastern parts rush on with so rampaging a flow, for it not only conveys torrents from many tributaries but rocks also. It is in consequence of its careering current that it is called the Tigris, because in the Persian tongue they mean the "Arrow" by this.

5.46 *Therefore,* just as in battle array, *the infantry were flanked by the cavalry and* they lifted their weaponry above their heads, so that *they forayed into the channel* without difficulty. And first among the foot to emerge at the far bank was the king, where he waved with his hands to show the shallows to his soldiers, whilst they were out of hearing. But *the water reached above their chests and they could barely keep a firm footing, since sometimes the slippery stones betrayed their steps and sometimes the swiftness of the current swept them into swimming. The task of those that bore burdens upon their shoulders was especially trying, since they could not right themselves and were swept into swirling vortices by their impeding packs and shields.* And whilst they all strove to retrieve the plunder, they came into conflict with one another more than with the river and the bunches of baggage that drifted about butted many of them under. The king instructed them to concentrate upon keeping hold of their arms, since he would replace anything else *that mattered.* But they were not in a state to accept either his council or what he ordered: their dread drowned him out, and also their mutual recriminations as one after another tottered. Finally, they rose up out of the river where a slackening of the current had revealed shallows with nothing except a few packs lacking.

5.47 *But Alexander devised a defence against the current's violence. He ordered all his troops firmly to link their hands together, so as to form a sort of barrage by bracing them one against another.* The army could have been annihilated had there been an attempt to overwhelm it by any of its enemies, but the king's consistently favourable fortune warded off his adversaries. Similarly, he crossed the Granicus whilst rank upon rank of infantry and cavalry stood riveted upon the far bank. So too he concentrated his forces in the Cilician narrows in the face of such multitudinous foes. Even that recklessness that he displayed in abundance cannot be considered of consequence, since there was never the opportunity to conclude that he had acted rashly. Had Mazaeus fallen upon them whilst they were crossing the watercourse, doubtless he would have surprised them when in disarray, but he did not start to charge them with his horse, until they had reached the riverbank and stood armed for the fray. Mazaeus had fielded no more than a thousand cavalry and Alexander, having ascertained their insufficiency, viewed them disdainfully and bade Ariston, the commander of his Paeonian cavalry, to charge them most vigorously. Those riders fought valiantly that day and Ariston especially. He thrust his lance straight through the throat of Satropates, the commander of the Persian cavalry, then catching him as he fled through the midst of the enemy, he hurled him from his horse and hacked off his head with his sword, though he struggled violently. Returning with his trophy from the decapitation, he laid it at the king's feet amidst loud acclamation, *declaring: "In my country, O king, for such a gift as this one is given a gold cup." "Yes," said Alexander, laughing, "An empty gift, but I shall drink your health in wine from one that is full up."*[91]

5.48 As the crossing had been treacherous and an ordeal for his men Alexander encamped and rested his army that day and the next, **then the day after that he ordered them to march on again.** But *that night* at about the time of the first watch the Moon in eclipse began to hide her heavenly brilliance and then the stain of blood defiled her entire radiance,[92] and those who were already nervous in the run-up to such a decisive collision were consumed by colossal superstitious awe, which engendered a certain sense of trepidation. They moaned that the gods were against their having been dragged to the ends of existence, where rivers refused to be forded, celestial bodies could not keep their characteristic incandescence and everywhere wilderness and wastelands were their environments. The blood of so many thousands *of men* was funding the wild aspirations of a single person, who hated his homeland, had disowned his father Philip and already in his own hubristic opinion was headed for Heaven. Matters were moving towards mutiny, when the king, quite unmoved by everything, summoned his commanders and a crowd of his senior soldiers to his headquarters tent. And Alexander bade that the Egyptian seers, whom he considered most expert in astronomy and astrology, should announce their judgement. But despite being sufficiently well aware that cyclical celestial bodies exhibit predictable fluctuations and that the Moon wanes either when it is shaded by the Earth or else when the Sun comes close to it *in the sky*, these sages did not enlighten the troopers with the wisdom that they themselves had come by. Rather they declared that the Sun symbolised the Greek side whereas the Moon signified the Persian, so that whenever she went into shadow, it presaged calamity and overthrow for that nation. And they specified examples of Persian kings of yore, for whom an eclipse of the Moon had made manifest divine disfavour in war. Nothing moves a mob more effectively than superstition. Though otherwise anarchic, wild and fickle, they better obey the seers than their leaders, when they are seized by a false sense of religion. Therefore this interpretation by the Egyptians, when communicated to the crowd, restored the optimism and loyalty of those who had been cowed.

5.49 Reckoning he ought *at once* to exploit their raised spirits, the king broke camp in the second watch of the night. The mountains called the Gordyaeans lay on his left and he had the Tigris on his right. After they had set out upon

---

[91] An anecdote from Plutarch, *Alexander* 39.1.

[92] A Lunar Eclipse occurred on 20th September 331BC (Julian) with totality beginning at around 9pm local time eleven days before the battle (Plutarch, *Alexander* 31.4). This is consistent with the inference above (end of section 5.44) that Alexander reached the Tigris fourteen days before the battle.

this march, scouts who had been sent ahead spying declared at dawn that Darius was arriving. Hence Alexander led his lines forward drawn up in fighting formation. But these were stragglers from the Persian concentration, just a thousand strong, who had given the impression of a colossal throng, since when the truth cannot be found fear compounds what is wrong. This being realised, the king led a few of his men in hot pursuit of the Persians as they fled back to their brothers, slaying some and seizing others. He sent horsemen ahead of him to perform a reconnaissance and in order to extinguish the fires that the Persians had set in the settlements in the same instance. For the fugitives had hastily cast torches into the roof-thatch and upon piles of grain and, although the fire had caught hold in the upper reaches, the lower parts were not yet aflame. Hence, when the fires were quenched, the majority of the grain remained edible and supplies of other provisions also grew plentiful. This in itself fired the enthusiasm of the troops in their pursuit of their adversaries, for since they were burning the land and laying it to waste, in order to stop them ere they set everything ablaze, there was need for considerable haste. Therefore what had been begun by necessity became sensible policy, for Mazaeus, who had been leisurely in setting the settlements alight previously, was now content to flee, relinquishing most things undamaged to his enemy. Alexander had determined that Darius lay no further than one hundred and fifty stades away, and so, being supplied with provisions to the point of satiety, he stayed for four days in the same locality.

5.50 Then dispatches from Darius were intercepted inciting the Greek allied troops either to slay or to betray their king and Alexander wondered whether he should recite them at an assembly, since he was satisfied that even these Greeks bore him sufficient goodwill and loyalty. But Parmenion deterred him, declaring that such offers would pollute the ears of the soldiers. A ruler is vulnerable to the treachery of even a single individual and greed makes nothing seem criminal. So the king broke camp, complying with the counsel of his general.

5.51 Whilst he was en route, *a eunuch from among those detainees that attended upon* the wife of Darius *announced to Alexander that she was weakening and barely breathing. Exhausted by the continual toil of travelling and with her spirit ailing, she had collapsed into the arms of her mother-in-law and her maiden offspring* in the course of miscarrying.[93] *Thereafter she* passed away *and another eunuch arrived bearing that announcement. Hardly less than if news of the death of his own mother had been sent, the king exclaimed many a lament and with welling tears, such as Darius might have shed, he went whither the mother of Darius sat beside the lifeless body in a tent. Here he relapsed into sorrow, when*

---

[93] Though not in either Curtius or Diodorus, the miscarriage is adduced by both Plutarch, *Alexander* 30.1 and Justin 11.12.6, which makes it likelier than not that it was in Cleitarchus: perhaps due to disease simulating pregnancy as in the case of Queen Mary Tudor or else the outcome of an illicit liaison during her captivity with Alexander.

he saw her laid low upon the ground. Reminded too of earlier ills by this fresh wound, Sisygambis enfolded the marriageable maidens in her embrace, a great solace in their mutual mourning, though it ought to have been their mother that did the consoling. Her tiny grandson was before her gaze, all the more pitiable because he was unaware of the cascades of calamity converging upon him most particularly.

Figure 5.5. The death of the wife of Darius (1696)

5.52 *It might have been thought that* **Alexander** *wept* compulsively *amidst his own family and that he did not offer but rather sought sympathy. Certainly, he abstained from nutrition and accorded her every* **funerary dignity** *in the fashion of the Persian nation,* deserving, by

Heracles, even now of reaping him a reputation for such temperance and compassion. **He had seen her on just a single occasion** *when he went to visit the mother of Darius rather than his wife on the day of their capture and her exceptional loveliness had vindicated his virtue instead of leading him into lustful rapture.*

5.53 *From among the eunuchs surrounding the queen and amid the commotion made by the mourners, Tyriotes slipped off* on horseback *through a gate that was but lightly guarded, since it faced away from the enemy's soldiers. He was seized by the sentries on reaching Darius' encampment and being led into the royal tent by these, he moaned and rent his raiment. When Darius set eyes upon him, he was apprehensive in anticipation of various species of adversity and being unsure about which he should have most anxiety he said: "Your expression portrays some untold tragedy, but have a care not to spare the ears of an unfortunate fellow; I have learnt to live lucklessly and it is frequently a comfort in calamity for a man to know his destiny. Are you not in fact going to announce what I most sorely suspect yet dread to utter: that my family have been debauched, which is to me and I believe also to all of them viler than torture?" To this Tyriotes retorted: "Actually, that's far from the truth of the matter, for the greatest respect that can be paid to queens by their own people has been accorded to your kinfolk by the conqueror. However, a little while ago your wife departed from this life."*

5.54 *Then indeed not just groaning but also shrieking was heard through the whole encampment. Nor did Darius doubt that she had been slain because she could not endure her defilement and manic with misery he moaned: "What heinous iniquity have I committed, Alexander? Which of your kin did I kill that you vengefully repay my brutality? You abhor me without even any provocation, but supposing that you wage war against me justly, are you consequently obliged to make women the targets of your aggression?" Tyriotes swore by the gods of his homeland that she had not been subjected to anything appalling. Just as Darius had not stifled his tears, Alexander too had been greatly grieved by her death and had not held back from bawling. But this itself in the mind of her doting husband fired up further anxiety and suspicion, for he inferred that mourning the loss of a captive must indeed have been inspired by habitual sexual molestation. Hence he dismissed all the onlookers and only retained Tyriotes. Now no longer crying, but rather sighing he said: "Do you not see, Tyriotes, that this is not the place for perjuries? The tools for torture are about to be brought in, but by the gods do not hold out for them, if you have any reverence for your sovereign. Being both youthful and her captor, did he not dare to do what I both wish to know but am ashamed to examine?"*

5.55 *The eunuch volunteered his body for interrogation under torture, but invoked the attestations[94] of the gods that the queen had remained unviolated and had retained her honour. Then, finally being brought to believe the eunuch's testimony, Darius veiled his head and wept a long while, until he wrenched the robe from his face and reached up his hands towards the heavens, declaring, tearful still:* "O ancestral gods of my country, I had rather that you should maintain my throne's stability, *so that I might properly requite my adversary,* but if now there must come an end to my sovereignty *to appease divine jealousy,* I pray that none other should in future be the king of Asia save he that is so just an enemy and so merciful in victory."[95]

5.56 *And so, despite having turned all his attentions towards war when his peace overtures had twice been spurned, being swayed by the forbearance shown by his opponent,* Darius dispatched *ten emissaries, his key kinsmen,* bearing fresh terms for a peace settlement. Alexander convened his council *and bade that these envoys be brought in and the eldest among them was their spokesman and said:* "Darius has *felt no compulsion to appeal to you for peace on a third occasion, but rather this has been elicited by your fairness and moderation. We gain* no impression of his mother, wife and children being incarcerated, except insofar as they and Darius stay separated. You are scarcely less careful of the chastity of those that remain than a father would be, recognising them as queens and suffering them to retain the semblance of their former dignity. *Your countenance conveys the sort of sentiment I saw in the face of Darius, when he dispatched our embassy, yet he is mourning the death of a wife, you the loss of an enemy. You should already be stood in battle formation, had your attention to her funeral not entailed your detention.* What wonder that Darius should seek to make peace with a man of such a friendly disposition? What need is there of warfare between those who have risen above their dissension? Previously, *as well as a twenty thousand talent bounty,* he intended the River Halys at the Lydian border to be the boundary of your hegemony. Now he cedes everything between the Hellespont and the Euphrates as the dowry of his daughter, whom he offers you in matrimony. *Let you hold on to his son Ochus as hostage for his fidelity and inaction, but* let his mother and two virgin daughters be returned to us. *For their three persons* he prays that you accept *in compensation* thrice ten thousand talents of gold from us. *As the son-in-law of Darius, your role shall be hereditary in sharing control of the whole country.*"

---

[94] There is a pun in the Latin of Curtius such that the eunuch, lacking *testes*, invokes the *testes* of the gods on his behalf.

[95] This prayer of Darius appears in similar forms in: Curtius 4.10.34; Plutarch, *Alexander* 30.6; Plutarch, *Moralia* 338E-F; Arrian, *Anabasis* 4.20.3.

5.57 "Had I not noted your moderate disposition, I would withhold from hailing this as the moment when you should not solely accept but ought actually to seize a settlement. Consider how much lies in your wake. Understand how much you have still to take. An overextended empire is perilous, for what you cannot reach is hard to hold. Have you not observed that overladen ships cannot be controlled? I am not at all sure that Darius has not suffered so many losses on account of the room for diminutions provided by excessively vast possessions. Some things are more readily wrested away than retained. By Heracles! How much easier it is for our hands to grasp a thing than that the thing be completely contained. In itself the death of Darius' wife could be cautionary in that you already have less ability to behave compassionately."

5.58 Alexander bade that the emissaries should withdraw from his tent for him to discuss with his council what they had urged in settlement. The king encouraged each councillor to express his sentiment. For ages no one dared to speak his mind, since it was unclear which way the king inclined. But at last Parmenion *mentioned that he had pressed previously for those prisoners detained at Damascus to be released to their ransomers, since a huge amount of money could be raised from those in fetters, whose handling was diverting many powerful warriors. And now too he earnestly advised that a solitary grandmother and a pair of girls should indeed be sold, being burdens both on the march and in battle order, in exchange for thirty thousand talents in gold. A rich realm could be reaped through negotiation, rather than hostilities, and nobody else had held the whole of the huge territories extending from the River Ister[96] to the Euphrates. Furthermore, Alexander ought to look back out of regard for Macedonia instead of staring forwards towards Bactria and India. He* concluded: **"If I were Alexander, I would accept this offer."**

5.59 The king *was displeased by this declamation, hence he* **replied** *at its conclusion:* **"So too should I, if I were Parmenion. That is, I would prefer funds to fame. But as it is, my name is Alexander and,** *being without a worry concerning penury,* **I remember that I am a ruler rather than a trader.** *Indeed, I have nothing at all to retail, but in particular I do not put my majesty up for sale. If it should please us to repatriate our prisoners, then it would be more honorable to give them as gifts, than ransom them for a fee, but thanks are worthless from an enemy."*

5.60 Thereafter, having recalled the delegation, he gave them his answer in the following fashion: "Tell Darius from me that my acts of kindness and clemency were due to my natural inclinations rather than any attempt to appear friendly *or to instigate diplomacy.* **I refrain habitually from warring with women and those I hold in captivity,** *but it befits him to arm himself, who has aggrieved me.* **Nevertheless, if he should ask for peace**

---

[96] The Danube.

in good faith, unambiguously, I might perhaps consider granting his plea. But just as a world with two suns would not work properly, so the lands of men cannot be kept in peace and tranquillity, whilst two kings share the sovereignty.[97] Therefore, if Darius desires peace, he must cede me the supremacy, *though he may live on in luxury and rule every satrapy under my warranty.* Alternatively, he must *shortly* do battle with me to see who shall have the monarchy, *but he should have no higher hopes than previously.* And when, in actuality, he has recently sent letters to my soldiers inciting them to treachery and has just tried to bribe my friends to do away with me, I must pursue him to perdition as an assassin who resorts to chicanery, rather than as a legitimate adversary."

5.61 "In truth the terms for peace that you have delivered, were I to agree them, would cede Darius the victory. He offers me what is behind the Euphrates with generosity. Are you therefore oblivious of where you are even now addressing me? I am beyond the Euphrates, surely? Hence my encampment is beyond the broadest boundary of the territory he promises as a dowry. So that I may know that it is yours to surrender, let you expel me from this territory. And Darius would give me his daughter with the same sort of generosity, though I know her to be betrothed to one who is his lackey. How highly indeed he honours me, if he prefers me to Mazaeus for propagating his dynasty! Go tell your king that both what he has lost and what he yet retains are the stakes in our hostilities, since for both of our domains it is war that shall set the boundaries and which shall see that each of us obtains whatever the fortune of the forthcoming day decrees." **The envoys *replied that, his heart being set upon war, he was acting with honesty in not beguiling them with hopes of a peace treaty. They begged to be allowed to return to their king immediately and advised Alexander that he too should make ready for butchery. Being then dismissed, they* reported that battle would be joined imminently.**

5.62 Darius did not delay in moving Mazaeus forward with three thousand cavalry to guard the routes via which his enemy's advance was likely. Alexander, having performed the rites for the body of Darius' wife in due fashion, left all the more cumbersome components of his expedition within the existing ramparts with a skeleton garrison and advanced rapidly towards the opposition. He had split his infantry into two wings and had positioned cavalry around both flanks with the baggage trailing behind the army's ranks. Next he sent Menidas ahead with veteran horsemen with the mission of determining Darius's location. But he, when he found Mazaeus ensconced nearby, did not dare to advance any further, and was able to announce only that he had heard the din of men and the whinnying of their mounts. Likewise Mazaeus, upon discerning the scouts in the distance, scurried back to camp and announced the arrival of their opponents.

---

[97] The metaphor of the "two suns" is curiously missing from Curtius, but clearly derived from Cleitarchus, since it is found in both Diodorus 17.54.5 and Justin 11.12.15.

5.63 Therefore Darius, who had chosen open ground for the fray, ordered his troops to take up their weapons and arranged them in battle array. On his left wing there were Bactrian cavalry about a thousand strong with the same number of Dahae horsemen plus four thousand from Arachosia and Susianê to complete the *front of the* throng. These were backed up by a hundred scythed chariots and Bessus sat behind these four-horse vehicle positions with eight thousand more mounted Bactrians. Two thousand Massagetae brought up the rear of the formation. To these he had adjoined footsoldiers from many races, not intermingled, but each with their national forces. Next Ariobarzanes and Orontobates led the Persians supported by the Mardians and the Sogdians. These men commanded individual divisions, but Orsines, a descendant of the "Seven Persians", who also traced his ancestry to Cyrus, that most renowned ruler, was their overall commander. These were backed up by other tribes, which not even the record made by their allies adequately describes. Next after these nations came Phradates leading fifty four-horse chariots together with considerable Caspian formations. To the rear of the chariots were the Indians and the rest of the Red Sea residents, there to make up numbers rather than to act in offence. The rear of this section of the front was occupied by other scythed chariots, to which were attached the foreign recruits. Next to these came the so-called "Lesser" Armenians and next to them the Babylonians and both the Belitae and those that dwelt amidst the mountains of the Cossaeans. After these went the Gortuae, actually a Euboean band, sometime recruits of the Medes, but now degenerate and ignorant of the customs of their homeland. Next to them Darius placed the Phrygians and the Cataonians. Thereafter the Parthians finished off this formation. Such was his left wing for the confrontation.

5.64 The right wing was held by the nationals of Greater Armenia together with the Cadusian, the Cappadocian, the Syrian and the Median nations. Here too a force of fifty scythed chariots took up their stations. The fighting strength of the entire field army comprised forty-five thousand cavalry and two hundred thousand infantry. Arrayed in this fashion they advanced ten stades and were then told to stand under arms awaiting their enemy.

5.65 Alexander's army was gripped by panic, the cause of which was not clear, for they began to be agitated and frantic as an obscure dread breached the breast of every soldier. A shimmer in the sky like that from late-summer stubble burning seemed to reflect flames and they supposed that this was the glow from the camp-fires of the Persian hosts as though they had chanced upon their outposts. If Mazaeus, who was holding the highway, had fallen upon them whilst they were in this state of alarm, he could have inflicted huge harm. As it was, whilst he lurked at ease upon an eminence that he had seized, content to sit there inviolate, Alexander, recognising his army's disquiet, issued the signal for them to halt in their tracks, ordering that they should set aside their arms and relax. And he admonished them that there was no cause for consternation, since they were still far from the opposition. Eventually, they calmed down, retrieving both their arms and their doughty disposition. And nothing seemed more prudent in their present position than to fortify an encampment at that same location.

5.66 The next day, either due to loss of nerve or through having been ordered only to observe, Mazaeus accompanied by his elite cavalry relinquished the lofty eminence overlooking the Macedonian encampment and returned to Darius' presence. The Macedonians seized the same height he had yielded; since it was more secure than the level ground and the fighting formations their foe fielded could be monitored from that mound. But a mist that had emerged from the humid hills in their environment, even though it did not obscure an overview, prevented the discernment of each regiment and its deployment. They had flooded the plain with their vast array and the din from so many thousands of men even filled the ears of those stood far away. The king's resolution began to waver in weighing up whether Parmenion's plan or his own were better; however, they had reached a point whence the army could not be withdrawn without calamity except through victory. Consequently, concealing his concerns, the king commanded the advance of the mercenary Paeonian cavalry. He had himself, as has been related, deployed his phalanx into two wings and he had designated his cavalry to protect these wings. And now the brightening daylight had dispersed the haze, plainly revealing his adversary's battle arrays. And his Macedonians, whether out of enthusiasm or to relieve the prelude's tedium, emitted a mighty rallying cry in fighting fashion. The Persians reciprocated so that the woods and the vales resounded with fearsome bellows. And now the Macedonians could no longer be dissuaded from charging upon their foes. Yet, reckoning it better to curtain his encampment upon that same elevation, Alexander bade that they throw up a fortification and when they rapidly completed this assignment, the king withdrew into his tent, whence he could survey the whole battlefront of his opponent.

5.67 Then indeed the entire form of the forthcoming contest was before his gaze. The arms and the banners of warriors and steeds made resplendent displays. Amongst the enemy everything was being made ready with meticulous care, as the fastidiousness of the commanders in riding up and down their lines made clear. And many inconsequential events, such as a murmur from the men, neighing from the nags and the glinting and glimmering of arms, disturbed a mind made anxious by the suspense. Therefore either due to genuine irresolution or else in order to put his officers to the test, the king convened a council to consult as to what course of action would be for the best. **Parmenion,** the most expert of his marshals in the art of war, **advised that a sneak attack rather than a battle was called for. Their adversaries could be surprised in the dead of night.** Having incompatible customs and mutually unintelligible tongues and being startled out of their sleep by an unforeseen fright, how could they possibly unite in the confusion of a nocturnal fight? But in broad daylight, the Macedonians would from the first be faced by the fearsome figures of the Scythians and the Bactrians: their faces furry and their hair unkempt, not to mention their extraordinarily huge height. Troops are more than reasonably upset by such silly and absurd sorts of threat. In that situation such a multitude could engulf a smaller force, for the fight was being fought in a wideopen plain, rather than in a narrow and constricted Cilician course. Practically everyone concurred with Parmenion and Polyperchon swore that victory was unequivocally vested in that plan. It was the latter upon whom **Alexander** fixed his gaze and to whom he **delivered a counter-statement**, since he had recently reproached Parmenion more stingingly than he had meant and was reluctant to repeat that admonishment: "The skills in which you would school me are theft and skulduggery, for their only prayer lies in secrecy. I shall not suffer my reputation repeatedly to be undermined either by the absence of Darius or a confined pass or nocturnal chicanery. **I am resolved to attack in broad daylight, as I prefer to risk regretting the outcome** of this fight, **than be shamed by stealing my victory**.[98] Additionally, it has been reported to me that the barbarians are standing at arms and watching vigilantly, so that it would not actually be possible to come upon them unexpectedly. Therefore it is for a pitched battle that I bid you to make ready." Then he sent them off to refresh themselves, having thus incited them against the enemy.

5.68 Darius, having inferred that his opponent would do as Parmenion had counselled, ordered that the steeds should stand bridled, that a large fraction of his army should stay armed and that the vigilance of the night watch should be redoubled. Consequently, his entire camp was effulgent with fire. In the company of his commanders and his relations he himself did the rounds of his regiments as they stood at their stations, invoking the Sun, Mithras and the sacred eternal flame to inspire them with courage in keeping with the record of their forbears and their immemorial fame. And certainly, said he, if the signs of divine support could be sensed by the human mind, then the gods stood behind them. They had, he added, recently struck a sudden terror into the minds of the Macedonians, who were still frenziedly casting aside their weapons and suitable suffering would soon be sought from these madmen by the deities of the domains of the Persians. Nor was their leader any saner than they, for in the way of a wild beast he had fixed his gaze upon his prey and was careering into the pitfall behind which this prize lay.

5.69 Amongst the Macedonians too there was similar apprehension, and they spent the night in fear, as if that were when the battle was in contention. Alexander, never in a greater state of agitation, bade that Aristander be called to preside over prayers and devotion. Robed in brilliant white, his head veiled, and holding out ahead of him the sacred fronds, the seer led the royal orisons to propitiate Zeus and Athena Nike *and then made offerings to Fear*.[99] Then, only when he had performed the sacrificial rite, **the king returned to his tent to rest for**

---

[98] See Plutarch, *Alexander* 31.7 for Alexander refusing to steal a victory.

[99] See Plutarch, *Alexander* 31.4 for the sacrifice to *Phobos*.

what was left of the night. But he could neither fall asleep nor relax: he fretted *whether he should launch his attacks from the crest of the ridge against the Persian right wing or else rush head-on upon the enemy, whilst pondering whether swerving his front against their left wing would be preferable, occasionally.* Eventually, at about the morning watch, his body being overburdened by his mind's anxiety, he slept exceptionally soundly. And already by daybreak Alexander's commanders had gathered to accept their orders, astonished by the unaccustomed silence enveloping the headquarters. *For on other occasions he had been in the habit of summoning them and sometimes chiding the tardy. Now* they were incredulous that he had actually failed to awake for the ultimate decisive tourney *and they began to believe that he was quailing in trepidation rather than sleeping restfully.* Yet none among his Bodyguards dared to enter his tent. *And now the moment was imminent, but without the orders of their commanders the troops could neither take up their arms nor form up by regiment.* After having waited a long while, Parmenion pronounced on his own authority that the soldiers should eat *and make ready.* But the king continued to slumber, though it had become necessary that the army should set forth urgently. Then, finally, Parmenion made entry to the king's tent, calling out his name repeatedly, but, when he could not rouse Alexander by voice alone, he shook him gently and confided: "It is fully light and our adversaries are advancing drawn up in fighting formation. Where's your lively disposition? Usually, indeed, you rouse the actual sentries."

5.70 Alexander retorted: "Do you suppose I could have slept before I had relieved my mind of all the anxieties that postponed my tranquillity?" *Then he ordered that the trumpet blast be blown that signalled the onset of hostilities.* And, when Parmenion relentlessly expressed his incredulity at Alexander's claim to have fallen asleep carefree, the king responded *grinning*: "It's not so surprising. When Darius was scorching the earth, devastating villages and spoiling provisions, it drove me round the bend, but now indeed what have I to fear, when he gives me a battle to contend? Now *that he has concentrated his contingents,* in a single day we shall make an end, curtailing the toil and risk that would otherwise extend. *By Heracles, he has fulfilled my heart's desire, but the reckoning behind this rationale shall subsequently transpire. Let you rejoin the regiments that you respectively lead. I shall join you imminently and explain how I wish you to proceed."* Alexander was only in the habit of donning a cuirass on very rare occasions and then at the urging of his Friends rather than through apprehension at entering into hazardous situations, but that time at any rate he assumed this bodily protection then went forth to meet his legions. Never before had they seen their king possessed of such alacrity and from his dauntless expression they conceived a firm expectation of victory.

Figure 5.6. Alexander and Aristander sacrifice to Fear by André Castaigne (1898)

5.71 After having *a section of* the rampart levelled, *Alexander ordered* that his forces march forth and that *his line of battle be assembled.* The king stationed the royal cavalry squadron, called the Agema, under the command of Cleitus, dubbed the Black, on his right wing. Adjoining them were the rest of the Friends led by Philotas, Parmenion's son, who also had overall command of the other seven squadrons successively flanking him. *Last of these was the squadron of Meleager, which was followed by the phalanx.* Behind *the phalanx in reserve* stood the Silver Shield[100] infantry under the command of Nicanor *another* son of Parmenion. Next in line lay the regiment *from Elimiotis* led by Coenus and after him the Lyncestian and Orestian regiment was posted *under Perdiccas. Meleager commanded* the next regiment *and after him* Polyperchon led *the Stymphaean contingent. Then came the foreign troops, whose commander, Amyntas, was absent.* Philip the son of Balacrus, *who had only recently been received into alliance,* was running these regiments. *Such was the composition of the right wing. On the left,* Craterus held the next command. Here were the combined Peloponnesian and Achaean cavalry, then the horsemen from *Phthiotis and* Malis and mounted Locrians *and Phocians* adjoining them, *all led by Erigyius of Mitylene.* Their flank was covered *by the ranks* of the Thessalian cavalry, commanded by Philip. *They far excelled the rest in*

---

[100] The *argyraspides*: the name in given at this juncture by both Diodorus and Curtius, the latter using the correct Greek term; hence it must be taken from Cleitarchus. They are also called *hypaspists*; it seems that they only became *argyraspides* when Alexander distributed silver embossed shields in India (Curtius 8.5.4), so Cleitarchus might be using the term anachronistically here.

their combat capability and in their horsemanship. Next to them the king stationed the Achaean mercenaries. And the ranks of the infantry were covered by the cavalry. Such was the left wing front. But in order that his shorter ranks could not be outflanked due to the numerical superiority of the enemy, the king *enclosed the back of his dispositions with robust battalions. He also* reinforced his flanks with reserves, not facing forwards, but rather towards the sides, *so that, if his foe should try to go around to attack behind his battle lines, they would stand ready to fight back. The Agrianians were here with Attalus as their commander and the Cretan bowmen were joined with them at this station. The hindmost ranks were rearward facing, so as to defend a ring around his entire formation. The Illyrians were in this location combined with the mercenary squadrons and there too he set the lightly armed Thracians in position.* And by these dispositions he made his ranks so adaptable that those that stood at the rear to resist encirclement could nevertheless turn around and be faced to the front. Hence the front was not better defended than the flanks, nor were the flanks better protected than the hindmost ranks.[101]

5.72 *Having thus configured his army,* Alexander instructed his soldiery that *if the barbarians sent their scythed chariots against them with a great din, then* they should silently open their ranks to receive them as they impetuously rushed on in, for he had no doubt that they would gallop through without doing injury, so long as their path were blocked by nobody. *However, if the chariots were sent forth without any clamouring, then* they were to panic them by beating their shields with their spears *and hollering and to stab their javelins up through the hides of the frightened horses from both sides. Those commanding the wings were bidden to space their soldiers such that they should neither be outflanked due to standing too near to one another nor rather make their rearmost ranks disappear. The baggage along with every detainee, amongst whom the mother and offspring of Darius were kept in custody, he placed upon the high hill hard by the battlefield leaving a skeleton guard. As was customary, Parmenion was put in charge of the left wing, whilst* a station on the right wing was taken by the king.

5.73 They had still not closed to within a javelin's flight, when Bion, a turncoat, rushed across to reach **Alexander** as fast as he might, declaring that Darius had driven iron spikes into the dust, where he thought that his foe's cavalry would make their thrust and he had marked the place with care, so that his own side could avoid the snare. The king, having called for the informer to be escorted, convened his captains and told them what had been reported, warning them to avoid the designated vicinity and to highlight the danger to their cavalry.[102]

---

[101] Cf. Frontinus, *Strategemata* 2.3.19.

[102] These kinds of spikes are called caltrops: cf. Polyaenus 4.3.17.

5.74 However, the army was unable to hear the king when he issued exhortations, for their ears were filled with the furore from the two opposing formations. But cantering between his commanders and his companions in the sight of all he *voiced these expostulations:* "After traversing so many lands in the hope of the victory for which we shall be contending, just this single struggle is outstanding. **Recall the Granicus River, the crags of Cilicia** and Syria and Egypt conquered in the course of our journey. These should be your inspiration for high hopes of huge glory. **Having had repeatedly to be rallied from flight, it will only be if they cannot flee that the Persians will stand and fight.** It is now the third day that, white with terror, they have stood rooted to the spot weighed down by their arms and armour. There is no better indication of their desperation, than that they have subjected their towns and their farms to incineration, thereby conceding that whatever they do not destroy is ours to enjoy. And *you should not be much afraid of the boastful names of obscure nations, for it is irrelevant to the outcome of the war which of their number are Scythians and which Cadusians.* Insofar as they have stayed unfound, they are bound to be unrenowned, for the valorous are never without their reputations, whereas shirkers levered from their lairs contribute nothing but their appellations. Through their valiance the Macedonians have guaranteed that there is no place in the whole world unaware of the bravery of their breed. Take a good look at the rabble in the ranks of our enemies. Some have nothing but a javelin, whilst others fling stones from a sling. Few indeed have proper panoplies. Therefore, *though more stand on their side, more on our side shall be engaging.* Neither shall I expect you valiantly to charge into this contest, unless I myself am the exemplar of courage for all the rest. You shall find me fighting before of our foremost banner. Ornamenting my body I bear many scars to attest to my valour. You know for yourselves that from the communal spoils I am almost alone in taking no share, but employ the prizes of victory for your care and accoutrement. But it is to the courageous that I have addressed this encouragement. Were there any here of a dissimilar disposition, I should have given them a different disquisition: that we have reached a point from which flight is not a possibility; that, after such expansive territory has been left in our tracks and we have put so many rivers and mountain ranges behind our backs, we must fight to make the journey to our own hearths in our home country." Thereby he inspired his commanders and the bystanders amongst the military.

5.75 Darius was on his left wing ensconced amidst mass formations of his soldiery, choice cavalry and elite infantry, and he had expressed contempt for the thin ranks of his adversary, reckoning that the extension of Alexander's wings had made his battlefront empty. But, being raised up in his chariot, with outstretched arms he swept his gaze right and left around his surrounding arrays, saying: "We, that just recently were the lords of lands washed by the Ocean on the one hand and extending to the Hellespont at the other end, must fight now not for glory but rather for our vitality and for what matters more to you than vitality: your very liberty. This day shall see re-established or finished an empire larger than any other age has witnessed. At the Granicus the least part of our manpower engaged the enemy. Being vanquished in Cilicia, Syria could give us sanctuary and the Tigris and the Euphrates were deep defences of our territory. But we have arrived at a place, from which, if thrown back, there is not even any space to flee. Everything in our rear has been consumed by these protracted hostilities. Our towns have lost their dwellers and our land lacks tillers. Our wives too and our children accompany our companies, ready prey for our adversaries, unless we interpose our bodies in defence of our dearest responsibilities."

5.76 "For my own part, I have fielded forces such as this almost immeasurable plain can scarcely contain. I have distributed arms and steeds and I have guaranteed that even so vast a multitude should not lack provisions and I have selected a location in which we can fully deploy our fighting divisions. Everything else lies within your power. You need merely dare to conquer, scorning their reputation, which is the most worthless weapon in confronting a brave warrior. What you have feared up until now as boldness was actually recklessness, which, having lost its initial impetus, like some bee that has shot its sting, becomes powerless. Furthermore, these plains have made manifest their sparseness, which the crags of Cilicia suppressed. Behold their thin lines, their widespread wings and their centre hollowed and frail, for he has averted his rearmost ranks from us, so that they are already turning tail. By Heracles, they can be trampled beneath the hooves of our horses, even if I send forth nothing but our scythed chariot forces. And we shall have won the war, if we win this fight, for they do not even have a chance at flight. The Euphrates over there and here the Tigris prohibit them from getting out of this."

5.77 "Furthermore, factors that formerly favoured them have now been turned about. Their army is laden with plunder, whereas ours is wieldy and lightly kitted out. Hence, hampered by loot lifted from us, we shall put them to the sword and the same thing as provides our victory shall also provide its reward. But if the reputation of their nation disturbs any of you, know that it is the Macedonian panoplies that are there and not their actual bodies. For we in our turn have shed their blood in large amounts and losses are more serious amongst modest headcounts. And as for Alexander, however imposing he may appear to the cowardly and craven, he is but a single being and, if you hold with my opinion, a reckless and irrational person, who owes more to our quaking than to his own dash and daring. But it is impossible for anything to prove lasting without being based upon reasoning. Though fair winds may seem to blow, they eventually cease to pillow rashness. Furthermore, the twists of fate are fast and unpredictable and Fortune's favours are never reliable. Perchance the gods have ordained our fate thus: that the Persian Empire, which they have raised to a pinnacle of power as it thrived through three decades plus two centuries, should be shaken rather than shattered by a shock of some gravity in order to remind us of our mortal frailties, which too easily slip from memory in the midst of prosperity. We were carrying out campaigning in Greece but recently. Now we are repulsing an assault upon us in our own country. We are tossed in our turn by Fortune's fickleness. Obviously, this Empire that is sought by both sides, one people will not possess. Nevertheless, even if no hope were left to us, we ought still to be spurred by dire necessity. For we have reached the worst extremity. My mother together with two daughters of mine and Ochus, conceived in the expectation of his inheritance of our dominions, and princes who are progeny of our royal houses and your commanders, kept fettered like felons. Except for what is left to me in you, I am the greater part held hostage. Rescue my flesh and blood from bondage, bring back those dear to me, my mother and offspring, for whom you yourselves do not shirk from dying. As for my wife, I lost her during her incarceration. But you may trust that all of them are even now holding out their hands to you in supplication, imploring the gods of our nation, entreating your aid, your pity and your devotion, to set them free from their shackles, from slavery and from humiliating submission. Or do you suppose them patient with their slavery to those of whom they disdain the government?"

5.78 "I see that the lines of the enemy are now advancing, but the closer I come to the contest the less content I can be with the words I have been pronouncing. By the gods of our country and by the eternal fire that is borne upon altars before us, and by the glow of the sun that ascends within the bounds of my empire and by the everlasting memory of Cyrus, who first wrenched the rulership from the Medes and the Lydians and apportioned it to the Persians, I beseech you to save from the utmost shame the people of Persia and our nation's name. Go forward in high spirits and full of confidence, in order that the glory got from your forefathers be left to your descendants. In your hands, by your right, you grip our liberty, our aspirations and our might. He who scorns death escapes mortality, but it always overtakes the most cowardly. A chariot conveys me, not only because of the customs of our country, but also to be seen the more conspicuously, and neither am I contrary to your copying me, whether I prove to set an example of cowardice or of bravery."

5.79 In the meantime **Alexander ordered his ranks to advance obliquely,** *both in order to circumvent the snares' vicinity and to intercept Darius, who had a wing to oversee. Darius too turned his own men in the same direction,* having bidden Bessus to urge the Massagetae cavalry on his left[103] to charge the flank of Alexander's wing formation. **Darius had the scythed chariots in front of his station, which upon his signal flung themselves collectively against the opposition. The charioteers galloped headlong towards the enemy,** *in order to fell more of the insufficiently forewarned warriors through their impetuosity. Accordingly some were lacerated by*

---

[103] Curtius 4.15.2 seems to say that the charge was against Alexander's left wing, but the Massagetae were stationed on Darius's extreme left wing near Bessus (Curtius 4.12.7).

the lances that lunged along far to the fore of the poles of the vehicles, whilst others were dissected by the scythes set on both sides of the curricles. Nor did the Macedonians give way steadily, but rather left their lines disorderly as they scattered readily. And additionally **Mazaeus, master of most of the cavalry,** *compounded the consternation by simultaneously sending his serried squadrons against the enemy.[104] And he ordered two thousand Cadusians and a thousand select Scythian horsemen to wheel around the flank of their adversary to capture the baggage ensconced in its den. For he considered that the captives, who were also being guarded, would break out of their bonds upon perceiving the approach of their countrymen.*

Figure 5.7. The charge of the scythed chariots by André Castaigne (1898)

5.80 But this did not escape the notice of Parmenion, who was on the left wing. Hence he hastily dispatched Polydamas, both to point out their peril and to seek orders as to what they should be doing. Alexander, upon hearing Polydamas out, replied: "Go tell Parmenion that, if we are victorious in this contention, we shall not only recover what is ours, but shall also seize what belongs to the opposition. Therefore let him not divert any men from his formation, but in order to be worthy of my father Philip and of me, let him scorn the loss of our luggage and fight the more valiantly." Meanwhile, **the barbarians having**

---

[104] From this point Curtius switches back and forth between the scythed chariot attack and the raid on the Macedonian base-camp, whereas Diodorus deals with the two actions successively. Since it is unlikely that Curtius would invent such alternations, whereas Diodorus had a strong motive to try to remove them in his ambition of producing a highly summarised account, I have concluded that the switchbacks are probably an authentic feature of Cleitarchus that Curtius reproduced.

ransacked the baggage train and many of its guards having been slain, the captives were struck from their chains and, snatching whatever weapons were to hand, they joined their own side's cavalrymen to beset the Macedonians, who were thus encircled by a second threat. *There was uproar and havoc amongst the tents at this rapid turn of events. The captive women attendant upon Sisygambis were joyous in announcing that Darius was victorious, their foes having been overthrown with great mayhem, even their baggage having ultimately been stripped from them. Most of them rushed to welcome the forces of their country, for they believed that the same outcome had been reached universally and that the Persians were running around pillaging in the aftermath of victory.* Yet Sisygambis, though the mother of Darius, remained emotionless and unmoving, when the captives exhorted her to raise her spirits from her grieving. *She uttered not one word and neither her pallor nor her expression altered, but* she sat unstirred, *I suppose* fearing to offend Fortune through premature jollity *or repudiate her gratitude for Alexander's generosity. And this she did in such a degree that those that beheld her were unsure of her loyalty.*

5.81 In the meantime Menidas, a commander of cavalry for Alexander, arrived with a few squadrons to bring the baggage succour – it is unknown whether on his own initiative or by the king's order. But he could not cope with the Cadusians and Scythians charging, for on scarcely skirmishing he fled back to the king, not so much the baggage's saviour as a witness to its forfeiture. Alexander's setbacks had already upset his plans and he was worried, not without justification, that attention to the recovery of their possessions might divert his troops from the main action. Hence he sent Aretes, the leader of the lancers that are called sarissaphoroi to contend with the Scythians. *Whilst this was happening,* the chariots, *which had thrown the ranks into confusion around the foremost standards, had* assailed the phalanx, *who linked shields and by drumming upon them with their spears raised a fearful din as commanded by the king. When their horses shied, most of the chariots veered about and careered back to collide with the ranks of their own side. Others were not deterred, but hurtled onward into the Macedonian lines and were received with stalwart resolve as* the troops channelled their ranks like valleys into which the chariots were trammelled. Wielding their spears *in concert,* they skewered *the flanks of* the horses *from both sides as they rushed recklessly on through these courses. Then they began to mob the chariots and to hurl forth their combatants. A huge number of crashed chariots and their crushed crews filled the field's expanse, for the charioteers could not control their terrified animals, which by incessantly thrashing their necks had not only cast off their yokes but had even overturned the vehicles. Those wounded dragged along the slain and could neither pull up in their panic nor progress due to the awful strain. Nevertheless,* a few of the chariots dodged their way through to the rear of the formation, condemning those they encountered to a wretched extinction, *for severed segments of men were strewn upon the soil. Such was the sharpness and velocity of the scythes, cunningly devised to despoil victims of their limbs, that arms were amputated with their shield and often slickly sliced necks sent heads tumbling upon the field with eyes wide open and a frozen expression or else slashes to the ribs left a fatal incision. Since those freshly injured perceived no pain from their lacerations, though maimed and drained, they did not even set aside their weapons, until they had so greatly bled that they fell forward stone dead.*

5.82 *As the main ranks closed they discharged their missiles using slings and bows and, after flinging their javelins, they came in contact and began to exchange blows. The cavalry were first into the fray and, the Macedonians being stationed on their own right, Darius, who held his own left in sway, flung his mounted kinsmen against them in his sight. These were men selected for bravery and loyalty, all one thousand of them being bound into a single chiliarchy.*[105] *Conscious that the king was overseeing their conduct, they faced all the missiles chucked his way with alacrity. Attached to them were the Apple Bearer infantry, as valorous as they were numerous, and additionally the Mardians and Cossaeans, famed for their dynamism and audacity, together with the entire palace guard and the bravest and best of the Indian soldiery. Collectively, they raised a resounding battle cry and engaged their opponents valiantly. Then the Macedonians were hard pressed by the enemy on account of Darius' numerical superiority.*

5.83 In the interim Aretes, having cut down the leader of the Scythians who were pillaging the baggage, set into them the more seriously since they were cowering. Then, directed by Darius, the Bactrians came upon the scene and tipped the fortune of the fighting. Hence many Macedonians fell at their first onset and still more fled back to the king. Thereupon the Persians gave a yell of such a sort as victors are wont to expel and fell fiercely upon their enemy there as though they had been put to flight everywhere. But Alexander upbraided those that were intimidated and exhorted his men, single-handedly reviving their contention of the tussle that had already begun to slacken. *Considering the successive successes for the opposition,* Alexander *knew that now was the moment for him to repair the fortunes of his forces by his personal intervention. Having finally restored the resolve of his troops, he* led the **royal squadron and the rest of the elite cavalry in a dashing charge towards Darius' position.** There had been a thinning of the Persian ranks facing his right wing, because the Bactrians had withdrawn from there to join the baggage fighting. Hence Alexander tore into the attenuated rows and burst through with a great slaughter of his foes.

---

[105] Greek term for a regiment of a thousand men.

Figure 5.8. Alexander's charge in the Battle of Arbela (~1880)

5.84 However, the leftmost Persians swung their lines up behind the focus of the fighting in the hope of being able to box in the king. And stuck in the middle, Alexander would have been in grave peril had not the Agrianian cavalry spurred on their steeds to assail the barbarians surrounding their ruler, compelling them to wheel and confront them by cutting into their rear. Their mutual battlefronts were in turbulence. Both before him and at his back Alexander faced opponents and those that beset him from behind, were themselves closely confined by the Agrianians. The Bactrians, who had been pillaging the baggage, were unable to reform their lines on their return. Several formations at once had broken away from the main fronts and were fighting wherever chance had clashed them together in the churn. The two kings, whose formations had virtually merged, gave fire to the fighting. Although the number of wounded was about the same on both sides, more of the Persians were perishing. **Darius was riding in a chariot *hurling javelins*,** whereas Alexander was mounted on horseback and both sovereigns were defended by krak troops, with no regard for their own preservation, for if their king were lost, they neither wished to survive nor had any hope of salvation. Each of these men reckoned it admirable to fall in battle before the eyes of his king. Yet they were exposed to the most peril whom their guards were best protecting, since everyone aspired to the distinction of killing a king.

PROELIVM AD ARBELAM INTER ALEXANDRVM ET DARIVM ET FVGA EJVS .

Figure 5.9. An eagle hangs over Alexander in the Battle of Arbela (1696)

5.85 Now, whether it was a mirage or the real thing, those around Alexander thought they spied an eagle hovering just a bit above the head of their king. It was unperturbed by either the din from the fighting or the shrieks of the dying, but seemed to be hanging around Alexander's horse rather than flying. Certainly, the seer Aristander, clad in a white robe and brandishing a laurel wreath in his right hand, persisted in pointing out the bird to the troops embroiled in the hostilities, deeming it undoubtedly an augury of their victory. In consequence, they, who shortly before had been filled with dismay, were inspired with confidence and fired with enthusiasm for the fray. And **as the kings converged, Alexander began to rain javelins upon Darius, whose charioteer,** *standing in front of him handling the horses,* **was transfixed by one such spear. And a great groan resounded amongst those that surrounded Darius, so that the Persians in the main and the Macedonians too did not doubt that the king himself had been slain.** *Therefore his kinsmen and his guards with their doleful wailing and undisciplined shouting and moaning threw practically the entire Persian battlefront into confusion, though it had until that point proved a match for its opposition.* The chariot was exposed by the flight of the troops on its left flank, so those to its right received it into the midst of their densely packed ranks. It is said that Darius, his sabre drawn, wavered as to whether by an honorable death to shun the shame of flight. But, conspicuous in his chariot, he thought it ignominious to forsake his forces, whilst they had not all abandoned the fight. And as he dithered undecided between hope and despair, **the Persians gradually gave ground and their lines began to tear.** Alexander, who had changed his horse again, having exhausted several steeds that day, was stabbing at the faces of those that still resisted and at the backs of those running away. *With the complete disintegration of his ranks, Darius became exposed on both his flanks, so it had already ceased to be a battle and become butchery, when* Darius himself wheeled his chariot to flee. **The victor was hot on the heels of the rout, but the dust kicked about by the Persian cavalry billowed up into the sky clouding visibility.** It was just as if they were roaming around in darkness, and only at the sound of a signal or a known voice would they coalesce. *Yet amidst the cries of the dying and the thunder of the cavalry,* they could clearly hear the cracking of the reins, with which the horses *that drew the chariot* were lashed repeatedly. *These were the only traces they could discern of the fleeing king, so they were unable to tell which way he was moving.*

5.86 *Yet on the Macedonian left wing, which, as previously stated, was in the charge of Parmenion, the affairs of the respective sides were in quite a different condition.* Mazaeus, the commander of the Persian right, had charged powerfully with virtually his entire cavalry and was pressing upon the flanks of the Macedonians quite severely. *Parmenion fought back fiercely with the Thessalian cavalry and for a while even seemed on the verge of victory, which was a testament to the Thessalians' fighting virtuosity. But Mazaeus had already begun to encircle the Macedonian battlefront through his numerical superiority, when* Parmenion ordered some horsemen to report to Alexander that they found themselves in a situation of considerable criticality: he would not be able to avert a collapse, unless he were reinforced rapidly. The king had already advanced a long way in the tracks of those Persians who were scuttling away and was close upon their backs, when he received Parmenion's dire communiqué. *He called upon his cavalry to rein in their mounts and the army checked its advance. The king gnashed his teeth that victory was being ripped from his grip, since Alexander was not so successful in his pursuit as Darius in giving him the slip.* Meanwhile Mazaeus had heard a rumour that his ruler had been bested by the Macedonian *and hence, despite being in the ascendancy, he was nevertheless alarmed by his side's situation, so he began to press his assault less vigorously.* Parmenion *was of course unaware of the cause for the spontaneous slackening of the attack, but he readily* took advantage of the opportunity to launch a fightback. He summoned the Thessalian cavalry *and queried: "Do you see that those, who were a moment ago savagely assailing us, are giving ground, scared by some sudden menace? Undoubtedly, some success of our sovereign has also secured us a chance to win. Slain*

Persians are strewn all about. Why are you lingering? Are you not even a match for such as have been put to rout?" The truth of what he was saying was plain to see and hope had even revived the weary, so they applied their spurs and surged upon the enemy. *And these no longer gave ground gradually, but at a faster pace, so that they were fleeing effectively, except that they had not turned face. Yet still being unaware of the circumstances of his sovereign on the right wing, Parmenion held back his men. Being thus afforded a gap in the fighting,* Mazaeus, ever the clever strategist, used the dust cloud to disappear and did not follow the other barbarians in withdrawing to the rear. Instead he took a longer and therefore safer detour in the opposite direction *and brought his troops into villages lying behind the Macedonian position.*[106] *Thence he crossed the Tigris via a circuitous course and entered Babylon with the remnants of his defeated force.*

5.87 *Darius had hastened with a handful of companions in his flight to reach the River Lycus, after crossing which he wondered whether he should break down the bridge, for it was reported that their foes were already approaching. But countless thousands of his men had not yet reached the rivercourse, so, if he destroyed the crossing, he saw that they would fall prey to the enemy force. Upon departing, having left the bridge standing, he is reliably reported to have said that he preferred to provide passage for his pursuers, than scupper the escape route of his survivors.* Darius himself, covering a vast distance in his flight, reached Arbela at about midnight.

5.88 Who could possibly grasp in his mind let alone verbally express such twists of fate: the wholesale slaughter of commanders and their contingents; the flight of the vanquished; the calamities that befell individuals and the entire state? Alas! Fortune congregated the events of practically an entire century onto one single date! Some fled by the shortest available route out of there, whilst others made for remote woodlands and tracks of which their pursuers were unaware. Cavalry and infantry were intermingled and unled; the armed were mixed up with the disarmed and the unscathed marched amongst many that bled. From then on compassion was consumed by dread and amidst mutual lamentation those that could not keep up were left for dead. *The fleeing Persians* were parched by thirst, particularly the injured and the spent, so that they sprawled facedown scattered along all the streams and gulped open-mouthed as onwards the waters went. Since, when the water became muddy, they still swallowed it avidly, the pressure of the slime distended their bellies quite promptly, such that

---

[106] Diodorus 17.61.1 attributes this evasive manoeuvre to Darius, but it is obvious by analogy with Curtius 4.16.7 and in view of the clear statements that Darius rode straight to Arbela that Cleitarchus actually wrote this of Mazaeus. Most likely some intermediary misread or otherwise incorrectly transmitted the name. Mazeus cannot readily have crossed the Tigris without crossing Darius's line of retreat except by going behind Macedonian lines, so this makes perfect sense.

their legs became sluggish and slack. Being then *overtaken by the enemy,* they *were goaded by renewed attack, so that the whole region became bedecked with bodies by the butchery.* Some, finding the nearby brooks occupied, turned further aside, to glean whatever hidden moisture trickled anywhere, and there was no pool so drained or so secluded that its thirsty trackers were eluded. And indeed from the villages closest to the road there resounded the wailing of women and of old men, calling in the barbarian fashion upon Darius, their sovereign till then.

5.89 As already related, Alexander had checked the charge of his forces and had arrived at the River Lycus, where the bridge was overladen, as the number of fugitives was enormous. Being hard pressed by their opponents, many of them threw themselves into the river's torrents. And heavily armed as well as fatigued by both the fight and their flight, they were swallowed up by the current's turbulence. Already the river, let alone the bridge, could not hold all those escaping, as regiment upon regiment kept mindlessly accumulating. For when men's minds are captured by consternation, they dread only that which initiated their trepidation. Being pressed by his men not to postpone the pursuit of his unpunished opponents, Alexander argued that their arms were either dulled or wearied, that their bodies were worn out from chasing with such persistence and that night would soon intercede. But really he was anxious about his left wing, which he supposed still to be standing and fighting, so he was bent upon offering them the support of their king. And he had already wheeled about, when riders sent by Parmenion reported that he was the victor in that sector too. However Alexander encountered no greater danger that day than whilst he was heading back to camp with his retinue. He was accompanied by just a disorderly few, who were exulting their victory, since they thought that all of their foes had fallen in the fighting or had fled the field impetuously. Then quite suddenly he was confronted by a body of cavalry, who reined back initially, but spurred their squadrons against him with hostility upon perceiving the meagreness of the Macedonian tally. The king was marching at the head of his unit, disregarding the risk rather than scorning it. And neither was he let down by the perpetual good fortune he enjoyed in every precarious circumstance. For when the leader of the cavalry, being keen for combat and consequently incautious, dashed towards him, the king transfixed him with his lance. And when he had toppled from his mount, the king skewered the next one and then several more men with the same weapon. His Friends too sailed in upon their disconcerted opponents. But the Persians were not slain without gaining recompense, for the entire battlefield saw no tougher contention than that engaged upon by this improvised battalion. When finally in the fading light, flight seemed safer than prolonging the fight, the Persian formation split up and withdrew *into the encroaching night.* After coming through this exceptional jeopardy, the king led his men back to camp in safety.

5.90 *Combining cavalry and infantry casualties,* ninety thousand of the Persians fell *in this battle insofar as the victors were capable of* *determining the total.* **The Macedonians dead numbered *fewer* than five hundred,** *but many more were wounded.* [107] Furthermore, this victory was attributable to the king's prowess rather than to his luck in the main. He won it with his brain rather than, as previously, through the intercession of the terrain. For he configured his forces most cleverly, as well as personally fighting most valiantly and with great perspicacity he disdained the loss of their baggage and personal property, since he perceived that victory would be decided at the front line of his army. And whilst the outcome of the contest remained in question, he behaved like the eventual champion. Thereafter, when he had daunted the enemy into stampeding, he pursued them judiciously rather than unrestrainedly, which is virtually incredible in view of his characteristic impetuosity. For, had he persisted in pressing upon the Persians as they withdrew, he would either have been defeated through his own fault or owed his victory to a viceroy's virtue. Lastly, had he been cowed in his confrontation with that considerable contingent of cavalry, he would, whilst on the crest of victory, have had either to flee disgracefully or to perish ignominiously.

5.91 *But neither should the commanders of Alexander's forces be defrauded of their share of the glory, for the injuries that they variously suffered are evidence of their bravery.* **Among the most eminent men, Hephaistion, who led the Bodyguards, was struck in the arm by a spear. Of the generals, Perdiccas and Coenus came near to being killed by arrows. So too was Menidas and others among the most senior fellows.** And if we wish fairly to assess the Macedonians that were present then, we shall allow that their king was wholly worthy of such men and his followers befitted so magnificent a sovereign. *And* **this was** *shown by* **the outcome of the battle near Arbela,** *for it was with this engagement that Alexander seized control of Asia on the twenty-sixth day of the month of Boedromion,[108] so the very next day was the fifth anniversary of the king's accession. This was so decisive a victory that none dared rebel thereafter, for the Persians after many years of their own mastery submissively accepted Alexander as their master.*

5.92 Back in Greece many of the cities *had become alarmed by the* **expansion of Macedonian dominance and** *had decided, whilst the* **Persian cause was still in existence,** *that they should seize the* **opportunity to recover their independence.** *They expected that Darius would support them and send them munificent moneys, so that they could enlist legions of mercenaries, whilst Alexander would not be able to divide his armies. If, alternatively, they looked on idly while the Persians*

---

[107] These figures are those given by Diodorus 17.61.3. Curtius 4.16.26 gives XL thousand Persian dead and fewer than CCC Macedonian casualties, but the numerical transmission in a Latin manuscript is more liable to corruption than the numbers expressed in words in Diodorus's Greek. For example, if XL in Curtius were a mistake for XC (which could very easily have happened), then Curtius would agree with Diodorus.

[108] Plutarch, *Camillus* 19.3.

were vanquished completely, the Greeks would stand alone and never again be able to reckon upon recovering their liberty. Additionally, a convulsion in Thrace that was quite timely appeared to grant the Greeks an ideal opportunity to make themselves free. Memnon, who had been made the marshal of Thrace, was a resolute fellow with a force of troops at his disposal. He suborned the barbarians, revolted against Alexander and raised a substantial army in no time at all, being blatantly bent on battle. Antipater was compelled to call upon his whole military and to cross Macedon and enter Thrace in order to campaign against Memnon. It was while the Regent was thus preoccupied that the Spartans, who had consistently denied the hegemony of Philip and Alexander, considered the time ripe to launch hostilities, so they issued a call to arms to the Greeks for the united defence of their liberties. Nevertheless, the Athenians demurred, since, above all the other Greeks, it was they that Alexander had preferred. However, most of the Peloponnesians along with some others came to an accord and cemented a pact to resolve things through the sword. They enlisted the cream of their youths according to their availability from each city and recruited more than twenty thousand infantry and two thousand cavalry into their army. The Spartans had primacy *and inducted their entire military* with their king, Agis, holding the overall supremacy.

5.93 *When* Antipater *learnt of the Greek aggression, he brought his Thracian offensive to an optimal conclusion and marched his whole force down into the Peloponnesian region. He incorporated troops from the loyal Greek cities and* augmented his army *to exceed forty thousand with ease. When a decisive battle took place at Megalopolis in the Peloponnese,[109]* Agis *charged into the focal point of the hostilities, cutting down his most resilient adversaries and driving back a large proportion of his enemies. Then the winners of this battle began to be put to flight, being cut down without reprisal, until they had led those too avidly hounding them right down onto level land. And there, at the first place they found in which they might stand and fight, they held their ground. Nevertheless, amongst all the Spartans their king retained pre-eminence, not just due to the splendour of his arms and person, but also in the vastness of his valiance, which was second to none. He was assaulted from all sides, sometimes hand-to-hand and sometimes from afar and for ages he swung his shield around to intercept every missile or else dodged them in a spar. But* his thighs were pierced by a lance in the end and haemorrhaging profusely they gave way whilst he still struggled to contend. *Therefore his guards rapidly removed him from the field, carrying him back to camp by*

---

[109] Curtius 6.1.1 opens here after a lacuna, introducing much more detail on the events. Probably Cleitarchus had given a lengthy introduction, explaining that Megalopolis was one of the few Peloponnesian cities to remain loyal to Macedon and that Antipater had come to its aid when it was close to surrender, engaging the army of the Spartan alliance in a narrow plain near the city.

raising him up on his shield, though he could barely bear the agony from the jolting of his injury.

5.94 *Yet* the Spartans did not abandon the struggle, *but as soon as they had got to ground that was more defensible,* they closed ranks and received a torrent of their opponents upon their line of battle. *History records that no other contest was ever so ferocious. Well-matched were the forces of the two peoples whose prowess in warfare was most notorious. The Spartans were fixated by their past achievements, whilst the Macedonians were intent upon their current accomplishments. The former fought for their liberty and the latter for their hegemony. The Spartans lacked their leader, whilst the Macedonians wanted for room to manoeuvre. Additionally, so many reversals on a single day respectively raised the hopes and compounded the fears of either set of soldiers, as if Fortune were deliberately evening up this contest between the bravest of warriors. However, the constricted nature of the site where the battle continued to take its course did not allow either of them to engage their entire force. Hence there were more men spectating than were actually fighting and those who were beyond the range of javelins and arrows in rotation were bellowing to fire up their fellows.* At length, the lines of the Spartan allies began to exhibit exhaustion, *for they could hardly hold up weapons that were slick with perspiration. Then they began to retreat and, being harried by the opposition,* they gave way *more obviously with the victors closely pursuing the broken. And the Macedonians rushed across all the ground that had been held by the Spartans, hounding after* Agis *in person. That king,* upon seeing his men fleeing and the foremost of his foes approaching, bade that his bearers escape to serve Sparta by setting him down. *And upon trying his legs to see whether they would obey his will, but feeling them letting him down, he sank to his knees donning his helmet hurriedly and brandished the spear in his right hand at his enemies using his shield to cover his body. Then he actually taunted his adversaries regarding which of them would deserve to despoil him as a casualty. But there was nobody at all that would venture to engage him in close combat. So* he was assailed from a distance by missiles, which he then hurled back felling some of his foes, until a long lance was implanted in his chest, *which he had been forced to expose. When it was yanked from the injury, he leant his bowed and dazed head upon his shield momentarily, then, as* breath and blood forsook him equally, *he collapsed dying to lie athwart his weaponry. Thus* he perished *in the ninth year of his sovereignty.*[110]

---

[110] Agis III succeeded his father, Archidamus III, to one of the dual Spartan kingships when the latter fell before the walls of Manduria in Italy in 338BC. It is possible that he ruled in 9 Attic years, if Archidamus died before the first New Moon after the Summer Solstice in 338BC (but Diodorus 16.63 & 16.88 suggests that it was on the same day as Chaeronea, which took place in August) and Megalopolis occurred after the same event in 331BC (which is likely).

5.95 Five thousand three hundred of the Spartans *and their allies* **fell and another** *three* **thousand** *five hundred* **of Antipater's army as well,** of whom fewer than a thousand were Macedonian.[111] However, hardly anyone returned to camp lacking any sort of laceration. This victory not only subdued the Spartans and those with whom they were allied, but all those who had been watching the outcome of the war from the sidelines were also thoroughly pacified. Nor was Antipater beguiled when those that offered him their congratulations betrayed dissenting sentiments in their facial expressions, but it was necessary that he allowed himself to be deluded, since he desired that the war be concluded. And although the outcome of the affair gave him some satisfaction, he nonetheless feared a grudging reaction, since he had exceeded the remit of a regent by such a major action. For despite that Alexander had desired the defeat of the enemy, he could not even manage to hold his tongue regarding the impropriety of Antipater's victory, reckoning that successes ceded to a deputy detracted from his own glory. Hence **Antipater**, who perfectly understood Alexander's psychology, did not dare personally **to impose the terms of his victory**, but **consulted a conference of the Greeks as to what it pleased them to decree.** Additionally, **the Regent** took as hostages a levy of the most prominent men among the Spartans totalling fifty.[112]

5.96 *Elsewhere in Europe, the uncle of the monarch of Macedon, that Alexander who was king of Epirus, had been invited into Italy, where the people of Tarentum had entreated his aid in combatting the Bruttii. He had been keen to charge in, as though the world had been partitioned, the East being allotted to Alexander the son of his sister, Olympias, and the West having fallen to him. And he considered that his opportunities would be no less in Italy, Sicily and Africa than those his nephew was encountering in Asia and Persia. Additionally, just as the Delphic Oracle had predicted a conspiracy against his nephew in Macedonia, so the Oracle of Zeus at Dodona had warned him to beware of the Acherusian River and the city of Pandosia. Since both lay in Epirus and Alexander was ignorant that identically named places existed in Italy, he had been the more eager to campaign overseas in order to dodge the dangers in his destiny. Therefore, when he arrived in Italy, he made war upon the Apulians initially, but he made peace and concluded an alliance with their king shortly, when he found out what was fated for their city.*

5.97 *Brundisium is a city held by the Apulians, though it was founded by the Aetolians, followers of Diomedes, that most glorious and noble leader, famed for his Trojan actions. However, they had been expelled by the Apulians. In consulting the oracles, the Aetolians had received a response that the place would belong in perpetuity to those that sought its return by embassy. Consequently, they had sent emissaries to propose with threats of belligerency that the*

---

[111] Curtius 6.1.16 states fewer than a thousand Macedonians fell, but the figure of 3500 casualties in Antipater's army given by Diodorus 17.63.3 is a more likely total. Possibly, 2500 of the casualties in Antipater's army were among his allied troops, so there need be no real inconsistency here.

[112] Jacoby Fragment 4 of Cleitarchus (Harpocration s.v. *homereuontas*) attributed to Book 5; cf. Diodorus 17.73.6.

Apulians should hand back their city. But the oracle became known to the Apulians, who slew every emissary and buried them within the bounds of the city, so that the site would indeed be theirs in perpetuity. Having thus fulfilled the prophecy, they had long held the city. When Alexander heard this history, he refrained from further hostility towards them out of respect for ancient prophecy. Then he engaged the Lucanians and the Bruttii in warfare, seizing several of their cities. With the Metapontines, the Poediculi and the Romans he concluded alliances and treaties. But the Bruttii and Lucanians gathered auxiliaries from neighbouring territories and with redoubled vehemence resumed their hostilities. In the course of this campaign the king was killed near to a Pandosia and a River Acheron as well, though he did not know the name of the fateful place before he fell and it was only as he was dying that he came to see that the threat of mortality that had led him to flee did not in fact lie in his home country. At public expense the citizens of Thurii ransomed and entombed his body.

5.98 Here ends the first part of the History Concerning Alexander, *which has recounted the events concerning that king up to the end of the fifth year of his reign.*

5. Book 6: October 2nd 331BC – July 330BC

The Escape of Darius and the Capture of Treasure at Arbela; Mennis and the Cave of Naphtha; The Occupation of Babylon; the Seizure of Susa; The Capture of the Susian Gates; Meeting with the Mutilated Greeks; The Burning of Persepolis; The Pursuit of Darius and his Murder by Bessus

6.1 *Here begins the second part of the history concerning Alexander by Cleitarchus of Alexandria at the start of the sixth year of the king's reign, which commenced in the course of the second year of the one hundred and twelfth Olympiad on the twenty-seventh day of the month Boedromion as the Athenians reckon in accordance with the regulation of the Lunar phases by the goddess Selene.*[113]

6.2 It was almost midnight when **Darius reached Arbela following the nearby fight.** There he found that Fortune had fetched up a large fraction of his friends and soldiers in their flight. Gathering them about him, he explained that he was in no doubt that it was the major cities and the farmland fertile in all sorts of resources that Alexander would make towards, for both his troops and their ruler were fixated upon rich and readily reaped rewards. As things stood this should prove to be Darius' deliverance, since **he would head into the wastes** with disencumbered contingents. **The upper satrapies, the further reaches of his realm, from which he could readily extract fresh warriors, were still intact.** So let that greediest of tribes go garnering his treasure and glutting itself with gold out of ravenous hunger, for they would soon become his plunder. Experience had taught him that fine furnishings, concubines and regiments of eunuchs were nothing other than burdens and impediments. Being likewise hindered, Alexander would be found wanting in those traits whereby he had formerly conquered.

6.3 This seemed a counsel of complete despair to everyone, since thereby they certainly forsook that wealthiest of cities, Babylon. Subsequently Susa would be seized and then the victor would overwhelm all his objectives in the war, the rest of the jewels of the realm. Yet Darius proceeded to construe that in episodes of adversity the course to pursue is not what is glorious to tell but what the practicalities compel. For war is waged with steel, not with gold, nor in the shelter of cities, but by the bold. Everything is ceded to the soldierly. So it was that their forefathers, though they had at first suffered regressions, had rapidly retrieved their former possessions. **Therefore**, either having bolstered

---

[113] The mention in the manuscripts of Diodorus 17.63.4 that the first part of his account of Alexander's reign ended here strongly suggests that he had found a similar division in his source, Cleitarchus; the date was 2nd October 331BC in the Julian Calendar, but Cleitarchus would have specified dates using Attic months according to strict Lunar regulation (i.e. not the so-called Archon calendar, which often strayed from strict Lunar regulation) with years identified according to the count of 4-year Olympiads starting in 776BC following Timaeus of Tauromenium.

their morale or because they accepted his authority rather than his strategy, **Darius entered upon the bounds of Media,** *so as to win a respite by far-flung flight.*

6.4 *He went first to Ecbatana and tarried there, mustering fugitives from the battle and refurbishing those that no longer carried their arms. He requisitioned the drafting of troops from the local inhabitants and despatched emissaries to his marshals and governors in Bactria and the upper satrapies asking that they reaffirm their allegiance.*

6.5 *In the wake of his victory* Alexander *arranged the burial of his dead and then, though Darius got there a little ahead, he* reached Arbela, *which had been abandoned to him.* On entering the town he found *it filled with a great stash of stocks together with Darius' gear and a tremendous treasure including a profusion of foreign finery and between three and four thousand talents of silver.*[114] As was said before, the valuables of the entire Persian host had been piled up in this post.[115] **Then, beset by a threat of contagion due to the stench of the corpses spread sprawled across the region, he hastened to advance his camp towards Babylon.** *Media was left on their left as they hurried on and* Arabia, renowned for its rich aromas, lay upon their right. Between the Tigris and Euphrates the route runs through cultivated country, which is so fecund and fertile that herds are kept from grazing lest they die of gluttony. The source of this productivity is the irrigation that flows from either river, for almost all the soil oozes with the water that canals deliver.

6.6 As for the rivers themselves, the mountains of Armenia are their sources, from which they pour forth like they arise on widely spaced courses. Around the Armenian ranges observers impart that they reach their greatest separation in running two thousand five hundred stades apart. When they start to slice through Media and the Gordyaean domains, they gradually converge, so that the further they flow the narrower is the intervening strand of land that remains. Where the rivers run closest together those that there abide call that land Mesopotamia,[116] since it is bounded by these watercourses on either side. Ultimately, after flowing through the Babylonian territory, these rivers empty into the Red Sea.[117] Upon the fourth day of his march Alexander reached the city of Mennis. At that place there is a chasm with a naphtha spring from which

---

[114] Curtius 5.1.10 has 4000 talents whereas Diodorus 17.64.3 gives 3000 talents, probably respectively rounding up and down some intermediate figure cited by Cleitarchus; there is another example where Diodorus 17.80.3 rounds down a figure for Alexander's main treasure to 180,000 talents that is rounded up to 190,000 talents by Justin 12.1.3.

[115] Curtius 4.9.9.

[116] Mesopotamia means literally "the country between the rivers" in Greek.

[117] The Red (Erythraean) Sea was the name of the Persian Gulf in ancient Greek geography.

such a huge amount of bitumen wells up as to corroborate the account that the vast walls of Babylon were mortared with tar from that fount.[118]

6.7 *Whenever Alexander was bathing, an Athenian named Athenophanes used to attend the king with the task of being entertaining. A boy called Stephanus, who could sing, but was not at all good-looking, was set to singing for the king during his Mennis bathing. Whereupon Athenophanes thought to suggest: "Why not make Stephanus the test of the naphtha's alleged zest? If it lights him up and is not straightaway put out, its potency would be shown beyond doubt." Amazingly, the boy agreed that this trial might proceed. Having smeared himself with naphtha in the bath he waited, while a lamp was lit so that he could be illuminated. When he quickly became engulfed in fire, the king was horrified and feared he would expire. And he might indeed have died, had the attendants at his side not used many ewers of water to quench the conflagration, though not without considerable exertion. Even so he was so badly burnt all over that it took a long time for him to recover.[119]*

6.8 Mazaeus accompanied by his adult offspring met **Alexander *and his whole army*** as the king **approached Babylon.** *As its satrap* he had fled from the battlefield to the city and now ceded its surrender and placed himself and his kin at Alexander's mercy. The king was thankful for his arrival, since the siege of so well fortified a city would have been an enormous operation. Moreover Mazaeus was a famous fellow and a formidable fighter, whose exploits had distinguished him in the recent battle, so others would see him as an exemplar to spur their own surrender. Therefore the king gave a welcome that was even cordial to him and his offspring. Nevertheless, he arranged his men in rectangular array with himself at their head and ordered them to advance as if they were going into combat.

6.9 A great number of the Babylonians had taken up vantage points on their battlements, being keen to catch a glimpse of their new king, yet even more of them had gone forth in order to greet him. Among the latter, Bagophanes, castellan of the citadel and the royal treasury, had strewn the entire route with flowers and garlands, so that Mazaeus should not surpass him in unction. He had set up silver altars in array along either side of the way and they were heaped, not merely with frankincense, but with all sorts of scents. As gifts there trailed in his train herds of horses and livestock. Leopards and lions too were borne forward in cages *under lock*. Next came the magicians chanting canticles after their manner and then the Chaldeans and of the Babylonians not just the seers but also the musicians with their local type of lyre. They customarily sing the praises of the king, whereas the Chaldeans make manifest the reasons for

---

[118] Although the site of Mennis is unknown, such bitumen springs were historically to be found in the vicinity of Kirkuk, circa 100km south of Arbela.

[119] This story survives in Plutarch, *Alexander* 35 and Strabo 16.1.15 in association with other stories of the naphtha/asphalt/bitumen spring encountered by Alexander in northern Iraq including its use for mortar in the walls of Babylon and its emission from a chasm, both mentioned by Curtius 5.1.16. Hammond, *Sources for Alexander the Great* p.68-69, thinks Cleitarchus is the likely common source, although this is conjectural.

the motions of the stars and the status of the cycle of the seasons. Last came the knights of Babylon, whose trappings as well as those of their steeds were a demonstration not so much of grandeur as of ostentation. **Alexander** attended by his men-at-arms bade that the citizen bodies should parade after the hindmost of his foot. He himself **entered the city** in a chariot and installed himself in the royal residence. On the next day he acquainted himself with Darius' furnishings and with his affluence.

Figure 6.1. Alexander's triumphal entry into Babylon (an engraving in the author's collection based on the painting by Charles Le Brun)

6.10 Yet *it was the splendour and antiquity of the city itself that drew the gaze not just of the king but also of his entire host and not without justification.* Babylon was founded by Semiramis, *rather than by Belus, as many have believed, though his basilica is among its sights. Her disposition made her eager for an exceptional deed and avid to exceed the fame of her predecessor on the throne.* She constructed the city wall from small baked bricks cemented with bitumen *that span a breadth of thirty-two feet and it is claimed that a pair of four-horse chariots upon it can freely pass as they meet.* This wall towers to a height of fifty cubits *and its towers are ten feet taller yet.* Three hundred and sixty-five stades are covered by its circuit *and they recall that each individual stade of the wall was made in a single day,* since it was her desire to match the days in a year, they say.[120] *There are a total of two hundred and fifty towers, which might seem small in*

---

[120] Jacoby Fragment 10 of Cleitarchus from Diodorus 2.7.3-4.

comparison with the length of the wall, but Semiramis saw that long stretches abut against marshland, which she considered a sufficient safeguard, so there no towers were planned. The built-up area of the city does not extend to the base of the fortifications, but a corridor runs between of two-plethron dimensions.[121] Of the whole area within the city, housing occupies only eighty *square* stades, *which are not merged into a single zone, but are strewn into many townships,* the rest being farmed and sown, *so that, if assailed by foreign forces, the besieged may receive from the city's own soil the requisite resources.*

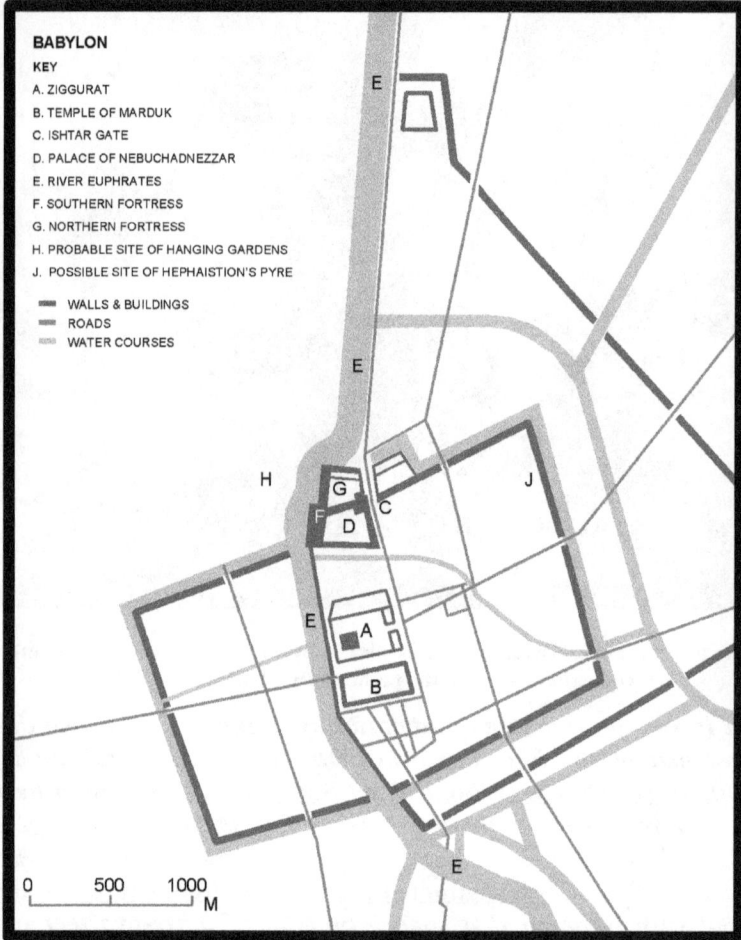

BABYLON

KEY

A. ZIGGURAT

B. TEMPLE OF MARDUK

C. ISHTAR GATE

D. PALACE OF NEBUCHADNEZZAR

E. RIVER EUPHRATES

F. SOUTHERN FORTRESS

G. NORTHERN FORTRESS

H. PROBABLE SITE OF HANGING GARDENS

J. POSSIBLE SITE OF HEPHAISTION'S PYRE

WALLS & BUILDINGS

ROADS

WATER COURSES

0   500   1000
                    M

Figure 6.2. Plan of Babylon (based on the excavations of Robert Koldewey)

6.11 The River Euphrates courses through the middle of the metropolis, *being trammelled between vast dykes. Nevertheless, the whole of these huge works is encompassed by ditches, delved deep to receive the river's*

---

[121] A *plethron* was about 30m.

spate. For when it overspills the crest of the embankment, it would wash away the housing, were it not intercepted by culverts and reservoirs, which are built of baked bricks with bitumen cementing everything. A stone bridge five stades long spans the narrowest neck of the river, linking the two sides of the city. *This too is mentioned among the marvels of the Orient, since the Euphrates deposits a great depth of sediment and even when this was deeply dredged to lay a foundation, it was hard to find firm footings for supporting the construction. Moreover, sands continually accumulate against the stone piers that carry the causeway's weight, hence impeding the river's flow, which, being dammed back so, roils even more violently than if the streaming of its course were free.* The span is twelve feet between each pair of piers, of which the masonry tightly coheres, aided by iron cramps, with lead sealing their joints. And cutwaters streamline the current from their points. The deck of this bridge has a breadth of thirty feet with colossal palm trunks and beams of cypress and cedar paving its street.

Figure 6.3. A bull modelled in the glazed bricks of the Ishtar Gate of ancient Babylon (excavated by Robert Koldewey)

6.12 *Semiramis built two royal enclosures upon the banks of the river at either end of the bridge with tall curtain walls of baked brick. The precinct that faces west[122] over the river has a circuit of sixty stades. Beasts of every sort are figured in the glaze of its bricks and they are made to seem lifelike by the skilful use of colour. Within its walls stands* **the citadel** *which*

---

[122] This is ambiguous in Diodorus 2.8.4, but it should mean "faces west from the perspective of a viewer on the river," which is my clarification to agree with the archaeology (see plan in Fig 6.2.).

has a perimeter of twenty stades *and its fortifications are taller and thicker that the others. The foundations of its towers are set thirty feet beneath the surface and the crest of its wall reaches up eighty feet in all. These walls and towers too are embellished with wild animals over four cubits tall, realistically portrayed by the masterful use of tints in the glaze. The ensemble depicts a hunt with Semiramis shown mounted on the point of loosing a javelin at a leopard and Ninus, her spouse, in the act of spearing a lion. The citadel has a triple portal, two of its gates being forged in bronze and swung by mechanisms. Across the river the perimeter of the other precinct is merely thirty stades and adorned with scenes from battles and chases. Those that muse over them reflect euphoric feelings in their faces.*

6.13 *At the centre of the city Semiramis set up a sanctuary of Belus, which long lapse of time has left in a state of dilapidation, yet it was once toweringly tall and served the Chaldeans as their station for astronomical observation, since stellar transits of the horizon were precisely viewed by virtue of its elevation.*[123] **Beyond the citadel lie the Hanging Gardens, which match the loftiness of the walls** *and are made heavenly by the shade of many monumental trees.* **Semiramis did not create these, but it is told that a king of Syria**[124] **that reigned in Babylon of old performed the feat of their construction for the sake of his spouse's satisfaction. She, being Persian, pined for the woods and glades of her native mountain landscape and persuaded the king to shape and to plant in the plains of that place an imitation of its natural charm and grace.** *So now from a distance in the eyes of those seeing the sights, these gardens look like actual woodland hangers on their homeland's heights.*

6.14 *The park stretches for four plethra on each side and its terraces ascend tier by tier as in a theatre along the approach in semblance of a hillside.* **The great weight of the planted terraces is borne by galleries inside, the highest of which is fifty cubits tall and level with the battlements of the city's curtain wall.** *No expense was spared in constructing* their piers, *which* are twenty-two feet thick with intervening passageways ten-foot broad.[125] **These corridors are roofed over with squared stone beams** *sixteen feet long and four-foot wide, which underpin a damp-seal of reeds in a massive matrix of bitumen that is in turn covered by two cemented courses of baked bricks with a top-layer of lead that reinforces its ability to keep moisture in. For* above *it* is set a sufficient bed of soil in which to rest the roots of the most tremendous trees in a terrace teeming with many spectacular species. The girth of their trunks reaches eight cubits and they soar to fifty feet high at their summits, fruiting as profusely as if they grew amidst their native thickets.

---

[123] This should be a reference to the Babylonian ziggurat, otherwise known as the Tower of Babel.

[124] It is a Cleitarchan quirk to refer to Assyria as Syria.

[125] Diodorus 2.10.4 has 22 feet and 10 feet; Curtius 5.1.34 gives 20 feet and 11 feet, but the Roman numerals in the Latin manuscripts are usually more vulnerable to corruption.

And the staggering of the galleries permits the light of day to reach into their royal suites and garrets. One chamber has apertures ascending to the topmost stage with mechanisms to raise river water for irrigating the foliage. And despite that time gradually grinds down not merely the monuments of mankind, but also those that Nature's behind, this huge heap, though riddled with the roots of so many trees and stacked with the burden of such grandiose groves, nonetheless continues to survive intact.

6.15 Alexander lingered longer in this city than elsewhere and in no other place was discipline more undermined amongst the military. Nothing is more corrupt than that city's immorality; nothing arouses illicit and unlimited lusts more systematically. Fathers and husbands condone the prostitution of their wives and offspring to guests, so long as a fee is forthcoming for such infamy. A fondness for frolicking at feasts among kings and nobles pervades the whole area of Persian domination, but the Babylonians are keenest of all on wine and what is entailed by intoxication. The feminine participants in these parties are initially modestly attired, but then stage-by-stage they divest their dress, progressively desecrating their demureness, until – with due respect to your sentiments – they slip out of their innermost garments.[126] Such entertainment is not left to the whores, but is delivered by ladies and lads, who consider it sociable to sell themselves as cheap paramours.

6.16 In the midst of such debauchery **the army that had conquered Asia was billeted and lavishly cosseted for thirty-four days,[127]** *since supplies were plenteous and the people were doting.* Yet in the aftermath it should undoubtedly have proven all the weaker in a crisis, had any enemy been forthcoming. However, continual refreshing of the army through augmentation mitigated such deterioration. *On the road after leaving Babylon* Alexander **was joined by Amyntas the son of Andromenes bringing six thousand Macedonian infantry and five hundred cavalry from the same country sent by Antipater. These were accompanied by six hundred Thracian horsemen together with three thousand five hundred Tri*b*allian[128] foot from the same nation. There also arrived from the Peloponnese a mercenary force of about four thousand infantry and three hundred and eighty cavalry. At the behest of their fathers fifty adolescent sons of the king's Friends had journeyed with Amyntas to train to become**

---

[126] It would be easy for a modern reader to suppose that the expressed disapproval stems from prudery. Actually, the problem is not nakedness itself, but that wives and daughters are exposed to insemination by strangers. It was a social priority for high-status Greek males to ensure the legitimacy of their heirs and the eligibility of their daughters (which necessitated their virginity). It was the affront to these axioms of Greek culture that prompted our author's outrage.

[127] Diodorus 17.64.4 says "more than thirty days", whilst Curtius 5.1.39 and Justin 11.14.8 both state precisely thirty-four.

[128] Trallian in the manuscripts of Diodorus 17.65.1, but the Triballians were a Thracian tribe who are elsewhere said to have fought for Alexander.

Bodyguards.[129] *For such as these serve their king at meals as he feeds; when he engages in battle they fetch him his steeds; they also escort him in the chase and take turns to stand sentry at the entrance to the royal resting place. These duties are the training and the apprenticeship for top commands and governorship. Having welcomed every new recruit, Alexander continued on his route.*

6.17 On leaving Babylon the king appointed Agathon of Pydna as castellan of the citadel with a garrison of seven hundred Macedonian soldiers *and three hundred mercenaries.* He also designated Apollodorus of Amphipolis and Menes of Pella as military governors of Babylonia and adjoining satrapies as far as Cilicia. They were assigned two thousand troops and one thousand talents with orders to enlist as many more soldiers as possible. *Alexander granted the Babylonian satrapy to the turncoat Mazaeus and ordered Bagophanes, who had surrendered the citadel, to serve under him.* Armenia was made over to Mithrenes, who had betrayed Sardis to the king. Then from the monies that had been relinquished to him at Babylon he made donatives of six hundred drachmae to each of the Macedonian cavalrymen, five hundred to each of his foreign horsemen, two hundred apiece to the Macedonian foot and two months' pay to every one of his mercenaries.

6.18 These matters being settled, *on the sixth day of his march* Alexander reached the region known as Sittacenê, a fecund land burgeoning with all sorts of supplies and provender, so during some days he protracted his stay. *He was keen to reconstitute his battle array, as well as to rest his warriors from the weariness of the way. But so that his soldiers should not mislay their mettle through lassitude,* he *set up a review board and* offered extraordinary commissions decided on the basis of military prowess and fortitude. *Those assessed to be the most valorous were individually to command a thousand of the soldiery. They were dubbed chiliarchs[130] and this was the first time that their forces had been regimented into such divisions, for formerly there had been battalions five hundred strong and the courageous had not been accorded the key commissions. A huge crowd of troops had gathered to participate in the selection, both to attest to the records of the candidates and to the fairness of the adjudication, for they could not but know whether the preferment were proper or a product of pretension.* The elder Atarrhias was

---

[129] The Greek of Diodorus 17.65.1 literally means "with a view to becoming Bodyguards", where the term for Bodyguards (*somatophylakes*) normally refers to the seven elite bodyguards, who were the highest officers of Alexander's court. Curtius 5.1.42 explains that these youths were in training to become the great commanders of the future, so Cleitarchus surely wrote that these were Pages looking to graduate as *somatophylakes* and not instant Bodyguards (as has usually been supposed.)

[130] Chiliarch is a Greek title preserved in the Latin of Curtius and meaning literally lord of a thousand.

adjudged the most resolute of all, who had single-handedly rallied the younger men at Halicarnassus, when they forsook the fight for its fall. Antigenes was ranked next after him and Philotas of Augaea took third place. Amyntas was given fourth and after him Antigonus followed by Amyntas Lyncestes, then Theodotus was given the seventh position and Hellenicus took the last commission. *Rewarding his captains with such recognition, he bound them to him by bonds of appreciation.*

6.19 *Alexander also effectuated many wholly advantageous alterations in the military practices of his predecessors.* For, whereas previously each cavalryman had been enrolled amongst members of his own tribe and sequestered from others, he abolished racial distinctions and assigned them to commanders not necessarily of their own tribe but rather handpicked by him. The sound of the trumpet that gave the signal when he wished to move camp could scarcely be heard by most amidst the tumult and din. Therefore he erected a pole above the headquarters that could be seen from every angle, from which a hoisted signal was clearly visible to all: flame by night and smoke during daylight. *Hence he honed his whole host into unhesitating allegiance to its leader and compliancy with his command, elevating its efficiency in consideration of what the coming contest would demand.*

6.20 And now the king *entered Susianê unopposed and as he* approached Susa *itself,* Abulites, the satrap of that region, sent *his son to meet him en route with* a promise of the surrender of the city. Perhaps he did this of his own volition, but some have written that he acted in accordance with an instruction from Darius to his faithful officials. They suggest the Persian sovereign hoped that the dazzling distractions and riches of the royal residences might retard Alexander's troupe, affording the fugitives a chance to regroup. The king extended a courteous welcome to the youth and under his guidance reached the River Choaspes, which is celebrated for the sweetness of the water that it conveys. There he was met by Abulites bearing gifts of regal richness. These presents included dromedary camels of exemplary swiftness and a dozen elephants acquired by Darius from India, now a buttress rather than the bane of the Macedonians that he had anticipated, now that the wealth of the vanquished was volunteered to the victors as Fortune had fated.

6.21 Upon entering the city Alexander took possession of a prodigious amount of money from its palace treasury, comprising forty thousand talents of gold and silver bullion and another nine thousand talents in minted gold darics. It had been hoarded over many reigns by successive sovereigns, so as to safeguard their descendants against the fickleness of Fortune. Or so they had supposed, yet but a single hour set it fully in a foreign sovereign's power. *Furthermore, he found phenomenal furnishings and* *fabulous things, including five thousand talents by weight[131] of purple cloth from Hermione,[132] which it appears had kept its freshness and brilliance despite having been stashed there for a hundred and ninety years. The reason is the use of honey in the purple tints and white olive oil in the white dyes, since these substances are seen to cleave to an unclouded clarity at equivalent antiquity.* My father Deinon has also recorded that the kings of Persia had water carted from the Nile and the Ister and ensconced amidst their treasures as a kind of corroboration of the enormity of their empire and the totality of their domination.

6.22 A curious incident transpired whilst the king was being shown the precious artefacts. Alexander seated himself upon the royal throne, which stood too tall for his stature. Seeing his feet dangling well above its footrest, one of the royal pages substituted a table for his footstool. On finding that it fitted the king found it fitting, yet a eunuch standing at hand and who had served Darius was seen to be crying, being saddened by the transformations that Fortune was applying. On noticing him, Alexander queried: "What wickedness have you witnessed that you are weeping?" And the eunuch responded: "Now I am your servant as formerly I belonged to Darius and I am submissive to my masters by dint of my condition, so it grieved me to see Darius' prized possession, from which he was served his meals, reduced to such a disrespected position." On hearing this, the king recollected how vast a revolution had been visited upon the Persian realm and he felt remorse for having transgressed against the gods of hospitality and that kindness to captives that was his usual policy. Therefore he called for the page that had put the table in place to take it away again. But Philotas was in attendance and he was moved to maintain: "This was not disrespect, for the thing was not done at your behest, but was engineered through the providential influence of some guardian angel. So do not undo his design, but accept as a propitious sign that the table from which your foe used lavishly to dine now forms your footstool." Hence the king chose to ordain that the table should remain to bolster his rule.

6.23 Alexander now aimed to enter within the bounds of Persia proper, so he set Susa in the hands of Archelaus with a garrison of three thousand. The custody of its citadel was consigned to Xenophilus and a thousand elderly Macedonians soldiers were assigned as his garrison. Callicrates was allocated the care of the treasury and Abulites was reinstated in the Susian satrapy. **Alexander** also **left the mother, the son and the daughters of Darius in the city of Susa,** *furnishing them with tutors to teach them the tongue of the Greeks.* And it chanced that the king had been sent a present of Macedonian

---

[131] A talent was a weight of about 26kg (equal to 6000 drachmae or 60 minas) with its most common usage being the largest monetary unit, when the weight was composed (usually implicitly) of silver.

[132] A port on the eastern side of the Peloponnese.

clothing and a great deal of purple material from Macedon together with those women whose work they were. He bade that these be entrusted to Sisygambis, for he lavished every honour upon her and even dealt her the devotion due from a son. And he bade that she should be made aware that, if the clothing met with her approbation, she might have her granddaughters familiarised with its production and he had lent her ladies who could give instruction. But the welling up at these words of her tears exposed that her spirit spurned such a presentation, since there is nothing that Persian ladies consider more humiliating than to have to set their hands to knitting.

6.24 Those that had presented the gifts reported Sisygambis' distress and it appeared proper to express regret and proffer solace. Therefore Alexander visited her in person and explained: "Mother, in these garments that form my dress you behold not merely a gift from my sisters but also work of their own creation. Thus I have been misled by the practices of my nation. I implore you to be careful not to interpret my ignorance as insolence. Wherever I have been aware of your customs, I have, I hope, observed them with diligence. I know, for instance, that amongst you it is forbidden for a son to be seated within sight of his mother unless she has sanctioned it. Hence on each visit to you I have held back until you have gestured that I might sit. Though you have repeatedly wished to do me homage through proskynesis, I have not allowed you to do this. And I apply to you the title due to Olympias as my most darling mother."

6.25 Having mollified the mother of Darius **Alexander marched on with his army and reached the River Tigris** *that the locals call the Pasitigris[133]* **at his fourth encampment. This river rises amidst the mountains of the Uxii and roils on rapidly for a thousand stades[134] through rocky gorges between forested banks in rough terrain. But then it slackens and becomes navigable by boats as it enters upon a level plain. After six hundred stades traversed tranquilly, it empties into the Persian Sea. The king crossed the river and entered the land of the Uxii** *accompanied by nine thousand infantry and archers from the Agrianians plus three thousand Greek mercenaries as well as a thousand Thracians. This territory borders upon Susianê but extends into the first part of Persia, leaving just a narrow corridor between the Persians and the Susians. This was a rich region, irrigated by widespread watercourses and fecund with multifarious fruits. At the harvest, by drying the ripe fruit, the merchantmen that ply the Tigris can convey to Babylonia all manner of sweetmeats to delight the gourmet.*

6.26 Alexander found that *the routes of* access had been secured *with many men* by Madates, *the governor of that region and a cousin of*

---

133 This was the ancient Eulaeus, which is the modern River Karun.

134 1000 stades in Diodorus 17.67.2, but only 50 in Curtius 5.3.1. The word *chilious* in the former is less likely to have been corrupted than the L in Curtius and 1000 stades better fits the geography.

Darius. This man was no chameleon, for he had determined to extend his loyalty to the very end. The king could see instantly that the sheer cliffs posed a great deal of difficulty, but a local man among the Uxii knew the country and confided the existence of a pinched and perilous path *that was directed away from the city.* If agreed, he would lead a few light-armed troops, who would ascend to a site above the heads of the enemy. When Alexander was pleased to approve this plan, he assigned a force *of fifteen hundred mercenaries and a thousand Agrianians* to be taken with the guidance of the man *by the backways under the captaincy of Tauron and he ordained that they should set forth after the setting of the sun.*

6.27 *The king himself* broke camp in the third watch and negotiated the narrows at about daybreak. After cutting canes for fashioning hurdles and breastwork, so that soldiers shifting up siege towers should be sheltered from missiles, he *instigated the investment of the city.* Every approach was sheer and riven by rocks and crags. Hence *the advance was repulsed* with many casualties, since they had to contend with the terrain as well as their enemies. *Nevertheless, they rallied and renewed the assault,* since their sovereign set himself amidst their front ranks, asking them whether the sackers of so many cities should not be ashamed to shirk from besetting so insignificant and unsung a citadel? Whilst he was chiding them, long-range missiles came marauding amongst them. His soldiers parried with a tortoise formation for his protection, when their efforts to urge his withdrawal met with rejection.

6.28 At last, Tauron manifested himself with his detachments at a vantage point overlooking the citadel of the city. The sight of him *both enfeebled their foes' nerve and also fired the Macedonians to fight with more verve.* The defenders were crushed *by the pincer movement, the impetus of their opponents being too powerful to repel. A few were of a mind to die, whilst* many thought to fly, *most of whom retired into the citadel.* Thence they sent thirty spokesmen to beg the king's pardon, but these received from him the grim response that there were no grounds for exoneration. Therefore, in trepidation of dire punishments as well, they sent persons by a hidden way unknown to their opponents to sway Sisygambis, the mother of Darius, into conciliating the king, since they were not unaware that he cared for her and indulged her as though he were her own offspring. Furthermore, Madates had married the daughter of her sister, so as to count as a kinsman of Darius.

6.29 For some while Sisygambis was loth to entertain the suppliants' petition, shaking her head to express that an appeal from her was inconsistent with her present position. She added that she was anxious not to compromise their conqueror's kind consideration and that she more often bore in mind that she was currently a captive than that she had been a queen of their nation. But being eventually converted to their cause, in a letter to Alexander she craved that he excuse her intercession in begging that he should excuse them too. Failing such lenity, then would he at least forgive her, for she was only pleading for the life of a relative and auxiliary, who no longer fought as his enemy but besought his mercy. In fact this single act sufficiently portrays the moderation and clemency of the king in those days, for he not only granted Madates amnesty, but he absolved and set at liberty both those who surrendered and those that he held in captivity. Moreover, in quitting the city, he left it intact and untaxed in the tilling of its territory. Had Darius been the victor, his mother could not have asked for more.

6.30 *Thus* Alexander *won his way through and soon* received all the cities of Uxianê, *which he incorporated in the satrapy of Susianê.* Then he divided his forces between himself and Parmenion, whom he bade pursue a path through the plains, whilst **the king** accompanied by disencumbered contingents seized the range of mountains, of which the ridge **ran right the way on into the Persian domains.** Having ravaged this entire region **Alexander** entered Persia upon the third day and **reached the gorge that the Persians call the Gates of Susianê on the fifth day. But Ariobarzanes held the passage with twenty-five thousand infantry** *and three hundred cavalry.* **Alexander at first thought to force the fairway, filtering forward through fine defiles. The cliffs were everywhere sheer and precipitous and the barbarians lined their crests above the range of missiles. Practicing passivity and a pretense of apprehension, the Persians allowed him to reach the narrowest part of the pass without opposition. But when they perceived that he continued to proceed, whilst paying them no heed, then indeed they rolled colossal boulders down the mountain shoulders. These, in commonly colliding with projecting rocks, were responsible for avalanche generations, such that they crushed not just single soldiers, but packed formations. Stones were also flung from slings and arrows were showered upon them from all directions.**

6.31 *Nor was this the most trying thing that these brave warriors were enduring, but rather that, in being butchered like beasts ensnared by a pit in that situation, they were denied any means of retaliation. Therefore their rage turned rabid and they seized upon projecting rocks in order to reach their foes by attempting to lift each other aloft, yet these blocks, when simultaneously wrenched by the hands of many men, collapsed upon those that had disturbed them. Hence they could neither stand nor struggle forward nor even be safe beneath tortoise formations, when such bulky blocks were being cast down by the barbarians. The king was anguished not merely by sorrow, but also by remorse, that he had imprudently pitched into that gorge with his whole force. Undefeated before that day, his every risk had been rewarded. He had careered into the conduits of Cilicia with impunity and in Pamphylia a novel pathway across the sea had been forded. But now his good fortune faltered and was held back, so that he had no other recourse but to retrace his track. Hence* Alexander, having issued the trumpet signal for retreat, bade his men *close ranks and* evacuate the gordge *by locking their shields overhead into a sheet.* For thirty stades they beat their retreat.[135]

6.32 The king encamped *in a place that was open on all sides, but set about defending the site with a palisade. There he not only commenced consultations on a course of action, but also made moves to summon seers out of a sense of superstition. But what would Aristander, the most credible of his diviners, be capable of prophesying in the present situation? Therefore, sidelining sacrifices as inopportune,* he commanded the convening of those familiar with the region. These locals proposed an unrestricted and risk-free roundabout route through Media at the expense of several days' journeying, but none knew of another road through the range ahead of him. But the king was ashamed to forsake his soldiers without burial, for it was conventional wisdom that scarcely any military duty was so sacrosanct as furnishing the dead with a funeral. But to beg for their bodies would have been discreditable, since it could convey that he had been bettered in battle. Hence he ordered that such captives as he had recently seized should be summoned and amongst these there came forward a fellow fitted out in skins who was fluent in both the Greek and Persian tongues.

6.33 He was a Lycian long ago deported to those parts as a prisoner of war, who had been a shepherd in these mountains since some years before. He had come to know the region well and so concurred that to lead a large force into Persia across the ridges of that range would be absurd. But there were tracks barely passable in single file through the wood, where foliage and intermeshed branches masked everything by forming an unbroken forest hood. And indeed Persia is upon that side ensconced by an unrelenting array of ridges. This range runs for a length of sixteen hundred stades with a breadth of one hundred and seventy, stretching all the way between the Caucasus and the Red Sea and, just where the mountains fade, the seething waves form a further barracade. A broad plain sinks down beyond the further foothills of the escarpments, where the fertile land is littered with cities and settlements. The River Araxes roils amidst those fields with the waters of many mountain spates, feeding the Medus, a less important river than that which it assimilates. Veering southwards to the sea, no other flow causes plants to flourish with more fecundity. Wherever it meanders is carpeted in flowers and its banks are plastered with plane trees and poplars, so that to those seeing them at some separation, they seem like a salient of the highland forestation. For the shaded stream is bound by a course carved deep into the ground, so the overhanging heights are lush with fronds and shoots due to the dampness that percolates to their roots. Asia in its entirety possesses no other region that is more salubrious, for its weather is abated upon the one side by the

---

[135] Diodorus 17.68.4 has 300 stades, but the difference between the words for 30 and 300 is small in Greek, so the xxx stades in Curtius 5.3.23 is preferable, also because it is more reasonable.

shading shelter of a range that is continuous and assuages the swelter, and upon the other by the adjacency of the sea that tenders the terrain its temperature stability.

6.34 *Having heard the internee's exposition, the king quizzed him as to whether he had learnt of the route through rumour or personal observation?* *He responded that, being a shepherd, he had traversed all those tracks and added that he had twice been waylaid, once by the Persians in Lycia and again by Alexander's brigade. This caused the king to recall a prophecy given out by* the Delphic[136] *oracle* of Apollo. Whilst Alexander was still a boy, *in some consultation it had been its intimation that he would be led along lanes leading into Persia by* a wolf, which might mean *a person of Lycian extraction.*[137] *Therefore* Alexander piled such promises of presents upon this person as were in proportion to the pressure from his present predicament and his prosperity's ability to apportion. *And he ordered him to arm himself in the Macedonian fashion. Then, praying for success,* the king bade him show him the way. Whatever its steepness and severity, he would surmount it with a small party, so as to emerge behind the enemy, *unless by any chance the chap were to construe that what he for the sake of his flock had got through, Alexander for the sake of his glory and eternal renown could not negotiate too? And yet the captive continued to caution the king concerning the difficulty of the route, especially for armed troops. Then Alexander retorted: "You can take it from me, indeed, that, wherever you may lead, none of those that follow shall refuse to go."*

6.35 Hence *he relinquished the custodianship of the camp to Craterus* with his customary command of infantrymen accompanied by the contingents led by Meleager and a thousand mounted bowmen. *He instructed him deliberately to light more fires than were required in order to maintain the semblance of the encampment, the better for the barbarians to believe that the king himself was still present.* However, if it chanced that Ariobarzanes should realise that he was infiltrating via those tortuous tracks and tried to interpose part of his forces upon the adopted trail, Craterus should distract him with intimidatory attacks causing him to concentrate his troops against the more pressing peril. Conversely, if the king should succeed in seizing the wooded escarpment unnoticed by their foes, then when Craterus heard the uproar due to the throes of the natives in encountering the king, he should not hesitate to advance by that way whence they had been repulsed the previous day. It would be deserted, since contending with Alexander would have drawn their opponents away.

---

[136] The information that this was the Pythia at Delphi comes from Plutarch, *Alexander* 37.1.

[137] This is a play on the Greek word for a wolf: *lykos.*

6.36 The king *himself* set out in *the third watch of* the night *upon the trail of the indicated route without even sounding any trumpet peals. He instructed his lightly armed troops to carry food for three days' meals. But,* as well as impassable reefs of rock and precipitous crags that repeatedly steered their steps astray, snowdrifts piled up by the wind frustrated their foray. *For they were swallowed up as if they had been pulled into imperceptible pits and when their fellow soldiers set about extricating them, they dragged in these rescuers more often than escaping with them. In view of the cloak of night as well as the obscurity of the territory and the unproven probity of the guide their disquiet was much increased.* If he had deceived his captors, they could each be trapped like a wild beast. The security of their sovereign and their personal safety depended upon both the loyalty and the life of a single detainee. *But eventually they crested the ridge. To the right ran the route to Ariobarzanes himself, which Alexander assigned to Philotas and Coenus with* Hephaistion *Amyntoros*[138] *and Polyperchon, who were accompanied by a disencumbered contingent of troops.* The king counselled them to advance gradually, since the land was most fertile and fecund with fodder and infantry were blended amongst their cavalry. He provided guides for their route from amongst those he held in captivity.

6.37 *Alexander himself pressed on with the hypaspists and the squadron dubbed the agema via a precipitous path, where he hit many hazards, but bypassed the positions of his opponents more widely. It was the middle of the day and their exhaustion dictated a delay for rest* under cover of the wood, *for as great a distance remained to be traversed as* the eighty stades that *they had already trod, though less arduous and steep. Therefore, the soldiers having been recuperated by dining and dozing, they rose to their feet upon the second watch.* The king traversed the rest of the route without inconvenience, except that, where the mountain ridge gradually gave way to level ground, the path was rent by a huge chasm carved out by a confluence of torrents. Beside this the branches of the trees were so intertwined and matted as to confront them with an unbroken fence. Hence they were gripped by an intense sense of despair, such that they could hardly hold back their tears. The darkness especially fed their tears, since the stars could not be glimpsed, even if they pierced the clouds, for the trees were thick with leafy shrouds. They lacked even the use of their hearing, since the forest was thrashed by the wind that clashed the branches so as to derive more din than was due to its howling.

---

[138] Manuscripts of Curtius 5.4.20 and 5.4.30 had Amyntas, but Polyaenus, *Stratagems* 4.3.27 appears to be following a Cleitarchan source in asserting that Philotas and Hephaistion were the commanders of the other pincer of the attack. Given that Hephaistion was the son of Amyntor (Arrian, *Indica* 18.3), it would seem possible that a reference to Hephaistion in Cleitarchus has been garbled by Curtius (cf. Arrian, *Anabasis* 3.18.6).

6.38 At last the long looked for light lessened all the terrors incited by the night. The cascade could be circumvented by a slight diversion and each man had begun to find his own way ahead. Hence *they emerged upon a lofty elevation, whence they overlooked the enemy position.* Upon a peal of trumpets, *these warriors promptly appeared behind the back of the Persians, who had not thought to dread such an attack. Some few that faced up to fighting back were cut down. Hence the combination of the groans of the dying and the pitiable appearance of those that were flying set in flight even those that still stood tight, before they had fought in the fray. The cacophony carried to the camp commanded by Craterus, who led forth his forces in a foray to seize those narrows in which the troops had faltered upon that previous day. Simultaneously, Philotas with Polyperchon,* Hephaistion **Amyntoros** *and Coenus, who had been ordered to pursue the alternative way, beset the barbarians as another threat.* But they made a memorable stand, despite that Macedonian arms flashed everywhere and disaster loomed at both their front and their rear. It may be supposed that necessity even hones timidity and that despair spurs hope to appear. Though they were themselves unarmed, they surrounded and seized their armed adversaries, tumbling them to the ground with them by the great weight of their bodies, and then they skewered many of them with their own armouries.

6.39 Nevertheless, *having slain the front ranks and seized the secondary positions, Alexander overran the rest, who abandoned their stations.* But Ariobarzanes, escorted by about forty knights and five thousand foot, shed much of his own men's blood as well as their enemies' in charging through the middle of the Macedonian lines and speeding off to seize possession of the city of Persepolis, the regional capital. However, its garrison denied him admittance and, being hotly pursued by his opponents, he resumed his armed resistance and was killed with all his fellow fugitives and adherents. Craterus too quickly came through by a forced march of his contingents.

6.40 The king stockaded a camp on the same site whence he had put his foes to flight, for despite that the rout of the enemy on every front had ceded him victory in the fight, his advance was arrested by the road, which was riven by deep and steep-sided trenches in many a location. Hence he no longer needed to proceed slowly and with caution due to the duplicitousness he suspected in his enemies, but because of the treacherousness he attributed to his situation. **As Alexander edged forward** on the road to Persepolis **a letter was delivered to him from Tiridates,** its governor and **the custodian of the royal monies, advising him that those within the city having heard that he was coming were wishing to plunder its repositories. He urged him to hasten to seize this vulnerable treasure,** for to surrender the city to Alexander would be his pleasure. He wrote that there was no hindrance on the highway except that between the king and Persepolis the River Araxes lay. Of all the virtues of that sovereign, none merits more approbation than his expedition. *Foresaking his footsoldiers, he rode all night and reached the Araxes with his cavalry at first light, despite such a distance inducing exhaustion. He demolished the neighbouring hamlets, rapidly erecting a bridge using their timbers supported upon stanchions of stone.*

6.41 Having crossed the river and being now not far from the city, the king was confronted by the wretched spectacle of a piteous parade of persons bearing fronds in supplication. *Ranking among the worst ever cases of affliction,* these were about eight hundred[139] mainly elderly Greeks, captured and carried away from their home nation by earlier kings of Persia. Each had suffered some sort of mutilation by their captors: some lacked feet and others were missing hands as a result of their amputation, whereas some had endured the severing of their noses and ears. *They had been branded with barbarian characters and retained for protracted derision by their overseers. But when their masters found that they too were faced with foreign domination, they failed to forbid the desire of their Greeks to go to greet the new lord of creation. They looked like outlandish phantoms rather than men, for nothing but their voices could be recognised by their countrymen, so* they wrung more tears from those soldiers round about than they themselves had poured out. *To be sure, amidst so many and varied individual fates, which was the most wretched could not be discerned. For though they were actually dissimilar in their suffering, they seemed a lot alike as far as onlookers were concerned. But when* they yelled out in unison that Zeus himself, the avenger of the Greeks, had at last opened his eyes to events, *all that beheld them felt that they shared in the same chastisements.* In hearing their appeal for *vengeance[140] and* succour Alexander was moved to weep more wantonly than any other. But having wiped away his tears, he respectfully called forward their leaders and bade them to be of good cheer, since he would guarantee that the chance for them to see their cities and wives was near.

6.42 The king constructed a camp enclosure two stades from the city. **The Greeks** came forth from its walls and **deliberated what it would be best to put to Alexander as their** *collective* **request.** *And when some favoured asking for a home in Asia, whilst others were pleased for each to be returning to his own homestead, Euctemon of Cymê addressed them in these words so it is said: "We, who were lately shy of emerging from darkness and imprisonment even to plead for aid, as it is now are desirous of exhibiting our mutilations, in which it is unclear whether our shame or our chagrin is greater, in Greece as though they were ornamentations. Indeed, he best*

---

[139] Didorus 17.69.3 and Justin 11.14.11 state "about 800", but Curtius, although seemingly following the same account, writes *ad IIII milia fere*. Most probably Curtius wrote "almost a thousand" and some other small word or mark has been corrupted to IIII, giving the numeral 4.

[140] See Justin 11.14.11.

---

bears a blight, who blots it out from sight and no refuge is so cosy for those in adversity as solitude and forgetfulness of their former prosperity. For those that confidently count upon their kinfolk being compassionate disregard how rapidly tears evaporate. No one's fondness is faithful for one whom he finds distasteful, for even as calamity causes us to complain, prosperity engenders disdain. Hence everyone considers his own state in deciding another's fate. If we were not mutually marred by mutilation, we would long since have succumbed to mutual revulsion. What wonder is it that the fortunate are always attracted to people in the same situation?"

Figure 6.4. Alexander meeting the mutilated Greeks (1696 edition of Curtius)

6.43 *"I implore you, let us seek a site where we can bury these half-eaten bodies. What a welcome in a word we would receive in returning to the wives whom we wedded in our youth! Will our offspring, at the peak of their powers and their deeds, accept those debilitated in dungeons as their colleagues in truth? And what fraction of us is capable of traversing so many lands? Far from Europe, carted to the ends of the East, aged and infirm, missing most of our feet and hands, are we so sure we shall be able to abide what has worn out the warriors from the winning side? What about the wives that chance encounters in captivity and keen necessity have wedded to us as our sole solace? Shall we drag them and their infants with us or shall we abandon them in this place? If they go with us, no one will want to know us.[141] Shall we therefore instantly forsake our current children, when it is uncertain whether we shall get to see our long-lost offspring? Instead, we should maintain our isolation among those who have begun to get used to our mutilation."*

6.44 *So spoke Euctemon, but the Athenian, Theaetetus, mounted some opposition: "No gentleman will judge his kin by their physical condition, especially when they were disfigured through the ferocity of their foes rather than at Nature's volition. He who is ashamed of his misfortunes is deserving of perdition. He thinks the worst of human nature and despairs of receiving a warm reception simply because he himself would confront his fellows with rejection. The gods are tendering you what you yourselves would never have dared to crave: your wives, your children, your homeland and whatever else men prize as much as their lives or will die to save. Why then do you not break out from this incarceration? At home they breathe another air and look at things in a different illumination. Even foreigners hanker for our customs, our cults and our common language. Yet you yourselves would voluntarily relinquish this heritage, although it is for no other cause that you suffer such desolation than that you are subjected to its deprivation. Emphatically, I would return to my household and my home country, availing myself of such regal philanthropy. But if a fondness for bedmates and their offspring that servitude has coerced you into adopting holds you in hesitation, you should forsake them if nothing is dearer to you than your own nation."*

6.45 *Few shared in this view. The rest were swayed by their habituation, which is stronger than the ties of nation.* They agreed that they should petition the king to supply them with a substitute Asian settlement and a hundred were sent to seek the king's consent. *Reckoning that they would*

---

[141] Euctemon is not suggesting special coldheartedness among his Greek relatives. There would have been a practical, legal problem in that their fathers would thereby in effect have acknowledged these illegitimate foreign offspring. That would have given them inheritance rights under Greek laws, making them a threat to the grownup sons at home. The response of the Greek families might well have been to refuse to acknowledge their fathers in the first place.

request what he himself had proposed to grant, Alexander announced: "I have bidden that beasts of burden be consigned to convey you and that a thousand drachmae be assigned to each of you. When you are back in Greece, my word ensures that none shall think his condition better than yours, save in the matter of your sores." With welling tears, they fixed their eyes upon the ground, neither daring to raise their gaze nor to make a sound. Finally, the king coaxed them for the cause of their trouble and Euctemon answered in much the same words as he had spoken at their council. Then, pitying not merely their misfortunes but also their misgivings, the king commanded that they be gifted three thousand drachmae per person. To this were added ten garments apiece, five for a man and five for a woman, and they were given two teams of oxen, fifty sheep and fifty medimni[142] of seedcorn, so that they could farm and plant the land that they got by Alexander's grant. *They were also exempted from the king's taxation and he mandated his ministers to prevent their molestation. Thus Alexander improved the propects of those preyed upon by adversity in line with his innate philanthropy.*

6.46 On the following day the king convened the commanders of his contingents. He asserted that *Persepolis was the imperial capital of the Persians:* "No city has been more aggressive towards the Greeks[143] than this, the ancient seat of the Persian kings. *It was from here that those huge hosts, firstly of Darius, then of Xerxes, wickedly waged war upon Europe.* Our forbears shall be avenged by its obliteration."[144] *In fact the barbarians had already forsaken their stronghold, being dispersed wheresoever dread had driven them, when* the king without lingering led in his phalanx. *He had stormed many cities stuffed with regal splendours, whilst others had submitted to his governance, but* the opulence of this metropolis surpassed all precedents. Here the barbarians had hoarded all of Persia's affluence. It was the wealthiest city under the sun: gold and silver were piled in heaps and there were vast numbers of vestments and furnishings that served no purpose but rank ostentation. Alexander allowed the looting of all but the palace quarter. In consequence the conquerors brandished their swords at one another, for he that had seized some more treasurable trophy was made their enemy *and of these they slew many.* Their lust for loot lasted from dawn to dusk

---

[142] A medimnus was around 55 litres.

[143] Alexander widens the scope of harmed Greeks to include victims of invasions of Europe launched from Persepolis, but coming immediately after the episode of the mutilated prisoners, it is clear that the king has them in mind as well.

[144] The implication of the timing is that Alexander was inspired to plan the destruction of Persepolis particularly as a result of the encounter with the mutilated Greeks, even if its eventual culmination at the instigation of Thais was decided on the spur of the moment (and in fact it may have been staged.)

and when they could not cope with all that they had nabbed, spoils were appraised rather than simply grabbed. They rent the royal robes of purple and gold by slitting with their swords *through a fold or crease* and vessels were vandalised with pick-axes, though each was a masterpiece. Nothing stayed intact nor was carried off complete and statues were maimed as they hacked from its seat whatever could be claimed.

6.47 *Not only greed but also brutality rampaged through the captured city. Those weighed down with silver and gold butchered the cheap carcasses of their captives, killing wherever they encountered those whose ransoms had once led them to be spared. Many therefore dodged the blows of their foes through suicides, donning their richest robes and plummeting from parapets along with their kids and their brides. Anticipating the apparent intentions of their enemies, some set their buildings ablaze, so as to incinerate themselves with their families. In the end the king commanded his men to spare* the persons and the attire of the women, *who* were *merely* made into thralls, but the vast villas and halls, famed throughout creation, fell victim to vandalism and obliteration. *Even as Persepolis had eclipsed every other city in its prosperity, so now it similarly surpassed the rest in its calamity.*

6.48 Alexander went up onto the terrace of the citadel and took possession of its treasure that had been hoarded from the royal revenues, since the time of Cyrus, the first king of the Persians. The vaults were crammed with silver and gold. When they equated the weight of the gold to its value in silver, there were one hundred and twenty thousand talents all told.[145] In addtion, six thousand talents were taken at Parsagada, a city that Cyrus had founded, now given up by its governor, Gobares. Alexander favoured ferrying some funds along with him to finance the forthcoming campaign and thought securely to stash in Susa whatever might remain. Hence he commanded that innumerable mules and three thousand camels be summoned from Susa itself as well as from Mesopotamia and Babylon, by means of which the king conveyed each thing to its appointed destination. *Alexander was irreconcilable against the local population: thinking them implacable, his plan for Persepolis was annihilation.*

6.49 The king detailed three thousand Macedonians to garrison the citadel of Persepolis and designated Nicarchides as its castellan. In addition, Tiridates was reinstated in the rank that he had held under Darius, since he had transferred

---

[145] As I write this in September 2011, the value of gold is $59.64/g and the value of silver is $1.33/g, so the ratio of their values by weight is 44.8. In Alexander's time this ratio was about 13. A talent was 6000 drachmae. On the Athenian standard (used for Alexander's currency) we know from surviving silver coins that a drachma was about 4.35g. Hence 120,000 talents of silver weighs 3132 metric tonnes and has a September 2011 value of $4170M, but if the treasure in Persepolis was mainly in the form of gold, then its present value could be as high as $14000M.

the treasure. Furthermore, a large proportion of the army and its baggage was left there under the direction of Craterus and Parmenion. Alexander himself with a thousand cavalry and a disencumbered contingent of infantry set off into the Persian hinterland at around the evening setting of the Pleiades.[146] Though assailed by many storms and almost unendurable weather conditions, he nevertheless pressed on to fulfil his ambitions. He ventured upon a route perpetually packed with snow that had set to ice from being so far below zero. The wilderness of these tracts and their trackless desolation intimidated the tired troops, who thought that they beheld the end of civilisation. They peered in complete perplexity at an utterly barren landscape that was devoid of any trace of human activity and they insisted that they should turn back again ere the weather should worsen and the light too should wane.

6.50 The king refrained from reproving his frightened soldiers, but leapt from his steed and began on foot to forge through the snows and across the hard-packed ice. First of all his Friends were shamed into pursuing him, followed by the commanders of his contingents and ultimately the rank and file. And the king was the first to cut himself some tracks by hacking at the ice with a pickaxe, whereupon the rest mimicked their monarch's style. At last, having passed through almost impassable forestation, they came back into contact with occasional traces of human occupation and scattered flocks of roving sheep and inhabitants who dwelt in isolated shacks, since they considered themselves secluded by the inaccessibility of the tracks. When these caught sight of the columns of their foes, they slew those of their fellows that were incapable of escape and fled into the trackless and snowbound mountain landscape. But then through the intercession of their countrymen in Alexander's custody they were gradually pacified and placed themselves at the king's mercy. Nor were those that surrendered dealt with severely.

6.51 After laying waste to the fields of Persia and putting in his power several settlements, the king next ventured among the Mardians, a truculent tribe greatly contrasting in their lifestyle with the rest of the Persian nations. They carve caves into the mountain features, wherein they conceal themselves with their wives and children, feasting upon the flesh of their flocks and of wild creatures. Even their women are not possessed of the gentler disposition that is Nature's tendency, but they wear their hair in shaggy tufts and the hems of their gowns hang above the knee. About their brows they bind a sling, which serves as a headdress as well as weaponry. Yet the same tide of Fortune also overwhelmed their community. Thus it was that thirty days after parading forth from Persepolis, Alexander likewise returned to the metropolis. Then he rewarded his Friends with presents and the rest too in proportion to each

---

[146] Plutarch, *Alexander* 37, states that Alexander was based at Persepolis for four months, which would be roughly February through May of 330BC. This 30-day roving expedition (southwards?) into the mountains during that period is dated by the evening setting of the Pleiades roughly to late March through April and is not explicitly recounted elsewhere than Curtius.

person's importance. Virtually everything that he had seized in that city was shared out as bounty.

6.52 *Some account is called for concerning the part of Persepolis occupied by the palaces in view of their splendour. This citadel is immense and is walled by a triple enclosure. The first circuit rising to sixteen cubits in all is crested with crenellations and rests upon elaborate foundations. Though the second wall is twice as tall, it is otherwise identical. The third enclosure has a rectangular layout and a sixty-cubit stature. The sturdiness of its stone is stout with the intention that it should long endure. Each façade features a portal with a bronze door and twenty-cubit poles of bronze lie alongside it for the sake of spectacle, whereas the door is such as to make the place secure.*

6.53 *The so-called Royal Crag that contains the sepulchres of the kings is situated some four plethra[147] to the east of the citadel. This is a cliff hollowed out halfway up to hold the tombs of many deceased sovereigns. These lack any other human access, save that they receive the burials of the dead by means of hoisting mechanisms. The sumptuously furnished lodgings of the kings and the marshals were spread across the citadel, which housed trusty treasuries for safeguarding the royal riches as well.*

6.54 But let us return to the course of events. Alexander's greatness of spirit was a trait in which he surpassed all other sovereigns: his steadfastness in the face of danger; his promptness and expedition in implementing his decisions; his conscientiousness towards those that capitulated and his clemency towards those that he had captured; he was not even enraptured by legal and general licentiousness. Yet his character was marred by a barely bearable infatuation with wine. Just when his adversary and rival for the rule of the realm was preparing to renew hostilities and whilst the conquered, being but lately subdued, remained resentful of his new regime, **Alexander held celebrations of his victories by** *dedicating lavish sacrifices to the deities and* **feasting his friends freely at all-day festivities,** *which were also frequented by females, though not such ladies as it was illicit to violate, but courtesans accustomed to accompanying the warriors with more coupling than was temperate.*

6.55 *Whilst the banqueting was well underway and a drunken hysteria had begun to possess the intoxicated attendees,* <u>an Athenian hetaera named Thais declared that Alexander would be most lauded among all the Hellenes, if it should please him to order that the palace of Persepolis</u>

Figure 6.5. Thais instigates the burning of Persepolis (G. Simoni)

be set ablaze.[148] *For there was an expectation that Alexander should raze this place among those Greeks whose cities had been obliterated by the barbarians in former days.* Let the king lead them in a comus to set the palace aglow and allow women's hands in a trice to overthrow the famous feats of their foe. And when the boozy bawd had aired her thoughts on such a serious design before men that were yet youthful and well the worse for wine, predictably several voices concurred, saying it were a thing worthy of the king and a shout to form the comus and light up torches was heard. *"Let us then avenge every last Greek shrine,"* the king answered, *"Let us incinerate the city,"* for he too had drunk immoderately and was fired up by their every word. All being sozzled, they surged up from their couches, calling for the composition of a comus of conquest in commemoration of Dionysus. Hence in their intoxication they set about the incineration of a city that they had spared when armed for confrontation.

6.56 *Immediately many a firebrand was brought to hand and female musicians from the banquet band accompanied the king as he led the throng with Thais the hetaera conducting the flutes, the pipes and the song.* Alexander was first to cast his blazing torch into the palace and Thais next, followed by the guests, the attendants and the courtesans. *A large proportion of* the entire palace *had been built of cedar, which* quickly caught fire, *fueling the propagation of the conflagration.* When the army, encamped not far from the city, espied the inferno, they rushed to render assistance, supposing it was happenstance. But on reaching the courtyard of the complex, they beheld the king himself bringing brands. So they set aside the water they had carried and themselves began to bung tinder upon the blaze. *And it was a most startling thing that the sacrilege that Xerxes, the Persian king, had perpetrated upon the Acropolis of Athens was avenged in kind by one woman alone, a compatriot of its citizens, in the course of revelling after many years had flown.*

6.57 Such was the demise of the seat of rule for the entire East, whither so many nations had looked for regulation, the home of such a succession of sovereigns and formerly a major menace to Greece. This was the city that had launched a fleet of a thousand vessels and had flooded Europe with her forces, bridging the sea with planking and digging defiles through mountains, then causing the sea to surge through the excavated courses.[149] *But not even the lengthy duration since its destruction has seen it rise again.* It was an embarrassment to the Macedonians that a city of such significance should have been razed by their ruler as a result of drunken revelling. Therefore the deed was deemed rather a result of deliberation and they brought themselves to believe that such had been

---

[148] Jacoby Fragment 11 of Cleitarchus from Athenaeus 13.37 (576 DE).

[149] The reference is to the carving of a ship canal through the isthmus of Mount Athos recounted by Herodotus 8.21-24.

the most appropriate approach to its levelling. Certainly, as soon as rest and repose had restored his senses from the throes of inebriation, Alexander himself repented, saying that the Greeks would instead have been better avenged upon the Persians had they been compelled to behold him sat upon the throne within Xerxes' own royal homestead. The next day he gave a present of thirty talents to the Lycian who had led him on that path by which Persia had been penetrated.

Figure 6.6. The ruins of Persepolis (an engraving published in 1685)

6.58 *All this having transpired, Alexander advanced upon the* other *cities of Persia, subduing some by force and winning others over through his clemency.*[150] Thence he moved into Media, where he was met by fresh reinforcements of troops from Cilicia, comprising five thousand infantry and a thousand cavalry with Platon of Athens commanding the combined body. Augmented by these forces, **Alexander set out in pursuit of Darius.**

---

[150] Alexander is now heading northwards past Parsargada and thence to Aspadana in southern Media, so there is no logic in associating the conquest of these Persian cities mentioned by Diodorus 17.73.1 with the late-winter campaign into the mountains (probably) south of Persepolis recounted by Curtius 5.6.12-20, which was explicitly antecedent to the incineration of the city.

Alexander the Great and the Conquest of the Persians

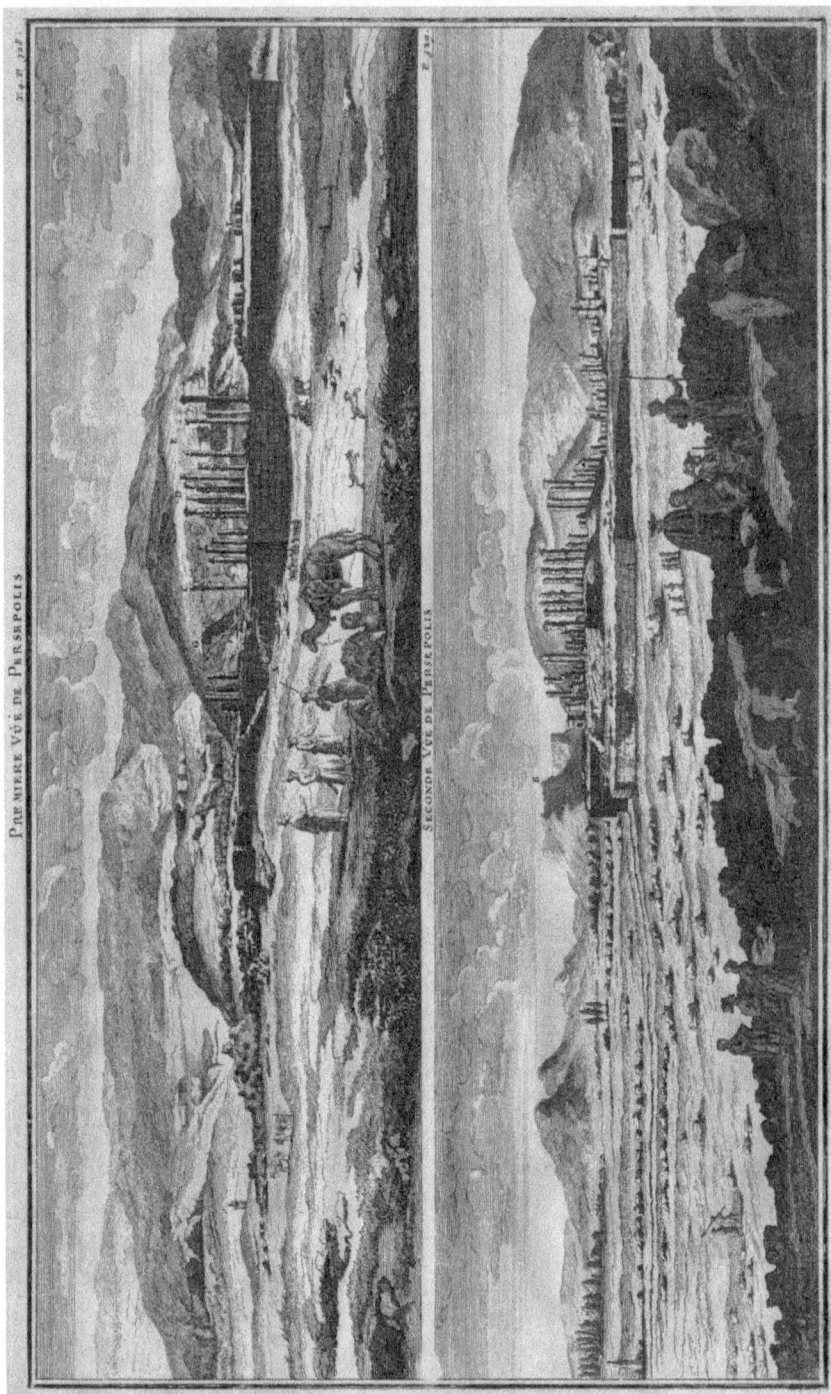

Figure 6.7. The first and second panoramas of the ruins of Persepolis by Cornelius de Bruyn, who visited the site in 1704 (1730 edition)

152

Figure 6.8. The third and fourth panoramas of the ruins of Persepolis by Cornelius de Bruyn, who visited the site in 1704 (1730 edition)

6.59 *The Persian monarch* was then tarrying at Ecbatana, which was the capital of Media. From there he had *proposed to go directly to Bactra, but,* fearful of interception *on account of Alexander's impetus, he modified* his policy and changed *his direction.* For, though Alexander yet lay fifteen hundred stades away, no separation now seemed to supply sufficient space when measured against the Macedonian's pace. Hence **Darius** was readying himself to fight more particularly than preparing for flight. He **was backed up by thirty thousand infantry, including** four thousand **Greeks**, who to the last stayed steadfast in their loyalty. He had also recruited companies of slingers and archers totalling four thousand men and additionally thirty-three hundred horsemen mainly of Bactrian origin. These were led by Bessus, who was satrap of the Bactrian region. With this array of troops Darius deviated a little from the military highway having bidden the baggage attendants and the sutlers to lead the way.

6.60 Having summoned an assembly Darius addressed them thus: "If fate had fastened me to the faint-hearted and to such as rate any sort of life above a distinguished estate among the departed, then I would rather maintain my silence than blather words of impotence. But having tested your faithfulness and your valiance further than I would have chosen, I ought all the more to strive to be worthy of such comrades, rather than doubt whether you remain of a like disposition. From among so many thousands you have stuck with me, though I was twice vanquished and twice forced to flee. It is your loyalty and your fidelity that lends my throne its credibility. Traitors and deserters now control my cities, not, by Heracles, because they are worthy of such dignity, but in order that their rewards should set your minds in a quandary. Yet you have preferred to bind yourselves to my fate rather than to the winner's destiny, making yourselves most deserving of rewards to be given by the gods on my behalf, if I should be unable to do so personally. And, by Heracles, you shall have your reward! No successors shall be so insensitive nor any record so callous as to fail to afford you fitting praise unto the Heavens!"

6.61 "Therefore, even if I had contemplated flight, from which my spirit completely cowers, bolstered by your bravery I would nevertheless have been roused to go to meet with these enemies of ours. Why indeed should I stay an exile in my own realm and flee before a foreign and alien ruler through the ends of my empire, when I have the chance to try the fortunes of warfare to either recover my losses or honourably expire? Unless perchance it should prove more fulfilling to dance attendance upon the decisions of the victor and emulate the example of Mazaeus and Mithrenes by being insecurely assigned the rule of a single province, always supposing Alexander now favours fawning upon his fame rather than indulging his anger?[151] May the gods forfend that anyone

---

[151] According to Diodorus 17.54.6 Alexander had already offered Darius the opportunity to retain his throne, provided that he acknowledged Alexander's overlordship. An imputation from this comment is that an offer for Darius to retain the satrapy of Persia was still on the table in 330BC.

should either remove or reinstate this diadem upon my brow or that I should lose my throne whilst I still respire, but let them rather allow my reign to last until the moment that I expire."

6.62 "If you adopt this spirit and this precept, there is not one of you for whom the promise of liberty will not be kept. None among you will be confronted by the disdain of the Macedonians or their haughty expressions. The right hand of each of you shall either extract vengeance for so many ills or bring them to an end. In truth I am myself the living proof of Fortune's accidents and not unjustifiably I look for milder swings in her trend. But if the gods do not side with just and righteous belligerency, they may nevertheless permit warriors to die with decency. By those auspicious ancestors of mine and yours, in their name, whose rule of the entire Orient has endowed them with enduring fame, by those warriors to whom these Macedonians once paid tribute, by those massed fleets of ships sent against Greece and all the many trophies amongst the royal loot, I beseech and implore you to embrace the courage befitting your reputation and that of your nation, so that you face up to whatsoever chance may bring with the same resolution with which you confronted the former suffering. I myself shall certainly secure enduring celebrity either through a notorious battle or a glorious victory."

6.63 As Darius spoke, the awful prospect of their imminent peril impacted upon the hearts and minds of everyone at once, so that they were at a loss for anything to say or suggest, whereupon Artabazus, the eldest of the Friends, who had been a guest of Philip (as I have often reported)[152], asserted: "We shall in very truth follow our sovereign into the battle, clad in our costliest dress and outfitted with the most potent arms that we possess and truly of a mind to anticipate victory, although also willing to accept fatality." The rest greeted these words with assent, but Nabarzanes, who was attending this same council, had hatched a hitherto unheard of plot with Bessus. They had resolved to arrest and fetter their sovereign with the support of the forces that they each commanded. Their thinking was that, should Alexander overtake them, surrendering the living king should win the victor's approbation, since he would certainly set great store by his seizure of Darius. Conversely, if they could outrun Alexander, then, having done away with Darius, they themselves might rule the realm and revive the struggle for its defence.

6.64 Such treason having long been contemplated, Nabarzanes was preparing the way for their wicked intentions when he stated: "I know that on first hearing, the opinion that I am about to express will not be such as pleases your ears, yet doctors too prescribe harsh remedies to cure the more serious diseases

---

Mazaeus had recently surrendered Babylon and retained its governance; Mithrenes had surrendered Sardis and had been given the Satrapy of Armenia in 331BC.

[152] Perhaps a remark by Cleitarchus preserved by Curtius 5.9.1, who wrote "as we have often said". It is also mentioned at Curtius 6.5.2.

and a pilot apprehending the wreck of his ship rescues whatever can be saved by jettisoning it. However, my advice is certainly not intended to cause you injury, but rather in order that you may rescue your realm through a sound strategy. The gods were against us from this war's inception and persistent Fortune perseveres with the Persians' persecution. There is a need for a new beginning and different divination. Let you for a little while cede the leadership and your sovereignty to another, who shall be called king only until Asia is abandoned by the enemy, then he shall restore the realm to you when he has secured victory."

6.65 "Moreover logic dictates that this shall soon come to be. Bactria remains unscathed and the Sacae and Indians are still subject to your authority: so many peoples, so many armies, so many thousands of infantry and cavalry standing ready to lend their strength for our recovery, such that more manpower remains to be deployed than has been destroyed amidst our military. Why should we like dumb beasts rush headlong into needless catastrophe? A valiant warrior rather spurns death than scorns his vitality. Frequently, cowards are caused by their intolerance of toil to squander their lives cheaply, but nothing is left untried by bravery. Considering that death brings complete finality, it is enough not to die lazily. Accordingly, if we wish to proceed to Bactra, which is our safest sanctuary, let us appoint the satrap of that country, Bessus, to an emergency monarchy. Then, when matters are resolved, he shall hand back to you, the rightful ruler, this trust of regency."

6.66 Hardly surprisingly, although it was still unclear just how much villainy lurked behind such disloyal language, Darius failed to contain his temper, yelling: "Most slinking of slaves, have you discovered the occasion that you have coveted for uncovering your treachery?" Drawing his sabre, it seemed he would have slain Nabarzanes, had not Bessus and his Bactrians hastily encircled him, as if to intercede with him, feigning dismay, but actually intent upon restraining him, if he would not give way. Meanwhile, Nabarzanes slunk away and Bessus soon went off to join him. They bade the forces under their command to set themselves apart from the rest of the army in order to instigate a private consultation. Adopting an attitude in keeping with their current circumstances, Artabazus began to calm Darius, repeatedly prompting him to be mindful of the emergency situation. Darius should bear with equanimity either silliness or vacillation from any sort of person, if they nevertheless supported his position. For Alexander was bearing down upon him, a menacing prospect even with all his forces at his disposal. What would be the outcome, if his followers in his flight should become estranged? It appeared to the king that Artabazus had a point and, despite having meant to move his base, whilst the hearts of all were wavering he kept to the same place. But being paralysed by both desolation and despair, he secluded himself in his royal lair.

6.67 Therefore divided loyalties arose amongst those in the camp, which became subject to a degree of anarchy in place of the former consensus that was in the interests of everybody. The commander of the Greek troops, Patron, called upon his men to snatch up their arms and stand ready to execute his instructions. The Persians had formed themselves into factions. The Bactrians backed Bessus, who sought to persuade the Persians to secede by reporting the riches of Bactra and its untouched territories, whilst also pointing out the impending peril for those that persisted with the performance of their duties. Practically all the Persians voiced the same objection: that it was treasonous to plot such a defection. In the meantime, Artabazus fulfilled all the leadership functions: he toured the tents of the Persians ceaselessly issuing exhortations, cautioning them individually and collectively, until it was sufficiently established that they would follow his command. Similarly, with some difficulty he induced Darius to take nourishment and to turn his mind to matters at hand.

6.68 But Bessus and Nabarzanes were burning with desire for dominance, so they plotted to implement the treachery of their earlier contrivance. They could not expect such supremacy, whilst Darius himself remained in authority, since among those peoples kingship confers exceptional majesty. At the mere mention of the king's name the barbarians are reduced to servility and the reverence he received in his heyday persists in his adversity. Yet the disloyal ambitions of the duo were inflated by the domain that was under their domination, which in arms and warriors as well as width of terrain was second to no other Persian nation. It constituted a third of Asia and the multitude of its young men matched the armies that Darius had mislaid. Therefore they not only despised Darius but even Alexander did not make them afraid, for thereby they would recover their empire's might, if they could but bring the satrapy in sight. After protracted consideration of every option, they favoured employing the biddably obedient Bactrian troops to arrest the king and then sending a message to Alexander declaring that Darius survived securely in their detention. If, as they feared, Alexander despised their treasonous actions, they would deal death to Darius and fall back upon Bactra with the forces from their factions.

6.69 However, it was impossible publicly to pinion Darius, since so many thousands of Persians would spring to his defence and it was intimidating too that the Greeks maintained their allegiance. Hence they adopted deception to proceed where force could not succeed by feigning contrition for their disaffection and excusing it to the king in terms of their consternation. However, they meanwhile introduced agitators amongst the Persians, who by turns utilised their aspirations and their fears to undermine the troops' affections, saying that they were exposing themselves to destruction and being dragged towards perdition, when Bactra beckoned beneficently to welcome them with wealth beyond their imagination. Whilst they were busied with this subversion, Artabazus came up to them, perhaps bidden by the king or else of his own accord, offering assurance that Darius had been mollified and that their former rank among his courtiers could be restored. At this they wept to wash themselves of suspicion, then implored Artabazus to plead their cause and convey their contrition.

6.70 Having thus reached the end of the night, Bessus and Nabarzanes in company with the Bactrian troops appeared in the courtyard of the headquarters just as it became light, veiling their secret treachery in the performance of a regular rite. Darius, having given the signal for getting underway, mounted upon his chariot in his familiar way. Nabarzanes and the other traitors prostrated themselves upon the ground, stooping to offer him reverence, whom they meant imminently to manacle, and even bursting into tears to protest their repentence. So readily indeed does the human conscience consent to pretence. In consequence, their humble pleas moved Darius, who was naturally kindhearted and sincere, not merely to believe their protestations, but even himself to shed a tear. Nevertheless, not even then did the conspirators conceive any compunction concerning their treasonous scheme, though they could perceive the mettle of the monarch and the man that they meant to deceive. He indeed, oblivious of this peril that neared, hastened to elude Alexander's grasp, his being the only hands that he feared.

6.71 However on the other hand, Patron, the leader of the Greeks, directed his men to don their panoplies that had up till then been stowed amongst the baggage and to be alert and attentive to his every command. He himself was dogging the king's chariot, hovering for a chance to speak with him, since he could perceive the impending perfidy of the satrap of Bactria. But Bessus, being fearful of just such a cautioning, did not budge from beside the chariot, behaving as a warden rather than a companion of the king. Hence Patron dithered for ages, often biting his tongue as he wavered between faithfulness and faintheartedness, whilst scrutinising Darius. When eventually the king's gaze alighted upon the Greek, he bade Bubaces, a eunuch among the nearest of his entourage to his chariot, to query whether he wished to speak. Patron confirmed his wish to talk to him, but without an audience. He was bidden nearer to converse without an interpreter, since Darius was not ignorant of the Greek tongue *and heard these words in confidence*: "Your majesty, out of fifty thousand Greeks we few are all that have come through, your comrades in every difficulty. And even in your present adversity, we who followed you in your prosperity shall similarly make for whatever lands you may fancy in place of our own hearths and our home country. We have become bound to you through the vicissitudes of your affairs. By these unbreakable bonds, my men urge and implore you to erect your tent amidst theirs and to suffer them to serve as your bodyguards. We have forsaken Greece and we have no stake in Bactra, so all our hopes are vested in you. Would that this were true of the others too! I need not continue. As a foreigner and an outsider I would not petition for the right to guard your person, if I believed that anyone else could assure your protection."

6.72 Despite that Bessus was ignorant of the Greek tongue, he was nevertheless spurred by the insight of an insider securely to assume that Patron had perpetrated an exposure. And that the Greek speech had been kept from the interpreters removed all doubt of the disclosure. But being, insofar as could be conceived from his countenance, scarcely distraught, Darius commenced querying Patron as to the cause of the advice that he had brought. Reckoning that this was not the occasion for further prevarication, Patron replied: "Bessus and Nabarzanes are intriguing against you. Your welfare and your life are in the utmost jeopardy and this day will be the last that either you or they see." And indeed Patron might have earned outstanding esteem by saving the king, although this thinking would indubitably be derided by those who are convinced that human affairs unfold and unwind by accident, else that a life runs its course consequent upon a combination of countless concealed causes long predestined according to laws with unalterable clauses.[153] As it happened, Darius answered that although he recognised the loyalty of the Greek legion, he would nonetheless never withdraw from among the men of his home region. For it was harder for him to vilify them than to allow them to beguile him. Whatever chance might instigate, he had rather suffer it among his countrymen than tergiversate. If his own soldiers did not wish to save him, then his end had come too late. Despairing of the king's welfare, Patron returned to those over whom he exercised authority, in order to prepare for every trial of loyalty.

6.73 But Bessus was possessed by a deep desire to despatch Darius right away. Yet fearing that he would fail to find favour with Alexander, unless Darius were delivered up alive, he arranged to delay his damnable design until the next night. Then he began to profess delight that Darius had diligently and prudently dodged the trap of a treacherous individual, who already had in view Alexander's might such that he would have made a present of the king's head to their opponent. He remarked that it was unremarkable that a man contracted for pay would make everything a matter of commerce. Without a hearth and family, an exile to all the world, he was a two-faced foe, trafficked at the dangling of a purse. As Bessus acquitted himself thus and invoked the gods of his country as testament to his loyalty, Darius expression conveyed his acquiescence, though he did not doubt the veracity of the Greek intelligence. But matters had reached the point that it was as perilous that his followers should be disbelieved as for Darius himself to be deceived. Those whose treachery or infidelity was feared numbered thirty thousand, when Patron had a mere four thousand men. If he should entrust his preservation to them, blackguarding the trustworthiness of his countrymen, then he perceived that he would provide a proper pretext for regicide. Therefore he preferred rather to be accosted undeservedly than justly. Nevertheless, when Bessus absolved himself of any subversive designs, Darius observed that it was clear that Alexander's sense of propriety was no less marked than his gallantry. They deceived themselves, who expected that he would reward them for perpetrating treachery, for there was none who would more vigorously vilify and avenge a violation of loyalty.

---

[153] An intricate observation worthy of a Cynic, although Curtius 5.11.10 is slightly corrupt.

6.74 And night was now nearing, when the Persians after their normal fashion set aside their arms and dashed off to fetch provender from *Thara* the closest settlement. But the Bactrians, as Bessus had bidden, still stood in their equipment. Meanwhile Darius bade that Artabazus be summoned and when he had disclosed what Patron had exposed, Artabazus was convinced that the king should convey himself into the Greek compound and that the Persians too would accompany him once word of his jeopardy were spread around. But Darius was now resigned to his fate and no longer heedful of healthy counsel. His sole solace in his travails, Artabazus, he beheld for the last time, hugging him whilst they were both overwhelmed with weeping, but ordering that he be dragged away as he continued to cling. Then, veiling his brow so as not to watch as Artabazus went away wailing as if from his funeral pyre, he threw himself face down into the mire. Whereupon indeed those that customarily comprised his bodyguard, whom it behoved to protect the king even at the risk of their lives, slunk away, reckoning that they would be no match for the armed men that they supposed would arrive without delay. Hence an intense sense of solitude descended within the tent, where just a few eunuchs, who had nowhere to go, still stood around their sovereign. But, dismissing this audience, Darius long contemplated alternative expedients.

6.75 Finally, feeling oppressed by the solitude from which he had sought solace but a bit before, he bade that Bubaces to be summoned. Fixing his gaze upon him, the king gave this command: "Leave me and look out for your own welfare. As is befitting you have been faithful to your king to the last. Here I shall await the verdict on my fate. Perchance you wonder why I do not take my own life? It is because I desire my death to be due to another's villainy rather than have it stain me." Upon these words, not just the pavilion but also the entire compound resounded with the eunuch's lamentation. Then others burst in upon the scene and, rending their raiment, they began to lament their king with plaintive and alien ululation. When this pandemonium pierced the ears of the Persians, they were transfixed by their fears so that they dared neither to seize their arms, in case they were confronted by the Bactrians, nor to appear impervious, lest they should seem disloyal in deserting Darius. Raucous and diverse disturbances resounded spontaneously and without coordination all around the compound.

6.76 *Bessus* and Narbazanes heard from their adherents, whom the lamentation had misled, that Darius was dead by his own hand. Hence they sped their steeds towards the scene with those they had appointed to perpetrate their perfidy in their band. And when they entered the royal tent, since the eunuchs disclosed that he had not died, they **ordered that Darius be seized and tied.** The king conveyed by a chariot but a little beforehand and reverenced by a sacred, sacrificial cult among the men of his land, was become the captive of his own lackeys without any foreign meddling **and thrust into a dingy cart, wholly hidden by a hide awning.** The king's funds and his furnishings were looted as if legitimised by hostilities, then they made good their escape burdened by the booty from this last of their iniquities.

6.77 Artabazus headed for Parthia with those that accepted his authority and the Greek soldiers, considering anything safer than being stalked by traitors. The Persians, who had been plied with promises by Bessus, mainly for want of anyone else to follow, attached themselves to the Bactrians, catching up with their column the day after the morrow. Yet, lest the king should lack any respect, **they fettered Darius with gold chain**, for Fortune formulated fresh mockeries for him again and again. And lest by chance he be recognised from any royal refinements, they had draped the wagon with shabby hides and the beasts were driven by peasants. In order that he could not be pointed out to the inquisitive amidst the column, his guards trailed at a distance.

6.78 Upon hearing that Darius had decamped from Ecbatana, **Alexander** abandoned the route whereby he was roving into Media and **pressed hard in the fugitive's pursuit.** He reached Tabae, a citadel in the furthest reaches of Paraetacenê, where deserters declared that Darius was heading for Bactra in full flight. Thereafter he got more authoritative information from Bagistanes, a Babylonian, who asserted that, though the king had not yet been fettered, he nevertheless stood in peril of being bound or murdered.

6.79 Having convened his commanders, Alexander declared: "The greatest of tasks but the briefest of labours remains to be undertaken. Darius is not far ahead, either deposed by his men or forsaken. Our victory is vested in his person and it is through velocity that such a prize will be won." All alike bellowed that they were ready to follow his lead: let him spare them neither toil nor peril in this deed. Hence he led his forces forward rapidly rather as if racing than marching, not even stopping at night to recuperate from the day's dashing. **He went onwards in this way for five hundred stades** and reached the village *of Thara* where Bessus had apprehended Darius. There Melon, Darius' interpreter, was captured. His frail frame had not been able to keep pace with the Persian army and, when waylaid by Alexander's rapidity, he pretended to be a turncoat. From him **Alexander learnt of the events** of note. **But rest was required by** those driven to exhaustion, so he augmented the **six thousand elite cavalry that accompanied him** with three hundred horsemen that were dubbed dimachae.[154] These wore weightier armour and, though each rode upon a steed, they fought on foot, when the matter and the moment made for a need.

6.80 Whilst Alexander was thus engaged, there came before him Orsilos and Mithracenes. They had deserted by dint of their detestation for the treachery of Bessus and they announced that the Persians lay five hundred stades away and that they would show him a shorter way. The king was gratified that deserters

---

[154] In the manuscripts of Curtius the word is *dimichas*, which is probably a slightly corrupted form of *dimachae*, Greek for "dual-fighters", since they evidently fought on foot as well as on horseback; Alexander is credited with having invented these troops by Pollux, *Onomast.* 1.10.

were coming over to him. Accordingly, at the onset of dusk led by these men he set out upon the route that they pointed out, having bidden the phalanx to follow as fast as they could. The king, forging forward in rectangular arrays, regulated the rate of advance so that the van could keep in contact with the rear. He had progressed three hundred stades, when *Brochubelus*,[155] the son of Mazaeus, sometime satrap of Syria, came before him. He too had deserted and declared that Bessus lay hardly more than two hundred stades away and that his forces, being panicked, were withdrawing in a disorderly and disorganised rout. They appeared to be on the point of heading for Hyrcania. If Alexander were to press his pursuit whilst they were straggling, he would overwhelm them. And he specified that Darius was still alive. Ever expeditious, Alexander was galvanised by the renegade into completing the chase, so kicking their spurs they made it a race.

6.81 Straightaway the commotion made by their enemies on the march became audible, but the vista was veiled in a cloud of dust, so Alexander reined in their onrush for a little while, whilst the dust settled. At that point they were sighted by the barbarians and themselves beheld the retreating columns, for which they would by no means have been a match, had Bessus fought battles with as much alacrity as he perpetrated treachery. For the barbarians were superior in both armour and numbers, added to which their fresh forces would have tangled with tired soldiers. But both the name and the fame of Alexander weighed most massively in war, such that they turned tail due to an attack of terror. To be sure, Bessus and the rest of the partners in his perfidy came up to the cart that carried Darius and began to harangue him into mounting a steed in order to seize the opportunity to flee from his enemy. But Darius declared that divine vengeance was visited upon them and appealed for asylum with Alexander, repudiating any desire to consort with traitors. Then, truly, also fired with fury, they hurled their spears at their sovereign and left him lacerated by many an injury. And so that they would not be able to keep going, they maimed the beasts too that drew the wagon and slew two slaves who had accompanied their king.

6.82 The murder having been committed, so as to split up the tracks from their flights, Nabarzanes made for Hyrcania, whilst Bessus bolted for Bactra escorted by a small number of knights. Bereft of their leaders and being led by either their hopes or their fears instead, the barbarians became increasingly widespread. There hung together a mere five hundred cavalry, who were as yet undecided as to whether they should stand or flee. Upon discovering the consternation amongst his foes, Alexander despatched Nicanor with a section of the cavalry to stem the stampede, whilst he himself followed on with their fellows. Almost three thousand that fought back were killed, but the rest of their army were rounded up in the manner of cattle without blood being spilled, since the king's command to refrain from slaughter was fulfilled. None among

---

[155] The name of Mazaeus' son may be corrupt in the manuscripts of Curtius.

those captured was able to identify the cart carrying Darius. Whenever a wagon was waylaid, it was individually scrutinised, but *as yet no observation of any trace of the king's disappearance was made.* Scarcely three thousand cavalry had kept pace with Alexander's rapidity. However, whole regiments of refugees gave themselves up to those that were following more slowly. Though it is barely believable to tell, the captives outnumbered those into whose custody they fell. So completely had calamity deprived the petrified of all rationality that they were unable correctly to recognise either the sparsity of their enemies or their own numerical superiority.

6.83 Meanwhile, lacking a wagoner, *the beasts that were hauling Darius had strayed* off the military highway and wandered for four stades until they drew to a halt in one of the valleys, exhausted by both the baking heat and their injuries. *There was a spring that lay not far away, which was pointed out to Polystratus, one of the Macedonians*, by well-informed persons. Spurred by thirst he got to it and, whilst quaffing water from his helmet, he espied the spears prodded into the body of each abandoned beast. Whilst he wondered why they had been stabbed instead of being nabbed, *he heard the moans of a man nearly deceased and discovered Darius lying within the wagon, his body perforated by many javelins.*

6.84 *The king called for something to slake his thirst, so Polystratus proferred water from his helmet. When a captive was fetched, recognising him from his voice as a compatriot, Darius confided: "It is at least a solace in my present sorrows that my speech shall be understood and that my last words will not be wasted."* Then **he bade that the following message be conveyed to Alexander:** *"Though I have done you no favours, I die most deeply in your debt, since* **in your conduct towards my mother and other family** *instead of any hostility* **royal standards have been met.** *Indeed I have been happier in my allotted enemy than in my kinsmen and the rest of those close to me. For my mother and children have been left alive by my foe, but I am slain by those I best know, to whom I have let my life and my lands go. And their reward for this shall be what you as victor wish to decree.* **I thank you in the only way the dying know, with my prayers to deities and regal gods on high and below that yours be the victory** *in every country and that your empire follow. For myself I seek the favour of a decent burial, which should be proper rather than impracticable. As regards revenge, now it is not mine alone but the common and particular cause of every king, which for you to ignore would be a perverse and perilous thing, since it is a question on the one hand of whether you are seen to act justly and on the other it is also a matter of expediency.* **Alexander, I offer my right hand to this soldier in your lieu, that he may convey this unparalleled pledge of royal loyalty to you."** *Then, in extending his hand to Polystratus, his spirit finally flew.*

Figure 6.9. The death of Darius (by André Castaigne, 1899)

Figure 6.10. Alexander cloaks the corpse of Darius (Antonio Tempesta, 1608)

6.85 *Alexander was told the story when he rode up presently and then he wept to see the body done to death so unworthily in view of its high dignity.* Therefore, unclasping his own cloak, he cast it upon the corpse of his erstwhile enemy. *Additionally,* **he ordered that his remains be** returned to Darius' mother to be **accorded a royal funeral,** then to be laid amidst the tombs of his forbears for his burial.

6.86 Yet certain persons have written that Alexander reached Darius whilst he was still breathing and condoled the king on his misfortunes; and that, when Darius told him that he should avenge his murder, Alexander acceded and set off in pursuit of the regicide. But as Bessus had a huge headstart and was retiring through the Bactrian countryside, Alexander curtailed this campaign and decided to head back again.

6.87 *Such was the situation in Asia. Yet in Europe the Spartans were compelled by their defeat in the decisive battle* near Megalopolis *to seek terms from* Antipater, who convened the Council of the Hellenic League *at Corinth* in order to refer a response to the Spartan diplomacy to its authority. But *after lengthy discussions* this body agreed no decisions save to allow the Spartans to send emissaries to Alexander *to expiate their indiscretions.* These were in addition to the **fifty hostages** who **were held by Antipater, selected from among the leading Lacedemonians and**

Spartans.[156] The Tegeans, excepting those that had incited their revolt, received pardons. The Achaeans and the Eleans were ordered to pay one hundred and twenty talents to the people of Megalopolis, whose city had been besieged by the rebel forces. *Such was the settlement of a war that broke out suddenly, but had actually ended ere Arbela saw Darius cede Alexander the victory.*

6.88 *These were the events concerning Alexander* in the sixth year of his reign.

---

[156] According to Harpocration, Cleitarchus had already mentioned the fifty hostages in Book 5, but Diodorus 17.73.6 suggests that the matter was reiterated here, perhaps to distinguish them from the envoys sent to Alexander.

6. Organisation and Sources

Tabulated References for the Reconstruction of Cleitarchus

Book 1: Spring 336BC – 15th October 335BC

Summary	Sources	References	Comment
Prologue: birth and ancestry of Alexander. Razing of the temple at Ephesus and descent from Aeacidae and Heraclidae.	Plutarch 2.1&3.3-5 Justin 12.16 Diodorus 17.1.5	Hammond THA 91 Sources 19-20	It has been thought that Cleitarchus opened his history with the assassination of Philip & Alexander's accession. However, a summary dealing with Alexander's birth & his youth may have been included. Hammond shows in *Sources* 19-20 that Plutarch's date for Alexander's birth comes from Timaeus, a contemporary of Cleitarchus. But Jacoby F7 of Cleitarchus from Clement of Alexandria says that both Timaeus & Cleitarchus gave 820 years for the period from the invasion of the Heraclidae to Alexander's crossing into Asia, whereas other Greek historians, such as Eratosthenes, gave wildly variant figures (cf. Jacoby F 36). This strongly indicates that Cleitarchus made use of Timaeus' work (cf. Pearson 216). If so, then Plutarch & Cicero are likely to be getting Timaeus' information on Alexander's birth via Cleitarchus. Perhaps Cleitarchus attributed the information to Timaeus. Hammond also attributes stress on Alexander's Aeacid ancestry to Cleitarchus & Jacoby F7 mentions the Heraclidae (cf. F36)
Philip sends his generals Parmenion, Amyntas & Attalus into Asia Minor	Justin 9.5.8-9	Hammond THA 93	Spring of 336BC
Philip celebrates marriage of daughter Cleopatra to Alexander of Epirus; Pausanias kills Philip in narrow passage, because he has ignored Pausanias' complaints against Attalus, who had raped him	Justin 9.6.1-8	Hammond THA 93	Summer of 336BC
Sons of Philip	Justin 9.8.1-3	Hammond THA 90-3	

Summary	Sources	References	Comment
Digression on the historical background in the Persian Empire: troubled prelude to the accession of Darius III to the throne	Justin 10 Diodorus 17.5.3-7.3		Hammond suggests this is from Diyllus in Diodorus and from Cleitarchus' father, Deinon, in Justin, but the material is similar and placed in the text in both such as to imply a common source. (cf. Jacoby F 33) Cleitarchus is the likely common source of Justin and Diodorus with a special interest in Persian events due to his father's work.
Accession & funeral of Philip; rebelliousness of Thebes; appointed general by assembly at Corinth	Justin 11.1.1-11.2.7 Diodorus 17.3-4	Hammond THA 94; Yardley & Heckel on Justin 83-5	Yardley & Heckel rightly reject Hammond's view that Diodorus used Diyllus here and prefer Cleitarchus
Balkan campaign: battle with Syrmus of the Triballi at the Danube	Plutarch 11.1-3 Justin 11.2.8 Diodorus 17.8.1	Hammond THA 94 & Sources 24; Yardley & Heckel on Justin 84-5	Spring-summer 335BC in extreme summary
Omens of the fall of Thebes	Arrian 1.9.8 Aelian VH 12.57	Hammond Sources 207	
Siege & destruction of Thebes & Council at which the destruction was proposed by the Plataeans and Phocians	Diodorus 17.8.2-14.4 Plutarch 11.4-6 Justin 11.3.1-11.4.6	Hammond THA 91-3 & Sources	
Alexander saves Pindar's house	Arrian 1.9.10 Aelian VH 13.7	Hammond Sources 207	
After razing of Thebes, its wealth (from selling Thebans into slavery…) just 440 talents & its citizens were stingy	Athenaeus 148 D-F (cf. Diodorus 17.14.4)	Jacoby, Fragment 1 of Cleitarchus	Attributed to Cleitarchus and Book 1 of Concerning Alexander – Diodorus *implies* 440 talents raised by selling the Thebans, but probably equals total proceeds
Reconciliation with Athenians upset by fate of Thebes	Plutarch 13 Justin 11.4.9-12	Hammond, Sources 27	
Visit to Delphi: Alexander declared invincible by the Pythia	Plutarch 14.4-5 Diodorus 17.93.4 [Livy 9.18] [SIG³ 251H, col. II, lines 9-10 (p.436-7)]	Hammond Sources 29 THA	Alexander is *aniketos* (invincible) & promised world-rule, cf. Siwa & Ammon. Livy too refers to the "invincible Alexander", though also the attacks on Alexander by Athenian orators, eg Hypereides, who called Alexander "king and invincible god" (ironically). Historicity of oracle visit supported by gift to shrine at this time of 150 gold coins of Philip from Alexander(?) Perhaps read of Xenophon's consultation of Delphi for *his* campaign against Persia. Pearson (Lost Histories p. 92) thinks Plutarch got Delphic visit from Onesicritus, but Cleitarchus used Onesicritus.

Book 2: 16th October 335BC – 5th October 334BC

Summary	Sources	References	Comment
Crossing to Asia and preparations; Alexander's gifts to his friends, Alexander took with him the most capable Thracian kings, dye on priests hands left marks foretelling victory on victims' livers	Justin 11.5.1-9 Plutarch 15.2-3 Front. Strat. 2.11.3 & 1.11.14	Hammond THA 95-6 Sources 31	
820 years from the invasion of the Heraclidae to Alexander crossing into Asia	Clement of Alexandria, Strom. I 139,4	Jacoby, Fragment 7 of Cleitarchus	Early Spring
Alexander casts a spear into the Asian shoreline	Justin 11.5.10-11 Diodorus 17.17.2		Hammond makes no suggestion for this against Justin, but this story is common to Justin and Diodorus, so Cleitarchus is overwhelmingly likely to be its source
Troops ordered not to ravage Asia, because it was their own property	Justin 11.6.1	Hammond THA 96	
Troop numbers: 32000 infantry, 4500 cavalry and 182 warships. Contrasting Alexander's world conquest with a small band of experienced troops with Darius' reliance on overwhelming strength	Justin 11.6.2-9	Hammond THA 96-7	Abbreviated(?) to 40,000 men in Frontinus, Stratagems 4.2.4 & Ampelius 16.2
Honouring the tombs of Achilles and the heroes (Patroclus) at Troy	Arrian 1.12.1 Diodorus 17.17.3 Justin 11.5.12 Plutarch 15.4 Aelian VH 9.38 & 12.7, cf. Cicero, Pro Archia poet. 24		Hammond does not explicitly identify this anecdote as Cleitarchus, but he does point out that Alexander's emulation of Achilles was probably a Cleitarchan theme (THA 64-5, 91, 109; Sources 48 n11). The story is common to Justin and Diodorus, which strongly suggests that Cleitarchus is its source
Battle of the Granicus	Diodorus 17.19.3-21.6 & 17.23.2	Hammond THA 16-17	Late spring - Thargelion according to Plutarch, Camillus 19.4 (~14th May to ~12th June 334BC) – Aelian, VH 2.25 may suggest 6th Thargelion, but this is perhaps an inaccurate Archon date

Alexander the Great and the Conquest of the Persians

Summary	Sources	References	Comment
Alexander takes the surrender of Magnesia, where lay the tomb of Themistocles (Athenian commander at Salamis) – digression on Themistocles at the court of Xerxes following his exile from Athens – he later drank bull's blood and died rather that lead Persian forces against Athens	Plutarch's Life of Themistocles 27.1-2 Cicero, Brut. 42-43	Jacoby, Fragments 33 & 34 of Cleitarchus	The surrender of Magnesia (Arrian 1.18.1) is the most likely occasion for Cleitarchus' digression on Themistocles, since the tomb of Themistocles was there. Cleitarchus' father Deinon had evidently told the story of Themistocles. It is possible that Cleitarchus drew a comparison between Themistocles' submission to Xerxes and Charidemus' allegiance to Darius, since they were both exiled Athenians serving Persian kings. Arrian (1.18.2) may implicitly be contradicting Cleitarchus when he makes a point of stating that Alexander stayed at Ephesus when Magnesia surrendered.
Miletus			Cleitarchan version lost?
Dismissed the fleet to encourage troops to fight more vigorously, when Darius reached the coast	Diodorus 23.1	Hammond THA 38	
Concentration of Persians at Halicarnassus. Memnon sends his wife (Barsine) and children to Darius for safety and trust	Diodorus 17.23.4-6	Hammond THA 39	
Halicarnassus	Diodorus 17.24.4-27.6	Hammond THA 39-40	Stalwart veterans and young shirkers – a Cleitarchan theme
Fortress of the Marmares on the border between Lycia and Pisidia	Diodorus 17.28	Hammond THA 40	Not recounted elsewhere – may be Chandir in Pamphylia
End of book 2	Diodorus 17.28.5		

Book 3: 6th October 334BC – 24th September 333BC

Summary	Sources	References	Comment
Alexander uncertain regarding future strategy	Plutarch 17.1-2	Hammond Sources 45-6	Alexander's policy is swayed by the ensuing oracles and miracles – mimics Herodotus in his account of Xerxes being swayed by dreams and oracles
Spring near Xanthus in Lydia casts forth a bronze tablet prophesying the overthrow of the Persians by the Greeks	Plutarch 17.2-3	Hammond Sources 46	
Sea gives way to Alexander on the Pamphylian coast; crowns statue of Theodectas at Phaselis during a comus	Plutarch 17.2-3 & 5	Hammond Sources 46-7, Tarn Sources 49	Cleitarchus following Callisthenes for the sea giving way? Tarn argues mentions of Alexander in a *comus* are from Cleitarchus.
Arrest of Alexander Lyncestes on charges of conspiracy due to information from a prisoner	Justin 11.7.1 Diodorus 17.32 Cf. Curtius 7.1.6		Justin's timing agrees with Curtius 7.1.6, who placed the arrest in his lost second book; Hammond makes no attribution.

Summary	Sources	References	Comment
Alexander cuts the Gordian knot with his sword	Arrian 2.3.7, Justin 11.7.3-16, Curtius 3.1.14-19, Plutarch 18.1-2	Hammond Sources 47 & 217 THA 97 & 128	Knot-solver "destined to become king of the inhabited Earth" in Plutarch – chimes with World-Ruler idea from Cleitarchus (cf. Siwa oracle below)
Death of Memnon	Plutarch 18.3, Curtius 3.2.1	C3.2.1=D17.30.7 Schwartz	Completes the encouragement of Alexander to attack Darius
Parade of Darius' forces before Babylon: Charidemus of Athens is pessimistic about their chances against the Macedonians and is executed	Curtius 3.2.2-19 Diodorus 17.30.1-31.2	Hammond THA 40-1 & 116	Resembles conference of Xerxes in Herodotus 7; Curtius directly references Herodotus 7.59
Dream of Darius misinterpreted by magi	Plutarch 18.4-5, Curtius 3.3.2-7	Hammond Sources 48	Hammond does not assign this passage in THA
Advance to Cilicia across Mount Taurus by a forced march on hearing of Darius' approach	Justin 11.8.1-2	Hammond THA 113	By association with Justin's version of Tarsus
Alexander tarries at Tarsus due to illness, after plunging into the Cydnus, but Darius thinks him intimidated	Plutarch 19 Curtius 3.5.1-3.6.3 Justin 11.8.3 Val. Max. 3.8 ext 6	Hammond Sources 48-9 THA 97-8 & 121	
Letter(s) from Olympias/Parmenion warning Alexander about Philip the Doctor and Alexander Lyncestes, who was arrested	Diodorus 17.32.1-2 Seneca *De Ira* 2.23 Val. Max. 3.8 ext 6 Curtius 3.6.4-16	Hammond THA 41	Note however that Justin 11.7.1 placed Lyncestes' arrest prior to the march to Gordium and Curtius gave it in his lost second book prior to Gordium (so too Arrian 1.25) – Diodorus may be conflating two different warning letters

Book 4: 25th September 333BC – 13th October 332BC

Summary	Sources	References	Comment
Alexander's visit to Anchiale; Sardanapalus died of old age after he had lost the sovereignty of the Syrians	Athenaeus 530A, cf. Plutarch *Moralia* 326F & 336C Cf. Curtius 3.7.2	Jacoby, Fragment 2 of Cleitarchus cf. Arrian 2.5.2-4	Attributed by Athenaeus to Book 4: context is Alexander's arrival before a monument and statue of Sardanapalus at Anchiale, 12 miles SW of Tarsus – here Cleitarchus is echoing his father Deinon's *Persica*, which may in turn have followed Ctesias' *Persica*. The story of Alexander's visit is also told by Athenaeus 530 A-B as a fragment of Aristobulus, so too Strabo 14.5.9 and Arrian 2.5.2-4 – this is also in Fragment 34 of Callisthenes Curtius 3.7.2 recounts Alexander's arrival at Soli, whereas his visit to Anchiale immediately preceded his arrival at Soli

Alexander the Great and the Conquest of the Persians

Summary	Sources	References	Comment
Battle of Issus: Darius defeated by Alexander	Cicero Ad f. 2.10.3 Curtius 3.8.13-3.11.27 Diodorus 17.32.3-17.38.2	Jacoby, Fragment 8 of Cleitarchus; Hammond THA 17 & 118; C3.11.7-11=D17.34.2-6 Schwartz; C3.11.20,23-6=D17.35.2,36.5,2,4 cf.J11.9.11-12 & C3.11.27=D17.36.6 Hamilton:C&D17	November 333BC
Alexander captures the chariot & bow of Darius	Plutarch 20.5-6	Hammond Sources 51	
Visit to the Persian Queens with Hephaistion, who is mistaken for Alexander	Arrian 2.12.6-7 Diodorus 17.37.5 Curtius 3.12.1-3.12.26 Justin 11.9.11-16 Plutarch 21.2-3 Val. Max. 4.7 ext 2	Hammond THA 19, 98, 118 Sources 50-52, 225; C3.12.15-17=D17.37.5-6 Hamilton:C&D17; C3.12.26=D17.38.2 Hamilton:C&D17	
Alexander sends Thessalian cavalry to capture the Persian treasure & women at Damascus & the defection of its governor	Curtius 3.12.27-13.17 Plutarch 24.1-2	Hammond Sources 53-54	
Alexander seduced by Persian luxury and falls in love with Barsine and advances into Syria	Justin 11.10.1-3 Plutarch 20.6-8 cf. Curtius 3.13.14	Hammond THA 98 Sources 51	Given the coincident mentions in Justin and Plutarch, it is very likely that Alexander's liaison with Barsine was mentioned here by Cleitarchus and Curtius's note of her capture surely marks the occasion for this in Cleitarchus's text
First peace offer from Darius: Diodorus uniquely suggests that Alexander concealed the real letter and presented a forgery	Curtius 4.1.7-14 Justin 11.12.1-2 Diodorus 17.39.1-3	Hammond THA 42, 99, 122	Diodorus appears to have wrongly summarised the second letter from Darius (delivered after Tyre) in place of the first and consequently thought that Alexander had misrepresented Darius's letter to his council in devising his indignant response.
Balonymus (Abdalonymus in J & C, Aralynomus in P Moralia) appointed king of Sidon	Diodorus 17.47.1-6 Curtius 4.1.16-26 Justin 11.10.8-9 (cf. Plutarch Moralia 340C-E)	Hammond THA 98, 119, 121; C4.1.15-26=D17.47.1-6 Hamilton:C&D17	Diodorus recounted this story at the end of the siege of Tyre and cited "Balonymus" – Hammond's belief that he was using Cleitarchus is probably correct, but I conjecture that Tyre (and possibly Paphos in Cyprus) was incorporated into the kingdom of Sidon at that point and that Diodorus's text was incorrectly corrected by an editor to attribute Tyre as the site of Diodorus's whole story.

Summary	Sources	References	Comment
Siege of Tyre	Diodorus 17.40.2-17.47.6 Justin 11.10.10-14 Curtius (most of) 4.2.2-4.4.19	Hammond THA 42, 98, 121, 119; C4.2.7=D17.40.4 Schwartz; C4.2.12=D17.41.3 -4 Schwartz; C4.2.18=D17.40.5 Schwartz; C4.2.20=D17.41.1 Schwartz; C4.3.6,9,11-12=D17.42.5-6,43.3 Schwartz; C4.3.22=D17.41.8 Hamilton:C&D17; C4.3.25-26=D17.44.1-3 Schwartz; C4.4.1-2=D17.45.7 Hamilton:C&D17; C4.4.10-12,17=D17.46.2-4 Schwartz	January-July 332BC
Tyrian dreamt that Apollo wished to abandon them, so they chained his statue	Diodorus 17.41.7 Curtius 4.3.21 (Plutarch 24.4)	Hammond THA 42, 119 Sources 55-6	
Phoenicians (especially Carthaginians) worship Cronos by burning a child as an offering	Schol. Plato Resp. 337A (Photius: Sardonios gelos); cf. Curtius 4.3.23	Jacoby, Fragment 9 of Cleitarchus, Hamilton Cleitarchus & Diodorus 17	Curtius relates that Tyrians proposed to resume the sacrifice of a freeborn boy to Saturn just after the arrival of Carthaginian envoys
Sea monster (whale?) temporarily beached upon the causeway	Curtius 4.4.3-5 Diodorus 17.41.5-6	Schwartz; C4.4.3-5=D17.41.5-6	Diodorus places this much earlier in the siege than Curtius, but Diodorus's ordering of events is suspect
Balonymus appointed King of Tyre (also Paphos as in Plutarch's Moralia?)	Diodorus 17.46.6 & 17.47.1-6 (cf. Plutarch Moralia 340C-E)	Hammond THA 98, 119, 121; C4.1.15-26=D17.47.1-6 Hamilton:C&D17	This was probably an extension of Abdalonymus's kingdom, which Diodorus thought a convenient place to recount his installation in Sidon as well, i.e. Tyre in D 17.47.1&5 is a mistake for Sidon, but Tyre is correct at D 17.46.6
"Now that we have described activity *concerning Alexander*, we shall turn our narrative in another direction"	Diodorus 17.47.6		Looks like a book-end from Cleitarchus, because it incorporates the title of his work: Concerning Alexander – cf. the ends of books 7 & 12

Book 5: 14th October 332BC – 1st October 331BC (Julian Calendar)

Summary	Sources	References	Comment
Agis hires mercenaries who had escaped from Issus and invades and conquers Crete	Diodorus 17.48.1-2 Curtius 4.1.39-40	C4.1.39-40=D17.48.1-2 Schwartz	

Summary	Sources	References	Comment
The rebel Macedonian, Amyntas son of Antiochus led 4000 troops to Egypt and overcame the local forces in battle, but his forces were destroyed in a surprise counter-attack, when scattered for looting	Curtius 4.1.27-33 Diodorus 17.48.2-5	C4.1.27-33=D17.48.2-4 Schwartz	Hammond THA thinks this is Diyllus, but it is clear that Curtius and Diodorus used a common source and it is not tenable that they independently selected the same episodes from two separate sources as Hammond has suggested. This is therefore very likely to be Cleitarchus. Diodorus relates this episode after Tyre.
The delegates of the League of Corinth vote at the Isthmian Games to send Alexander golden crowns via 15 envoys	Curtius 4.5.11-12 Diodorus 17.48.6	C4.5.11=D17.48.6 Schwartz	Hammond THA thinks this is Diyllus, but the exact agreement of Curtius and Diodorus is suggestive of Cleitarchus
Capture of the pirate, Aristonicus of Methymna, at Chios	Curtius 4.5.19-22		This is Cleitarchus, because the delivery of Aristonicus to Alexander at Alexandria (see below) was related by Cicero, who is a source for other fragments of Cleitarchus
Second peace offer from Darius: Parmenion suggests acceptance of terms offered in a letter from Darius	Curtius 4.5.1-8 Justin 11.12.3-4 Arrian 2.25.2 (Plutarch 29.4) Val Max 6.4 ext3 cf. Diodorus 17.39	Hammond THA99-100, 122 Sources 62, 225	Diodorus appears to edit out this offer, but implies it was in his source by speaking of other daughter of Darius under third offer (he gives some of the contents of the second letter when citing the first after Issus). Plutarch places his anecdote in the run-up to Gaugamela (i.e. where Cleitarchus probably recorded Darius' third offer).
Siege of Gaza: Alexander struck by an arrow, the city is stormed and Alexander is struck in the leg, Alexander emulates Achilles by dragging Betis behind his chariot	Curtius 4.6.1-12(?) & 4.6.17-30	Hammond Sources 57 THA 128;	Falls November 332BC – Curtius 4.6.12-16 resembles Fragment 5 of Hegesias, but this may be Cleitarchus using Hegesias as his source.
Alexander sends Amyntas son of Andromenes with 10 triremes to Macedonia Occupation of Egypt		C4.6.30=D17.49.1 Schwartz	Enthroned as Pharaoh in Memphis (Alexander Romance) December 332BC
Settles affairs in Egypt and decides to visit the Temple of Ammon (at Siwa) – meets envoys from Cyrene		C4.7.1,5,9=D17.49.2-4 Schwartz	
Enters the desert - water gives out after 4 days - a great storm provides drinking water		C4.7.12-14=D17.49.4-5 Schwartz	
Description of the oasis, its people and its situation - visit to the oracle at Siwa: Alexander, son of Ammon, would be invincible (invictus[Lat] = aniketos[Gk]) and rule all lands	Curtius 4.7.25-28 Diodorus 17.49.3-17.51.4 Justin 11.11.2-10 Plutarch 26.6-27.4 Val. Max. 9.5 ext 1	Hammond THA 43, 92, 122 Sources 58-61; C4.7.16-17,20-28=D17.50.3-51.3 Schwartz	Plutarch's version is coloured with an item from Callisthenes, a letter from Alexander to Olympias and the confusion of Paidion with Paidios, but his reference to Cambyses might be from Cleitarchus

Organisation & Sources

Summary	Sources	References	Comment
Foundation of Alexandria	Plutarch 26.5-6 Curtius 4.8.1-6 Diodorus 17.52.1-3 Justin 11.11.11-13 Arrian 3.2.1 Val. Max. 1.4 ext 1	Hammond THA 44, 99, 128 Sources 59, 226	April 331BC Cf. Strabo 792
Pirate (captured at Chios) brought before Alexander (by Hegelochus)	St Augustine *De Civ. Dei* IV, 4. 25 (from a lost passage of Cicero *The Republic* III .24), cf. Arrian 3.2.4, Curtius 4.5.19-22		The rhetorical style of the passage, its origins via Cicero (a source of other fragments of Cleitarchus) and the location in Egypt (Arrian says Egypt, probably at Alexandria, which was later Cleitarchus' home) all suggest Cleitarchus as source. The pirate is Aristonicus of Methymna, whose capture is mentioned by Curtius, probably following Cleitarchus
Alexander's return march up the Levantine littoral: Story about the ultra-handsome Theias Byblios, who fell in love with his daughter Myrra	Stobaeus *Flor.* IV, 20, 73	Jacoby, Fragment 3 of Cleitarchus Brown, Clitarchus p.149	Attributed by Stobaeus to Book 5: presumably relates to a visit of Alexander to Byblos, an ancient Phoenician port to the north of Sidon – may reflect worship of Adonis at Byblos – must reflect Alexander's return to the vicinity after Egypt, if it is placed in Book 5
Darius hears news of Alexander's return from Egypt – his preparations for war including 200 scythed chariots		C4.9.4-5=D17.53.1-2 Hamilton: C&D17	
Run-up to Gaugamela, march into Mesopotamia	Diodorus 17.53.3-4, 17.55	Hammond THA 44-45	In Diodorus the 3rd peace offer precedes the Tigris crossing
Crossing of the Tigris	Diodorus 17.55 Curtius 4.9.14-21	Hammond THA 45	
Ariston, captain of the Paeonians, slays Satropates, cuts off his head and lays it at Alexander's feet	Curtius 4.9.24-25 Plutarch 39.1-2	Hamilton Plutarch Alex liii (lix in 2nd edition)	
Lunar eclipse	Curtius 4.10.1-8		20th September 331BC (Julian)
On the death of Queen Stateira - reported to Darius by a eunuch	Plutarch 30 Curtius 4.10.18-34 Diodorus 17.54.6	Hammond Sources 63-64	Gallantry with Darius' women as with meeting in Darius' tent after Issus
Third peace offer from Darius: an embassy	Curtius 4.11.1-22 Diodorus17.54.1-5 Justin 11.12.7-16	Hammond THA 45, 99, 122	Diodorus & Curtius have Parmenion urge acceptance on this occasion, but it is not unlikely he did so at both the second and third offers
Disposition and size of the Persian army	Curtius 4.12.5-13 Arrian 3.8.6 (Diodorus 17.39.4 & 17.53.2-3)	Hammond THA 42, 44 Sources 231	There is a distinction to be made between the host of up to a million raised by Darius at Babylon and the army of a quarter of a million that he fielded at Arbela/Gaugamela
Parmenion counsels a night attack	Arrian 3.10.1, Curtius 4.13.4-10 Plutarch 31.5-7	Hammond Sources 38, 232	

Alexander the Great and the Conquest of the Persians

Summary	Sources	References	Comment
Alexander and Aristander sacrifice to fear	Curtius 4.13.15 Plutarch 31.4	Hammond Sources 38, 65	(Note however that many Aristander stories seem to come from Aristobulus)
Alexander oversleeps before Gaugamela	Justin 11.13.1-3 Diodorus 17.56 Curtius 4.13.16-24 Plutarch 32.1-2	Hammond THA 20, 100, 122-3 Sources 38	
The order of battle of Alexander's forces		C4.13.26-29=D17.57.1-4 Schwartz	
Battle of Gaugamela (Arbela in Cleitarchus)	Curtius 4.14.1-26, 4.16.8-9 Diodorus 17.57.5-17.61 & parts of Plutarch 33.1-11, Arrian 6.11.4 (for use of Arbela) Front. Strat. 2.3.19	Hammond THA 20, 123, 128 Sources 39-40 & 270	1st October 331BC (fixed by Lunar eclipse) – Cleitarchus in particular located the battle close to Arbela, though it was ~70 miles away. Hamilton, "Cleitarchus & Diodorus 17", p128 thinks Curtius used Ptolemy for parts of his account.
The attack of the scythed chariots and its defeat		C4.15.16-17=D17.58.4-5 Schwartz	
Attack on Alexanders's camp by Scythians – Sisyngambris remains aloof		C4.15.9-11=D17.59.6-7 Schwartz	
Darius' charioteer slain by spear (thrown by Alexander) – Persians suppose Darius slain – Persian flight instigated		C4.15.28-29,32=D17.60.2-4 Schwartz	
Wounds of Hephaistion, Perdiccas, Coenus & Menidas		C4.16.31-32=D17.61.3 Schwartz	
Persian casualties	Arrian 3.15.6	Hammond Sources 232	
Alexander proclaimed king of Asia, abolishes tyrannies in Greece, promises to rebuild Plataea, sends some spoils to Croton in Italy	Plutarch 34.1-2 (Justin 11.14.6-7 cf. Curtius 4.10.34)	Hammond Sources 66-68	
Uprising of the Spartans in Greece; heroism of King Agis of Sparta	Diodorus 17.63.4 Justin 12.1.6-11 Curtius 6.1.1-16 (& 6.3.2 in a speech) Front Strat. 2.11.4	Hammond THA 46; Yardley & Heckel on Justin 37 & 183-8	Hammond's view (THA 113) that J's account is inconsistent with D is unconvincing

Summary	Sources	References	Comment
Antipater refers the fate of Sparta to the League of Corinth. Sparta receives permission to send envoys to Alexander. Fifty representatives sent to Alexander by the Lacedaemonians.	Harpocration: homereuontas Curtius 6.1.16-20 Diodorus 17.73.5-6	Jacoby, Fragment 4 of Cleitarchus Hammond THA 133	Attributed by Harpocration to Book 5: happened after Antipater defeated Agis at Megalopolis in 331BC – it is therefore certain that Cleitarchus gave an account of the Spartan rebellion in Greece at this point, which is when it probably actually took place (although 330BC is not impossible). C & J postponed mention of events in Europe until after the death of Darius (D until after Gaugamela); Curtius stated that he was deliberately doing so at 5.1.1-2. Hammond thought the matter of the League came from Diyllus, but the details are very similar in D & C, so it is likely to be from Cleitarchus
This was the end of the first of the two parts of Cleitarchus' history of Alexander. It was the fifth anniversary (according to Lunar reckoning) of Alexander's accession. Events in Europe, such as the death of Alexander of Epirus, given in Justin 12.2, may have been related by Cleitarchus at this point, but this is conjectural. It is however interesting that Curtius 8.1.37 mentions a complaint by Alexander of Epirus (whilst he died of a wound according to Livy) that he had encountered men in Italy, whilst his nephew was up against women in Persia (cf. Gellius, NA 17.21.33, Livy 9.19.10-11). This section of Livy has some Cleitarchan elements, such as referring to the "Invincible Alexander" (see Hammond THA 112 on Cleitarchus as Livy's likely source)			

Book 6: 2nd October 331BC – July 330BC

Summary	Sources	References	Comment
Capture of Persian camp and treasures at Arbela	Diodorus 17.64.1-3 Curtius 5.1.10-11	Hammond THA 54; C5.1.10-11=D17.64.3 Schwartz	
Visit to Mennis in Babylonia – the cave of Naphtha – anointing and igniting the boy Stephanus	Curtius 5.1.16 Plutarch 35 Strabo 16.1.15	Hammond Sources 68-69	
Babylon: description of the city – walls 365 stades in circumference and 50 cubits tall – the Hanging Gardens were built by "a later Syrian king" than Semiramis for his wife	Diodorus 2.7.3-4 & 2.10 Curtius 5.1.24-35	Jacoby, Fragment 10 of Cleitarchus, P. Schnabel, Berossus, 1923, Ch III, Pearson p.230; C5.1.25-26=D2.7.3-4 Schwartz; C5.1.34-35=D2.10.4,1 Schwartz	Cleitarchus corrects the wall height of 50 fathoms cited by Ctesias in his Persica - Nearchus fragment 3a/b notes Alexander's rivalry with Semiramis in marching across the Kedrosian desert

Alexander the Great and the Conquest of the Persians

Summary	Sources	References	Comment
Dissolute nature of Babylonians; relaxation of army at Babylon for 34 days	Diodorus 17.64.4-17.65.1 Curtius 5.1.36-39 & 5.1.40-45, Justin 11.14.8	Hammond THA 54; C5.1.40-42=D17.65.1 Schwartz; C5.1.43-45=D17.64.5-6 Schwartz	Curtius 5.1.36-39 is attributed to Diyllus in THA 129-130, but Hammond is clearly mistaken, because the 34 days is common to Curtius and Justin and so must be Cleitarchus; the appointments of Agathon etc to commands at Babylon and the arrival of 50 sons of the Macedonian nobility are common to D & C, therefore Cleitarchus; probably all in C about Babylon is Cleitarchus
Reorganisation of the army in Sittacene	Diodorus 17.64.2 Curtius 5.2.1	C5.2.1-7=D17.65.2-4 cf.D17.27.1-2 Schwartz	Strong resemblance between C & D, though D is heavily summarised
Susa – Abulites sends forth his son – 40,000 talents found there, mother and children of Darius left there, Alexander uses a stool to rest his feet upon when sitting in Darius' throne	Plutarch 36.1-2 Diodorus 17.65.5, 17.66.3-5, 17.67.1 Curtius 5.2.13-17 Justin 11.14.9	Hammond THA 55 Sources 70; C5.2.8, 12-15=D17.65.5, 66.2-7 Schwartz	Plutarch quotes Cleitarchus' father Deinon in 36.2 – this probably follows such a quote by Cleitarchus himself. Hammond thinks Diodorus is following Diyllus at this point in THA, but the throne story is from the same source in C & D, which is therefore Cleitarchus
Alexander gives Sisygambis purple cloth	Curtius 5.2.18-22	Hammond THA 130-131	
Uxii and campaign against Madates – Sisygambis obtains a pardon for Madates	Curtius 5.3.1-15 Diodorus 17.67.2-5	Hammond THA 55-56, 130-131; C5.3.1.2,4-5,10 =D17.67.1-2,4-5 Schwartz	
Campaign against Ariobarzanes – Susian Gates – a Lycian leads Alexander around them by a narrow path through the woods	Curtius 5.3.16-5.4.34 Diodorus 17.68.1-7 Plutarch 37.1 Front. Strat. 2.5.17 Polyaenus 4.3.27	Hammond THA 56, 131 Sources 70 Hamilton Plutarch Alex liii; C5.3.17-18,23&C5.4.2-4,10,12,18=D17.68.1-6 Schwartz	The story of the Lycian guide and the connection made with an earlier oracle is widespread in the sourecs
Advance to the Araxes	Curtius 5.5.1 Diodorus 17.69.1	Hammond THA 131	
Letter from Tiridates	Curtius 5.5.2-4 Diodorus 17.69.1-2	C5.5.2-4=D17.69.1-2 Schwartz	
Alexander meets 800 mutilated Greeks who do not wish to return home	Diodorus 17.69.2-9 Curtius 5.5.5-24 Justin 11.14.11-12	Hammond THA 56, 101, 131; C5.5.5-9,12,23-24=D17.69.2-8 cf.J11.14.11-12 Schwartz	
Capture of Persepolis followed by a Winter campaign in Persis	Curtius 5.6.1-20 Diodorus 17.70.1-17.71.7 & 17.73.1	Hammond THA 132; C5.6.1-5,8,9=D17.70.1-71.2 Schwartz	The campaign is only detailed by C, who places it at the evening setting of the Pleiades (April 330BC), and mentioned after the burning of the palace in one sentence by D

Summary	Sources	References	Comment
Burning of Persepolis incited by Thais the Athenian courtesan: a *comus*	Athenaeus 576D-E Diodorus 17.72.1-6 Curtius 5.7.1-7 Plutarch 38.1-4	Jacoby, Fragment 11 of Cleitarchus Hammond THA 56, 131-132 Sources 72-73 Hamilton Plutarch Alex liii	May 330BC
Pursuit and death of Darius	Curtius 5.8.1-5.13.25 Justin 11.15 Diodorus 17.73.2-3 Plutarch 42.3-43.3	Hammond THA 57, 101, 132-133 Sources 74-76 Hamilton Plutarch Alex liii	At the death of Darius Trogus ended his Book XI and Curtius ended his Book V, further vindicating the view that this was the conclusion of Book VI of Cleitarchus
Antipater refers the fate of Sparta to the League of Corinth. Sparta receives permission to send envoys to Alexander.	Curtius 6.1.16-20 Diodorus 17.73.5-6		Cleitarchus may also have reiterated the matter of the 50 hostages, perhaps to distinguish them from the envoys sent to Alexander

Book 7: July 330BC – June 329BC

Summary	Sources	References	Comment
Advance to Hecatompylus. Persuasion of the army to join in the pursuit of Bessus, who declares himself king and adopts royal regalia as Artaxerxes.	Curtius 6.2.15-6.4.1 Diodorus 17.74.3-17.75.1 Justin 12.3.2-3 (Plutarch 47.1-2) King Bessus: Diodorus 17.74.1 Curtius 6.6.13	(Hammond Sources 80); C6.2.15=D17.75.1 Schwartz	Hammond THA 58 & 134 argues Diyllus as the source for Curtius and Diodorus. But the details are very similar in Justin too, so the common source must be Cleitarchus. Hammond worries that Plutarch has a slightly different order of events and indeed Plutarch attributes his version to a letter from Alexander to Antipater, so it is doubtful whether Plutarch followed Cleitarchus here.
Entry into and description of Hyrcania and the Caspian Sea	Diodorus 17.75 Curtius 6.4.1-22	Hammond THA 58 & 135; C6.4.3-6=D17.75.2 Schwartz; C6.4.18,22=D17.7 5.3,6 Schwartz	Onesicritus may be the ultimate source of the natural history details – Aristobulus is unlikely despite noting oaks in Hyrcania
Caspian Sea equal to the Euxine (Black Sea)	Pliny NH 6.36-38 Plutarch 44.1-2	Jacoby, Fragment 12 of Cleitarchus Hammond Sources 77	This resembles a comment by Patrocles, a geographer who wrote circa 280BC and was cited by Eratosthenes, but it is possible that the comments are independent of one another or that Cleitarchus inspired Patrocles.
The isthmus between the Caspian and the Euxine is subject to inundation from either sea	Strabo 11.1.5	Jacoby, Fragment 13 of Cleitarchus, Brown, Clitarchus p.140	The "isthmus" in question is the region of the Caucasus Mountains, neither low-lying nor narrow – Brown suggests this was inspired by Polycleitus' error of confusing the Sea of Azov with the Aral Sea

Alexander the Great and the Conquest of the Persians

Summary	Sources	References	Comment
Wonders of Hyrcania: the wasp (*tenthredon*) of the hill-country	Demetrius, De Eloc. 304 Diodorus 17.75.7	Jacoby, Fragment 14 of Cleitarchus	Diodorus has *anthredon*; Tarn (vol 2, Sources, p.90 n.3) notes that Diodorus uses a peculiar phrase μεγίστην ἐπιφάνειαν and a rare verb κηροπλαστεῖν in describing this bee-like creature; the same combination occurs in one other place in Diodorus 19.2.9 in a passage Tarn attributes to Timaeus. Tarn poses the question of whether Cleitarchus is using Timaeus; our answer must be yes, given the other evidence of his doing so.
Surrender of Persian commanders (Phrataphernes, Phradates, Artabazus)	Curtius 6.4.23-24 & 6.5.1-5 Diodorus 17.76.1	Hammond THA 135	
Surrender of the Greek mercenaries	Curtius 6.5.10 Diodorus 17.76.2	Hammond THA 135	
Attack on the Mardi: theft and restitution of Bucephalus	Curtius 6.5.11-21 Diodorus 17.76.3-8	Hammond THA 135; C6.5.11-12,18-21=D17.76.3-8 Schwartz	
Surrender of Nabarzanes: entry of Bagoas into Alexander's service	Curtius 6.5.22-23 (Diodorus 17.76.1)	Hammond THA 157	
Visit of Thalestris, Queen of the Amazons, who had journeyed from the River Thermodon to conceive a child by Alexander in Hyrcania	Plutarch 46.1 Strabo 11.5.4 Curtius 6.5.24-32 Diodorus 17.77.1-3 Justin 12.3.3-7	Jacoby, Fragments 15-16 of Cleitarch. Hammond THA 59, 102 & 135 Sources 81 (Jacoby Fragment 32?); C6.5.24-26,30-32=D17.77.1-3 cf. J12.3.5-7 & Strabo11.5.4 Schwartz	The Thermodon is in northern Asia Minor, which anomaly Cleitarchus explained by making the Caucasus region very narrow. The story may have originated with Onesicritus, but could have been embellished by Cleitarchus. (Brown, Clitarchus p.149 suggests Jacoby Fragment 32 was background to the Amazon story)
Alexander's adoption of Persian dress (purple tunic with a vertical white stripe, zona belt, diadem, sceptre) and luxury: 365 concubines from Darius' harem. Macedonian resentments assuaged by gifts from Alexander.	Curtius 6.6.1-12 Diodorus 17.77.4-7 & 17.78.1 Justin 12.3.8-12 Metz 2	Hammond THA 59, 102-3, 136; Pearson 221 (Plutarch, Artaxerxes 27 for Deinon)	Here again is seen the Cleitarchan propensity for making things equal to the days in a year; probably inspired by Deinon - Pearson. The Metz Epitome opens here, replete with Cleitarchan stories. F. Dicaearchus (Athenaeus 13.5 [557]) citing 350 concubines

Organisation & Sources

Summary	Sources	References	Comment
Alexander burns surplus baggage and wagons to avoid the encumbrance in crossing the mountains into India	Curtius 6.6. Plutarch 57.1-2 Polyaenus 4.3.10	Hamilton Plutarch Alex liii	Plutarch associates this with the invasion of India & Polyaenus likewise; but Curtius is more likely correct. The confusion is probably due to the geographical disparity that Cleitarchus regarded southern Afghanistan from the Helmand River eastwards as part of India. Hence in Cleitarchan tradition this really was the first transit across montains into India.
Revolt of Satibarzanes, who flees to Bactra with 2000 cavalry. Alexander storms a rock occupied by rebels.	Diodorus 17.78.1 Curtius 6.6.20-34 (Justin 12.4.1) Metz 3	Hammond THA 59, 136	The Metz has Ariobazanes and states he fled to India – perhaps this is an error for Barzaentes as at Curtius 6.6.36 (which is suggested by Elizabeth Baynham in Antichthon 29, p.71).
Dimnus conspiracy: execution of Philotas	Curtius 6.7-6.11 Diodorus 17.79-80 Justin 12.5.2-3 Plutarch 49	Hammond Sources 87 Hamilton Plutarch Alex liii	Hammond THA 59 argues Diodorus is from Diyllus mainly because he differs from Curtius in saying Alexander "learnt everything" from Dimnus, but Cleitarchus probably said *behaviour* of Dimnus spoke eloquently of his guilt & Diodorus is summarising clumsily. Compelling points of similarity on incidental details between D & C are: Cebalinus hidden in the armoury; Alexander is informed while bathing & Philotas is executed "in the manner of his country, Macedon". Hammond concedes (in Sources) that Curtius must be from Cleitarchus: it is too vividly detailed for a general history, e.g. Diyllus or Duris. Plutarch's version resembles Cleitarchus, but not on Alexander hiding behind a curtain where Plutarch is less likely to be using Cleitarchus than Curtius 6.11.12, who has Alexander not present during the torture.

Alexander the Great and the Conquest of the Persians

Summary	Sources	References	Comment
Execution of Alexander Lyncestes	Curtius 7.1.1-9 Diodorus 17.80.2	C7.1.5-9 =D17.80.2 Schwartz	Hammond THA 138 suggests Diyllus, but his argument about the timing of Lyncestes' arrest being later in Diodorus than in Curtius overlooks the fact that Justin 11.7.1 suggests that the Cleitarchan tradition placed Lyncestes' arrest prior to the march to Gordium (as in Arrian). It looks as if Diodorus mentioned Lyncestes' arrest a few months late, perhaps connecting it with warnings in a letter from Olympias, which might have taken months to reach Alexander. Curtius & Diodorus follow the same source for Lyncestes' execution & the detail in Curtius seems too extensive for sourcing from a general history. (Hammond's view that C & D shared Diyllus as a secondary source is statistically implausible: it implies they independently made the same choice for most episodes between Cleitarchus & Diyllus: it is more likely that matches between C & D means both used Cleitarchus.)
Assassination of Parmenion: Polydamas' camel trek	Curtius 7.2.11-34 Diodorus 17.80.3 Strabo 15.2.10	C7.2.18=D17.80.3 Schwartz	Detailed correspondence between Curtius and Diodorus implies Cleitarchus was the source for the completion of the story of the downfall of Parmenion
Alexander forms a disciplinary regiment by reading the letters which the troops sent home to Macedonia to identify malcontents	Justin 12.5.4-8 Diodorus 17.80.4 Curtius 7.2.35-38 Polyaenus 4.3.19	Hammond THA 103; C7.2.35-37=D17.80.4 cf. J12.5.4-8 Schwartz	Hammond thinks that the version in Diodorus comes from Diyllus, but its close resemblance to the version in Justin is clear evidence that this material came from Cleitarchus. Hammond THA 139 fails to attribute the corresponding passage in Curtius, but it is Cleitarchus, since it is connected with the execution of Parmenion as in the other accounts.
The march against the Euergetae: origin of the name Euergetae (Benefactors) for the Ariaspi (Arimaspi in Cleitarchus) in their succour for Cyrus' army	Diodorus 17.81.1-2 Curtius 7.3.1-4 Metz 4	Hammond THA 60; C7.3.1,3=D17.81.1 -2 Schwartz	From Deinon? Strong correspondences between Diodorus and Curtius
Land of the Paropamisadae	Curtius 7.3.5-18 Diodorus 17.82 Metz 4	Hammond THA 60, 139; C7.3.5-18=D17.82 Schwartz	

Summary	Sources	References	Comment
Crossing the "Caucasus" (Hindu Kush) in 16 or 17 days; Rock of Prometheus; foundation of an Alexandria; advance into Bactria in pursuit of Bessus	Curtius 7.3.19-23 Diodorus 17.83.1-2 Metz 4 (for the foundation)	Hammond THA 60, 139; C7.3.22-23=D17.83.1-2 Schwartz	Diodorus 17.83.3 has a terminal one-liner, Καὶ τὰ μὲν περὶ Ἀλέξανδρον ἐν τούτοις ἦν ("These were the concerns of Alexander"), which may indicate the end of Book 7 of Cleitarchus. A similar formula ended Bk 6 at 17.73.4 and exactly the same formula ends Bk 12. Similar formulae are used in other books of Diodorus, but this one may echo Cleitarchus, because it contains the title of his history (Περὶ Αλεξάνδρου - Pearson p.213).

Book 8: July 329BC – Autumn 328BC

Summary	Sources	References	Comment
Bessus and Bagodaras (D) or Cobares (C) quarrel at a banquet	Curtius 7.4.1-19 Diodorus 17.83.7	Hammond THA 139	Digressions and accounts of events elsewhere often mark a book boundary in Cleitarchus.
Alexander receives news from Greece of the Spartan revolt, of Scythians coming to the aid of Bessus and of the combat between Erigyius and Satibarzanes	Curtius 7.4.32-40 Diodorus 17.83.4-6	Hammond THA 140 Heckel & Yardley on Justin 184; C7.4.33,38=D17.83.4-6 Schwartz	Spartan news is only in C: was this the arrival of the Spartan envoys/hostages in Alexander's camp? Their departure seems to have been delayed (preparing to leave in Summer 330BC - Aischines 3.133).
Advance to the Oxus: march through a desert with the loss of many men – anecdote of Alexander refusing water brought in skins	Diodorus, List of Contents for 17 Curtius 7.5.9-12 Front. Strat. 1.7.7		The anecdote being in Frontinus and Curtius tends to confirm that it is Cleitarchan
Betrayal by Spitamenes, Dataphernes & Catanes of Bessus and his dispatch to Alexander as a prisoner	Curtius 7.5.19-26 Diodorus 17.83.8-9 Justin 12.5.10-11 Metz 5-6	Hammond THA 61, 140-141	It appears that Curtius correctly reflects Cleitarchus by breaking up the downfall, torture and execution of Bessus into several mini-episodes. The Metz similarly divides the betrayal to Alexander from the eventual execution
Branchidae	Curtius 7.5.28-35 (in the long lacuna in Diodorus 17, but listed in contents), Strabo 11.11.4, Plutarch Moralia 557B(?)	Hammond THA 141; C7.5.28-35 cf. Dκ Schwartz Aelian, ap. Suda s.v. Branchidae Strabo 14.1.5	Perhaps Cleitarchus gave the Branchidae story as a doublet with the destruction of Bessus: Persian and Greek traitors similarly destroyed (so Pearson).
Bessus delivered to Alexander in fetters; Alexander hands him over to Oxathres for interim torture but postpones his execution.	Curtius 7.5.36-43 Diodorus 17.83.8-9 Justin 12.5.10-11 Metz 5-6		The handing over to Oxathres is explicit in Curtius, Justin and Diodorus

Alexander the Great and the Conquest of the Persians

Summary	Sources	References	Comment
Alexander wounded by an arrow of which the point remained fixed in the middle of his leg; the rebels sent envoys to apologise the next day; rivalry between the cavalry and the infantry over bearing Alexander's litter	Curtius 7.6.6-9	Hammond THA 142	
Advance to Maracanda – circumference of 70 stades with many rivers flowing around it	Curtius 7.6.10 Metz 7		With Diodorus missing in the great lacuna (and Justin being very thin and episodic here), the Metz Epitome (7-43) provides key corroboration that much of Curtius is from Cleitarchus, wherever there is close correspondence between Curtius and the Metz. This is vital, because it appears that Curtius sometimes resorted to other sources. This applies until the middle of Book 10, where Diodorus resumes.
Plan to found a stronghold on the Tanais to subdue the region	Curtius 7.6.13		News of this plan probably instigated the ensuing revolts.
First news of the revolt of Spitamenes & Catanes	Curtius 7.6.24 Metz 9	Hammond THA 143	Alexander destroys several rebel cities.
Foundation of Alexandria on the River Tanais (Alexandria Eschate) with a circumference of 60 stades in 17 days	Curtius 7.6.25-27; Justin 12.5.12 Metz 8		Hammond THA 142 discusses Aristobulus, but the detailed correspondence of Curtius with Justin is a clear indication of Cleitarchus. Tanais is a Cleitarchan name for this river (through confusion with the Don). Actually the Syr-Darya.
Emperor of the Scythians sends his brother Carthasis to prevent Alexander crossing the Tanais. Speech of Alexander & augury of Aristander in Curtius. Plan for an attack on the Scythians.	Metz 8 Curtius 7.7.1-29	Hammond THA 143-4	Carthasis is in Curtius and the Metz has "Carcasim"
Insurrection of Spitamenes: routing and destruction of the Macedonian column under Menedemus. (2000 infantry and 300 cavalry are dead.)	Metz 9 Curtius 7.7.30-39	Hammond THA 143	Alexander spends the night sleepless – watches Scythian fires in Curtius, reflecting upon wrongs against him in the Metz
Alexander's attack across the Tanais via 2000 rafts (Metz) or 12000 (Curtius)	Metz 10-12 Curtius 7.8.1-9.16 (Diodorus – contents)	Hammond THA 143-4, Pearson (Lost Histories) 222	X may have been dropped from XII in the Metz. Curtius gives Scythian envoys' words verbatim from his source – arrows, shouts, markers of Dionysus are common; Pearson notes parallels with aphorisms attributed to Cleitarchus
Visit of envoys of the Sacae	Curtius 7.9.17-19	Hammond THA 143-4	Escorted by Bagoas as Alexander's Greeter?
Alexander's return to Maracanda to counterattack Spitamenes who flees; burying of Greek dead and erection of a monument to Menedemus.	Metz 13 Curtius 7.9.20-22	Hammond THA 143	Reached Maracanda on the 4th day – bones covered with mound-monuments in the Metz

Organisation & Sources

Summary	Sources	References	Comment
Pardoning of Sogdian prisoners (chieftains) who sang on their way to execution	Curtius 7.10.1-9 (Diodorus – contents)	Hammond THA 144; C7.10.4-9 cf. Dκβ Schwartz	
Alexander defeated the Sogdiani & slew over 120,000	(Diodorus – contents)	Hammond THA 61	Hammond notes that Theophylactus Simmocata burnt 120,000 & Goukowsky thought Cleitarchus his likely source
Return to Bactria – orders Bessus to Ecbatana for splitting and chopping up – founds towns (6 or 12?) to curb the conquered nations (in SE Sogdiana near Margania)	Metz 14 Curtius 7.10.10-16 Justin 12.5.13	Hammond THA 103 on Justin; C7.10.15-16 cf. Dκδ Schwartz	Crosses rivers Ochus and Oxus at Metz 14 and Curtius 7.10.15 (Hammond THA 144 thinks this is Aristobulus) – emendations of Margania to Margiana (Merv) are wrong.
Sogdian Rock (Rock of Arimazes in C or Ariobazanen in M or Ariamazes in S or Ariomazes in Polyaenus)	Metz 15-18 Curtius 7.11.1-25 Polyaenus 4.3.29 (Diodorus – contents) Strabo 11.11.4	Hammond THA 144-145	Both Curtius and the Metz Epitome seem to make this a climactic event of the campaigning year in 328BC – hence this should close Book 8 of Cleitarchus as well as Book 7 of Curtius. Curtius 7.11.28 *appears* to differ from the Metz, but this is probably just a transmission error (Hammond THA 144-145 thinks Curtius' account is Aristobulus then Cleitarchus.) Commonalities with the Metz include a cavern on the ascent path, 20 (Metz) or 30 (Curtius) stadia high, 300 climbers signalling with white cloths, iron wedges, ropes.

Book 9: Autumn 328BC – May 327BC

Summary	Sources	References	Comment
Offer of daughter in marriage by the Scythian king. First campaign against Massagetae, Dahae – 3 columns through Sogdiana	Curtius 8.1.1-10	Hammond THA 145	
The hunt in Basista (Bazaira in Curtius) and the abundance of game there	Curtius 8.1.11-19 (Diodorus – contents)	Hammond THA 145; C8.1.11-19 cf. Dκσ Schwartz	Hammond thinks this is Onesicritus (but this is no bar to it being in Cleitarchus)
Killing of Cleitus at Maracanda – Alexander persuaded to forgive himself by Callisthenes	Curtius 8.1.19-8.2.12 Justin 12.6 Arrian 4.9.2-6 (Diodorus – contents)	Hammond THA 104,146 Hammond Sources 242	Arrian has legomena about Alexander's attempted suicide, concern over Lanike's reaction and a forgotten sacrifice to Dionysus
Winter in Bactrian Nautacene (Metz)	Curtius 8.2.13-18 Metz 19		
Treaty with Sisimithres, who had fathered 2 sons and 3 daughters through incest with his mother, after a siege of his rock.	Curtius 8.2.19-33 Metz 19 Plutarch 58.3 Strabo 11.11.4	Hammond THA 146	Hammond Sources is silent on the mention of Sisimthres by Plutarch
Death of Philippus.	Curtius 8.2.34-39	Hammond THA 146-7	Hammond THA thinks Philippus is from Onesicritus (but this is no bar to it being in Cleitarchus too)

Summary	Sources	References	Comment
Beheading of Spitamenes by his wife assisted by a slave boy – delivery of head to Alexander and his gratitude and her expulsion from camp	Curtius 8.3.1-15 Metz 20-23	Hammond THA 147	
Dahae surrender Dataphernes (& Catanes?)	Metz 23 Curtius 8.3.16-17 Justin 12.6.18		Curtius 8.5.2 says that Catanes was subsequently killed in battle. Hammond is unsure of the source for this, but its presence in the Metz suggests Cleitarchus.
The proskynesis experiment	Curtius 8.5.5-24 Justin 12.7.1-3 Val. Max. 7.2 ext 11	Hammond THA 148 says speeches are Curtius' own invention, Alexander hides behind curtain like Agrippina in Tacitus Ann. 13.5.2 (but also like Alexander with Philotas [Plutarch 49], which suggests Cleitarchus) Hammond THA 103-4 for Justin: "most likely Cleitarchus"	This is postponed until the point of departure for India in Curtius. However Cleitarchus evidently placed it here, because Justin agrees with Diodorus by putting the award of silver shields to the hypaspists after Callisthenes' arrest, rather than before as in Curtius. Arrian gave the proskynesis experiment and the arrest of Callisthenes following on from the death of Cleitus, but points out (4.22.2) that the pages' conspiracy occurred at Bactra just prior to the invasion of India. It may be that Cleitarchus was correct in placing the proskynesis experiment at this point and chose to tell the whole story *en bloc*.
The conspiracy of the pages and the arrest and execution of Callisthenes	Curtius 8.6.1-8.8.23 Justin 12.7.2 (Diodorus – contents)		Hammond is unsure of the source for Curtius and Justin, but Diodorus' contents list confirms that this material was in Cleitarchus. It is possible that Curtius used other sources as well.
Campaign against the Nautaces and the destruction of the army in a hail storm	Metz 24-27 Curtius 8.4.1-15 (Diodorus – contents)	Hammond THA 147	
Saves a common soldier after the snow storm	Val. Max. 5.1 ext 1a Frontinus, Strat. 4.6.3 Curtius 8.4.15-17	Hammond THA 147	
Visit to (rock of) Chorienes (perhaps a re-visit to Sisimithres, but Cleitarchus now used his title rather than his name – yet it looks as though Cleitarchus believed him to be a distinct individual)	Metz 28 Curtius 8.4.21 has "cohortandus" in MSS wrongly changed to Oxyartes by Aldus		The Metz manuscript read "corianus"; Chorienes is from Arrian 4.21; Brunt & Heckel suggest that Chorienes is an official title of Sisimithres from the name of the area he ruled. Justin 12.6.18 mentions the surrender of the "Chorasmians"

274

Summary	Sources	References	Comment
Marriage to Roxane	Metz 28-31 Curtius 8.4.20-30 (Diodorus – contents)	Hammond THA 146	Metz & Diodorus mention marriages of Alexander's companions – hence probably from Cleitarchus

Book 10: June 327BC – June 326BC

Summary	Sources	References	Comment
Orders formation of 30,000 "Epigoni"	Curtius 8.5.1		This is Cleitarchan, since their arrival at Susa in 324BC is in Diodorus 17.108.1-3
Preparations for India: distribution of silver shields etc. - 120,000 men followed Alexander into India (Curtius only)	Justin 12.7.4-5 Curtius 8.5.4	Hammond THA 104, 147-8; C8.5.4 cf. DΛα, J12.7.5 Schwartz	Hammond seems inconsistent in recognising that J is using Cleitarchus, but expressing uncertainty over C – the 120,000 men may have been derived from Nearchus by Cleitarchus (see Arrian Indica 19.5 – Plutarch 66.2 gives 120,000 foot)
Digression on India: mention of processions of the kings in which trees are drawn along on four-wheeled carriages and tame birds (the Orion and the Catreus) decorate their branches and sing – "…some birds are like sirens" may reflect Cleitarchus' father Deinon's belief that there were sirens to be found in India (Pliny NH 10.136)	Strabo 15.1.69 Aelian NA 17.22-23 Curtius 8.9.23-26	Jacoby, Fragments 20-22 of Cleitarchus, Brown, Clitarchus p.148	Curtius 8.9.8 mentions the River Iomanes (Jumna), which elsewhere (e.g. Arrian Indica 8.5-6) is mentioned by Megasthenes. Hammond THA 148 also notes that Curtius 8.9 includes material that was not known until after Alexander's time (e.g. Megasthenes' info on the Ganges region), yet at least some of it is from Cleitarchus. This is *suggestive* of use of Megasthenes by Cleitarchus, but Megasthenes dates to 1st decade of 3rd century BC. Cf. digression on Pandaea below.
Invasion of India: march from Bactra, Alexander greeted as third son of Zeus to enter India following Heracles and Dionysus, destruction of a city occupied by his initial opponents as an example	(Diodorus – contents) Curtius 8.10.1-6 Metz 32-35	Hammond THA 148; C8.10.5-6 cf. DΛβ Schwartz	
Alexander visits Nysa finds the ivy of Dionysus - citizens of Nysa intimidated into surrendering (probable mention of Acuphis and Alexander's request for 100 of his best men), then Alexander climbs Meron, the adjacent mountain, sacred to Dionysus with streaming waters and fruitful trees.	Schol. Apoll. Rhod. 2.904 Diodorus (in the great lacuna but listed in Contents of 17) cf. Arrian 5.1.1-6 Justin 12.7.6-7 Curtius 8.10.7-18, Metz 36-38	Jacoby, Fragment 17 of Cleitarchus Hammond THA 104 &148	See also Arrian's Indica 1.5-6, which has several mentions of Nysa and its legend of Dionysus – also Strabo 15.1.7-8 & Plutarch, Alex. 58.4-5
Dionysiac revels of companions (a *comus*)	Arrian 5.2.7, Justin 12.7.8	Hammond Sources 250	A legomenon

Alexander the Great and the Conquest of the Persians

Summary	Sources	References	Comment
Mazaga in kingdom of Assacenus & slaughter of the Indian mercenaries – Alexander wounded in leg - Cleitarchus especially noted that the siege engines and their missiles terrified the defenders into surrendering, since they seemed supernatural – Alexander may have been seduced by Cleophis and she had a son, whom she named Alexander – Cleitarchus wrote that the mercenaries opposed the surrender, but then requested that they be allowed to leave the town – Cleitarchus did not give an excuse for Alexander's attack on them	Diodorus 84 (emerging from the great lacuna), Metz 39-45, Justin 12.7.9-11, Plutarch 59.3-4, Curtius 8.10.19-36 Polyaenus 4.3.20	Hammond Sources 106 Hammond THA 52-3, 104 & 149	Arrian blamed the slaughter of the mercenaries on their plan to slip away without Alexander's leave
Aornus – Heracles' failure to capture it due to an earthquake & Alexander's longing to outdo his ancestor – 100 stades in circumference, 16 high – poor old local man with two sons guided Alexander's assault – filled chasm in 7 days & nights	Metz 46-7, Curtius 8.11.1-25, Diodorus 17.85.1-86.1, Justin 12.7.12-13, Plutarch 58.3 on other Alexander	Hammond THA 53, 104-5 & 149; C8.11.2=D17.85.1-2, J12.7.12 Schwartz; C8.11.3-4=D17.85.4-5 Schwartz; C8.11.7-8,25=D17.85.3,8-9&D17.86.1 Schwartz	Hammond thinks Curtius supplemented his account from Chares (see Jacoby fragment 16 of Chares) especially for the heroic acts of the king, another Alexander and Charus (Strabo 15.1.8 says Alexander's flatterers reported that Heracles had thrice failed to take Aornus)
Aphrices (D) or Erices (C) blocks Alexander's advance with an army of 20,000, but his own men bring his head to Alexander	Diodorus 17.86.2-3, Curtius 8.12.1-3	Hammond THA 53, 149-150; C8.12.1-3=D17.86.2 Schwartz	Aphrices may have been the brother of Assacenus
Hephaistion's bridge of boats across the Indus	Metz 48, Curtius 8.12.4, Diodorus 17.86.3		Not explicitly attributed by Hammond but subsumed into the adjoining Cleitarchan passages
Mophis ruler of Taxila and son of dead Taxiles advances against Alexander seemingly in battle array, but joins forces and donates treasure and 56 or 58 elephants	Metz 49-52, Curtius 8.12.4-18 Diodorus 17.86.4-7 Plutarch 59.3	Hammond THA 53-4 & 149-50 Hammond Sources 106; C8.12.4-10,14=D17.86.3-7 Schwartz	Mophis is the probable Cleitarchan form, since the Metz (Motis) and Diodorus agree (the form Omphis in Curtius may be from elsewhere) – Curtius 8.12.17-18 is attributed to Onesicritus by Devine & Hammond, but Cleitarchus may well have repeated it.

Summary	Sources	References	Comment
The Battle Against Porus (Cleitarchus may not have named the battle after the river Hydaspes – modern Jhelum) initial diversionary tactics – precipitated by rumoured approach of Abisares (the name is probably corrupt in Diodorus, who gives both Embisarus 87.2 and Sasibisares 90.4) – Alexander's horse wounded (C, J, M), elephants arrayed like towers in a circuit wall, trampled or seized opponents with their trunks and dashed them to the ground, were attacked with missiles, axes and Kopis swords, then trampled their own men. Concentration of archers upon Porus – Porus slid off kneeling elephant, which was killed by missiles when it tried to protect its master. Porus asked how he wished to be treated – Porus replied that Alexander should consult his feelings as a king	Diodorus 17.87-88, Metz 53-61 (Justin 12.8.1-7) Curtius 8.13-14, Polyaenus 4.3.22 (cf. Strabo 15.1.42 on elephants protecting their masters in warfare) Front. Strat. 1.4.9 & 1.4.9a	Hammond THA 22-3, 54, 62, 150; C8.14.3=D17.87.5 Schwartz, Merkelbach thinks the letter from Porus in ME 56-58 is from a separate letter collection, but this is dubious	Perhaps the first half of May (Heckel & Yardley on Justin p.246), though Arrian 5.9.4 suggests late June after the solstice. Hammond's view that the version of the battle in Cleitarchus was as naïve as that in D is suspect, because of the details given by the Metz and Polyaenus. Hammond (THA 105) thinks J differs from D, but the Metz and D have common details such as concentration of bowmen on Porus and the Metz and J share the wounding/killing of Bucephalus: it seems more that D, J and the Metz are retaining different details from a lengthy original. Hammond thinks C supplemented his version from other sources. The Letter from Porus in ME 56-58 is faintly echoed in Pseudo-Callisthenes 3.2
Casualties	Metz 61, Diodorus 17.89.1-3		
Report of the revolt of Baryaxes in Media (Arrian 6.29.3) following the replacement of Oxydates as its Satrap by Arsaces (Curtius 8.3.17) or Atropates (Arrian 4.18.3) in early 327BC. Cleitarchus explained that Baryaxes had worn the tiara upright, which signified a claim to the throne of the Persians and Medes. (A location at the start of book 10 is also feasible, but Baryaxes probably waited for Alexander to be safely distant in India before he struck.)	Schol. Aristoph. Av. 487	Jacoby, Fragment 5 of Cleitarchus	The revolt of Baryaxes, though known to us solely through Arrian, is the only likely reason for Cleitarchus to have needed to explain the significance of the upright tiara at this juncture (the Fragment is specific that this was related in Book 10). A corollary is that Cleitarchus did not mention that Bessus had worn the tiara upright. Also Cleitarchus may have noted the arrest of Baryaxes by Atropates, who brought him to Alexander for execution at Pasargadae early in 324BC. This would place it in Book 12.

Book 11: July 326BC – Spring 325BC

Summary	Sources	References	Comment
Alexander plans to visit the ends of India and the Ocean – orders ships built with timber from neighbouring mountains – sacrificed to Helios – disbursements of gold coinage as reward to officers and proportionate rewards to troops (C only)	Metz 63, Curtius 9.1.3-4 Diodorus 17.89.4-5, 17.90.3-6	C9.1.1,3-4,6=D17.89.3-6&D17.90.1 Schwartz	This is evidence of a Cleitarchan discussion of Alexander's plans. Geographical and other digressions are characteristic of a new book in Cleitarchus. The coinage may be the famous Porus decadrachms (see Holt on the Elephant Medallions)

Alexander the Great and the Conquest of the Persians

Summary	Sources	References	Comment
Foundation of a city to honour the dead Bucephalus – the naming seems to have happened later just before the voyage down to the Indus	Arrian 5.14.4, Metz 62, Curtius 9.1.6, Justin 12.8.8 Diodorus 17.90.6 & 17.95.5	Hammond Sources 257	Some details in Arrian may be from Chares. Hammond's view (THA 54 & 62) that the foundation of Bucephala in D was from a different source is contradicted by the evidence of the Metz, which concludes this episode with the foundation.
The serpents of India reach sixteen cubits in length	Aelian, NA 17.2 Diodorus 17.90.1 Curtius 9.1.4	Jacoby, Fragment 18 of Cleitarchus	This is probably lifted by Cleitarchus from the account of Nearchus (Arrian, Indica 15.19)
Indian monkeys mistaken for an army: a curious technique using mirrors for the capture of monkeys (there may be confusion between arboreal monkeys and baboons here)	Aelian, NA 17.25 Diodorus 17.90.2-3	Jacoby, Fragment 19 of Cleitarchus, Brown, Clitarchus p.144	This probably derives from Onesicritus, because there is a more intelligible version in Strabo 15.1.29 (however, Aristobulus and Nearchus cannot be ruled out as Strabo's source – see Pearson 223-4, Hamilton C&A 451 and Brown AJP 71, p144, n9)
After he recovered from his wounds, Porus invited to Macedon in Metz Epitome: re-instatement as king & Friend of Alexander	Curtius 8.14.5 Diodorus 17.89.6 Justin 12.8.7 Metz 61 & 64		Curtius and Metz preview this at the end of the battle, but Diodorus & the Metz put the actual event here in Cleitarchus
Abisares sends envoys, but Alexander replies that he will pursue him if he does not come in person	Curtius 9.1.7-8, Metz 65-6 Diodorus 17.90.4	Hammond THA 62-3, 151	
Crosses a rapid river (the Acesines?) and marches east into forests: the height, extent and trunk circumference of the banyan tree, small multicoloured snakes with deadly bites	Diodorus 17.90.5-7 Curtius 9.1.9-12 Aelian, NA 17.2	Pearson 225; C9.1.8-12=D17.90.4-7 Schwartz, Jacoby F18 (on the snakes)	Cleitarchus is plagiarising Nearchus on the banyan (Arrian, Indica 11.7) and Onesicritus (Strabo 15.1.21)
Hephaistion sent to deal with the rebel Porus, a cousin of the conquered Porus	Diodorus 17.91.1-2	Hammond THA 63, 151; C9.1.24-33=D17.91.4-	
Marches on across a desert and across the Hyraotis (Hydraotis) past a grove of wild peafowl; campaign against the Adrestians (city surrenders) & campaign against Cathaeans (sacked city & 2 surrendered cities) – custom of cremating wives on the pyres of their husbands to forestall poisoning	Diodorus 17.91.2-4 & 19.33 Curtius 9.1.13-23 Justin 12.8.9 Polyaenus 4.3.30	D17.92.3 Schwartz	Cleitarchus is again following Onesicritus (see Strabo 15.1.30) on the custom of Suttee - Polyaenus names the Cathaean capital of Sangala as the sacked city – supplication with fronds at third Cathaean city
Surrender of Sopithes with his sons: sets dogs on a lion	Curtius 9.1.24-36, Metz 66-7 Diodorus 17.91.4-92.3	Hammond THA 63, 151; C9.1.24-33=D17.91.4- D17.92.3 Schwartz	Cf. Strabo 15.1.31 & Isidore of Seville, Etymologiae 12.2.28.
Campaign of Hephaistion – his return.	Diodorus 17.93.1 Curtius 9.1.35		

Organisation & Sources

Summary	Sources	References	Comment
Realm of Phegeus: 12 days from the Ganges which was 32 stades wide (30 in M) – warnings of an army of 200,000 infantry, 20,000 cavalry, 2000 chariots and up to 3000 elephants under Xandrames (D) or Aggrammes (C) or Sacram (M), king of the Gandaridae (D & P) or Candaras (M) or Gangaridae (C & J) or Gandridae (P Moralia 327B) and also the Prasii (C) or Praisii (P) or Praesidae (J) or Tabraesians (D) or Persidas (M) beyond the Hyphasis (7 stades wide in D) and at the Ganges. Alexander asks Porus to validate these figures. Alexander is undeterred, recalling that the Pythia had called him invincible.	Metz 68-9, Curtius 9.2.1-9 Diodorus 17.93 Justin 12.8.9 (Plutarch 62.1 has the same width for the Ganges)	Hammond THA 63, 151	Plutarch & Diodorus are probably not getting the width of the Ganges from Megasthenes (pace Bradford Welles), because Strabo 15.1.35 quotes a width of 100 stades from Megasthenes. Xandrames was king of the Nanda kingdom, probably the same as Nandrus in Justin 15.4.16.
Mutiny on the Hyphasis and retreat to the Acesines – exhaustion of the soldiers is a Cleitarchan feature – speech to soldiers - armour wearing out – Greek clothing gone and replaced by Indian stuff – dressed stone altars of extraordinary size (50 cubits tall in D) were built and the camp was enlarged to thrice its size with 5 cubit long beds/couches in huts as wonders for posterity	Metz 69, Curtius 9.2.10-9.3.19 Diodorus 17.94.1-17.95.2 Justin 12.8.10-17 (Plutarch 62.3 also mentions the upscalings, but of different things)	Hammond THA 63-4, 151-2; C9.3.10-11=D17.94.2 Schwartz; C9.3.19=D17.95.1 -2, J12.8.16 Schwartz; C9.3.19=D17.95.1 -2, J12.8.16 Schwartz	Speeches of Alexander (9.2.12-34) and Coenus (9.3.5-15) might be Curtius' inventions, but Diodorus 17.94.5 agrees there was a speech to the troops (speech was to the officers in A). Unclear whether Alexander's sulk in tent was mentioned by Cleitarchus (it is in C, who may have taken it from Ptolemy or elsewhere, but not in D, J, M – it is also in A & P). Whether Cleitarchus noted Coenus' role is also uncertain.
Alexander retraces his advance to the Acesines and is joined by reinforcements who bring 25,000 suits of armour inlaid with gold and silver - a fleet has been built by Porus and Taxiles at the Acesines: 800 service ships and 200 open galleys (D), 800 biremes & 300 penarias (Metz); 1000 ships in Curtius – Alexander names the cities he had earlier founded on opposite river banks: Nicaea & Bucephala [Coenus dies (C only)]	Metz 70, Curtius 9.3.20-24 Diodorus 17.95.3-5 (Justin 12.9.1 also reports a return only to the Acesines)	C9.3.20,23=D17.9 5.3,5 Schwartz	It seems to be a Cleitarchan error to state that Alexander returned only to the Acesines, when in fact he went back to the Hydaspes (according to Aristobulus and others). Hammond (THA p.62 & 152) thinks this material is from Diyllus, but ship numbers and other details match between D, C & M, so this is still Cleitarchus
Death of Alexander's infant son (or child) by Roxane	Metz 70		The Metz is the sole surviving source for this

Alexander the Great and the Conquest of the Persians

Summary	Sources	References	Comment
Voyage down the Acesines to its junction with the Hydaspes with Hephaistion & Craterus commanding the bulk of the army which marched down the bank	Diodorus 96.1 Justin 12.9.1 Curtius 9.3.24-9.4.1		Alexander sailed down the Hydaspes, which flowed into the Acesines, which in turn flowed into the Indus (Arrian 6.14.4-5).Cleitarchus' confusion on this point is evidence that he was not with the expedition in India, else he would not have made such an error. Hammond thinks this is Diyllus, but D, C & J essentially agree, though all are brief and omit different details.
Digression on an Indian salt-mine	Strabo 5.2.6 (& 15.1.30)	Jacoby, Fragment 28 of Cleitarchus	Likely to have been occasioned by a visit of Alexander to the ancient salt mines at Khewra in the SE foothills of the Salt Range 15km north of the Hydaspes (Jhelum) River. A fragment of Onesicritus (Strabo 15.1.30) mentions a mountain of salt in the kingdom of Sopeithes. Arrian 6.2.2 says that Hephaistion was to hurry to the capital of King Sopeithes at the start of the voyage down the Hydaspes. (It is dubious whether Sopeithes is the same as the Sophytes/Sopeithes, who ruled an Indian kingdom further east.)
At junction of the Acesines with the Hydaspes Alexander took the surrender of the Sibi (C) or Ibi (D), who were descended from followers of Heracles - Defeated Agalasseis (Agesinas etc in MSS of J?)	Diodorus 17.96.2-5 Justin 12.9.2 Curtius 9.4.1-8	C9.4.1-2,5=D17.96.1-3 Schwartz	The footsteps of Heracles is a Cleitarchan theme. Hammond THA 153 thinks this is a mixture of Diyllus and Cleitarchus, but there is a good level of agreement between D & C and foundation by Heracles is also in J. Hammond's argument (THA 64) that D gives different accounts of the failure of Heracles to take Aornus is not credible.
Sailed to confluence with the Indus – near wrecking of the flagship in rapids – Alexander says he has done battle with the river like Achilles (Iliad 21.228-382)	Diodorus 17.97.1-3 Curtius 9.4.8-14	Hammond THA 64-5, 153; C9.4.8-14=D17.97.1-3 Schwartz	Emulation of Achilles is a Cleitarchan theme – D said Alexander jumped into the river and swam to safety, but Curtius that he merely disrobed to be ready to swim
Letter from the Indian philosophers	Metz 71-4; cf. Pap. Hamb. 129	Merkelbach thinks the letter from the Indian Philosophers in ME 71-74 is from a separate letter collection, but this is dubious	Similar letter in Philo of Alexandria, Every Good Man Is Free, Section 96. Similar letter among the letters of St Ambrosius XXXVII (11), 34/35, Migne, Patrologia Latina XVI col 1139 (letter in Pseudo-Callisthenes 3.5 differs substantially)

192

Summary	Sources	References	Comment
Campaign against the Oxydracae & Malli - Alexander suffers an arrow wound to the chest when leading the storming of a town of the Oxydracae & Malli (Mandri/Mambros in J) – Cleitarchus said Ptolemy & Peucestas (A & C) & Limnaeus (P: wrongly Timaeus in C) & Leonnatus (A & C – Metz had Legatus) & Aristonus (C) saved Alexander (Syracousas in D; Sugambri in J; Sudracae in C; Sydracai or Oxydrakai Strabo; Oxydracae in A & Pausanias, oxudrac in Metz) - Alexander showered with missiles, jumps down inside wall, ladders collapse under weight of Macedonians, Alexander shelters next to tree, drops to knees	Curtius 9.4.15-9.5.21 Arrian 6.11.3 & 6.11.8, Metz 75-8 Plutarch Moralia 327B & 343D & 344D Diodorus 17.98.1-99.4 Justin12.9.3-12 Pausanias 1.6.2	Jacoby, Fragment 24 of Cleitarchus Hammond Sources 270 Hammond THA 65, 153-4	c. November 326BC, the Metz mentions both the Oxydracae (oxudrac) and the Malli – so probably Cleitarchus – Oxydracae is probably Cleitarchan since it is in Arrian (where he disputes the "Vulgate" version), some manuscripts of Strabo. Pausanias (where he tells Cleitarchan stories) and the Metz – Timagenes also had Ptolemy present
Risky treatment: Alexander's wound enlarged by Critobulus to remove the barbed arrow – Alexander faints, then slowly recovers	Curtius 9.5.22-30 Diodorus 17.99.4 Justin 12.9.13	Hammond THA 154 (wrongly Critodemus in Arrian 6.11.1, cf. Indica 18.7)	D & J are very brief; Pliny NH 7.37.37 notes that Critobulus was even more famous for having extracted an arrow from Philip II's eye in 354BC.
Revolt of the Greeks settled in Bactria (since they heard tell that Alexander had died from the Mallian wound)	Diodorus 17.99.5-6 Curtius 9.7.1-11	Hammond THA 66 (for 99.5 only), 154	Diodorus confuses this rebellion with another after Alexander's death (probably due to his account of a subsequent rebellion of Bactrian colonists at 18.7.1). The version in C is probably Cleitarchus. Since Cleitarchus habitually ended books with news from elsewhere, this report from his work of events in Bactria is the best indication of the boundary between his 11th and 12th books. Also chapter 17.99 in Diodorus and chapter 12.9 in Justin end here.

Book 12: Spring 325BC – June 324BC

Summary	Sources	References	Comment
Surrender of Indians - Alexander held a banquet – the contest between Coragus (D) or Coratas (C) and Dioxippus and the latter's suicide	Diodorus 17.100.1-101.6 Curtius 9.7.12-26 Aelian VH 10.22	Hammond THA 66, 154-5; C9.7 16-26=D17.100.2-D17.101.6 Schwartz	The story of Dioxippus is exclusive to D & C among the main sources, so is clearly from Cleitarchus
Submission of Sambastae(D) or Sabarcae(C), 60,000 infantry, 6000 cavalry & 500 chariots – impressed by the fleet into thinking another Dionysus was coming - Sodrae & Massani – founds an Alexandria on Indus	Diodorus 17.102.1-4 Curtius 9.8.4-8	C9.8.4-8=D17.102.1-4 Schwartz	

Alexander the Great and the Conquest of the Persians

Summary	Sources	References	Comment
Subjugation of the Musicani. Trial of Teriloltes and Oxyartes. Conviction & execution of the former – acquittal and enlargement of realm of latter.	Diodorus 17.102.5 Curtius 9.8.9-10	Hammond THA 155	The trials were probably in Cleitarchus, though only found in C (compare and contrast with Arrian 6.15.3) D subsumes the later revolt and crucifixion of Musicanus into a single sentence entry at the arrival of Alexander in his realm (is D following Cleitarchus or does Curtius better reflect Cleitarchus?)
Dispatch of Polyperchon (& Craterus) to Babylonia with an army	Justin 12.10.1	Yardley & Heckel on Justin 260-1	This mention in J is the only indication that Cleitarchus recorded the return of a large contingent of the army with Craterus to the west – probably from the kingdom of Musicanus and before the war with Sambus. Hammond THA 106 has a curious explanation that this line is misplaced in J
Invasion of the kingdom of Porticanus – storming and burning of two cities – capture and slaying of Porticanus as he sheltered within a stronghold	Diodorus 17.102.5 Curtius 9.8.11-12	Hammond THA 155	Porticanus is Cleitarchan – he is Oxycanus in Arrian 6.16.1
The kingdom of Sambus (Ambus in Justin 12.10.2): 80,000 Indians slain by Alexander (Curtius names Cleitarchus as his source for this) – Sambus escaped to the east with thirty elephants in D but surrendered (gave up the fight?) in C	Curtius 9.8.13-15 Diodorus 17.102.6	Jacoby, Fragment 25 of Cleitarchus, Hammond THA 67, 155; C9.8.13-15=D17.102.6 Schwartz	The Sambus at the Mallian siege in Metz 75 is almost certainly a different person. The number was DCCC *milia* rather than LXXX *milia* in manuscripts of Curtius, but is emended on the basis of Diodorus
Revolt and suppression of the Brahmins and their supplication with branches	Diodorus 17.102.7		Supplication with branches is recalls the surrender of Mazaga
Revolt, capture by Pithon and crucifixion of Musicanus	Curtius 9.8.16	Hammond THA 155	It is uncertain whether this was in Cleitarchus, but it is in the same paragraph as a direct quote of Cleitarchus
The Indian town of Harmatelia, the last city of the Brahmins, refuses to submit and is attacked by 500 Agriani. Ptolemy receives a wound from a poisoned hand weapon (sword in C or arrow in J) and his life was saved by Alexander who was shown an antidote herb in a dream – followed by a eulogy of Ptolemy	Diodorus 17.103 Curtius 9.8.18-28 Justin 12.10.2-3 (cf. Strabo 15.2.7 who places this among the Oreitae) [Cic. de divinatione. 2.135 – Schwartz on Curtius]	Hamilton Cleitarchus & Diodorus 17, Hammond THA 67, 105, 155; C9.8.17-28=D17.103, J12.10.2-3 cf. Cic. de divin. 2.135 Schwartz	Definitely Cleitarchus, because the eulogy is common to Diodorus and Curtius. The mention by Curtius that Ptolemy was believed to be an illegitimate son of Philip is echoed by Pausanias 1.6.2 in a Cleitarchan context and thus probably also goes back to Cleitarchus. Dreaming cures was a standard technique in Greek medicine. Alexander had been taught herbal medicine by Aristotle according to Plutarch 8.1.

Organisation & Sources

Summary	Sources	References	Comment
Interview with the Indian philosophers, who were asked why they had induced King Sambus to revolt *inter alia*	Metz 78-84, Plutarch 64-5, cf. Pap. Berol. 13044	Merkelbach thinks the interview with the gymnosophists is from a separate letter collection, but this is dubious	Plutarch mentions that the 10 gymnosophists were captured after instigating the revolt of King Sabbas (probably Sambus in Curtius & Ambus in Justin). Hammond traces some of Plutarch to Onesicritus & Megasthenes, but this may nevertheless be via Cleitarchus, since it is in the Metz
Digression on the Indians (called Mandi) of Pandaea(?) – their women can bear children from the age of 7 and become old at 40 – Pandaea is the southernmost part of India extending to the sea, which Heracles gave to his daughter of that name to rule: he divided it into 365 villages, one of which would pay the royal tax each day of the year	Pliny NH 7.28-29 Polyaenus 1.3.4 Arrian Indica 9 (cf. Solinus 52.6-17)	Jacoby, Fragment 23 of Cleitarchus	Pliny co-attributes this fragment to Megasthenes & he is the source for a parallel description in Arrian's Indica, which adds the story of Pandaea. Polyaenus gives the Pandaea story in what has been thought a fragment of Megasthenes, but the usage of the number 365 in his version is highly characteristic of Cleitarchus. Solinus has a garbled version linked with Nysa. (Mandi from Pliny is similar to Mandri, which is J's name for the Malli) – Tarn, Alexander the Great II, Sources & Studies p.52 appears to confuse Pandaea with the Panchaea of Euhemerus (Brown, Onesicritus p.66 ff.)
Patala and the Patalii – pursuit of their king Soeris and a sojourn upon an island in the channel of the Indus (the island of Patala – "insulam catacam" in the Metz?), whilst seeking fresh guides	Metz 84 Curtius 9.8.28-30 (Diodorus 17.104.2 mentions Patala when Alexander returns from the Ocean)	Hammond THA 155	Reached "Patalene" about the rising of the Dog Star, i.e. mid-July 325BC (Strabo 15.1.17 from Aristobulus)
Sailing on 400 stades to visit the Ocean: during a stop Alexander's cavalry have to gallop to escape the returning tide (evidently a tidal bore) which dashed ships together – Alexander's sacrifices to Oceanus and Tethys on islands (one in the river and one out in the ocean)	Strabo 7.2.1-2, Metz 85-6, Curtius 9.9.1-27, Justin 12.10.4-5, Diodorus 17.104.1	Jacoby, Fragment 26 of Cleitarchus	Hammond THA 67 & 155 thinks D follows Diyllus & fails to attribute Curtius' account, except to note that he used a different source to Arrian and probably did not use Diyllus. But that a fragment of Cleitarchus in Strabo recorded the bore makes it likely that Curtius used Cleitarchus & the Metz agrees with C on details.
Return to Patala (mooring at a salt lake which diseased the skin of swimmers – C only) Nearchus as admiral and Onesicritus as chief pilot appointed to lead fleet along the coast keeping India on their right as far as the mouth of the Euphrates recording all they saw – burnt damaged ships	Diodorus 17.104.3 Curtius 9.10.3-4		

Alexander the Great and the Conquest of the Persians

Summary	Sources	References	Comment
Submission of the Abritae (D) or Arabitae (C) & the Kedrosian tribesmen	Diodorus 17.104.4 Curtius 9.10.5	C9.10.5-11,17-18,27=D17.104.4-D17.106.1 Schwartz	
Three columns under Leonnatus, Ptolemy and Alexander himself – founds an Alexandria at a sheltered harbour	Diodorus 17.104.4-8 Curtius 9.10.6-7	Hammond THA 155-6; C9.10.5-11,17-18,27=D17.104.4-D17.106.1 Schwartz	The city at Rhambakia in Arrian 6.21.5 – perhaps "Barce" (*parcem/bartem/bastemostem*) in Justin 12.10.6
The Oreitae inhabit the land separated from India by the River Arabis/Arabus and expose their dead naked to be eaten by wild animals… on the coast of Kedrosia an unfriendly and brutish people eat nothing but fish, which they tear to pieces with their nails and dry in the sun to make bread – their houses are roofed with whale ribs and scales	Pliny NH 7.30 cf. Diodorus 17.105.1-5 Curtius 9.10.6-10	Jacoby, Fragment 27 of Cleitarchus, Hammond THA 70, 156; C9.10.5-11,17-18,27=D17.104.4-D17.106.1 Schwartz	?Autumn 325BC The story of the fish eaters seems gleaned from Nearchus (cf. Strabo 15.2.2)
The march through Gedrosia (Kedrosia in Cleitarchus) - many deaths in Kedrosia – Alexander had ordered wells to be dug at regular intervals to provide water, but the army was threatened by starvation - Alexander sent to the satraps who made supplies abundantly available – Leonnatus attacked by Oreitae	Diodorus 17.105.6-8 Arrian 6.24.4 Plutarch 66.2-3 Curtius 9.10.11-21 Justin 12.10.7	Hammond Sources 124-5 & 275 Hamilton Plutarch Alex liii; C9.10.5-11,17-18,27=D17.104.4-D17.106.1 Schwartz	Arrian legomenon – Plutarch says that only a quarter of the army survived the desert, but he may have read that 30,000 infantry came through and (wrongly) compared this figure with Alexander's army of 120,000 in India – it is not clear that the Cleitarchan vulgate mentioned the men who returned with Craterus
Festivities in Carmania – seven day comus	Arrian 6.28.1-2 Diodorus 17.106.1 Curtius 9.10.22-28 Plutarch 67	Hammond Sources 125 & 278 THA 156 Hamilton Plutarch Alex liii; C9.10.5-11,17-18,27=D17.104.4-D17.106.1 Schwartz	Arrian legomenon
The purging of the Satraps – first Astaspes – then Cleander & Sitalces and the rebels Ozines & Zariaspes	Curtius 9.10.19-21, 10.1.1-9, Diodorus 17.106.2-3 Justin 12.10.8		Hammond THA 70 &156 is unsure of D's & C's sources for the purging of satraps except that they were different to Arrian's
Return of Nearchus & Onesicritus – meeting with in theatre at Salmous - stories including: an island where a horse was worth a talent of gold, school of whales etc. – fleet ordered to sail to the Euphrates (kiss with Bagoas in this theatre may have been noted – Plutarch 67)	Pliny, NH 6.198 Diodorus 17.106.4-7 Curtius 10.1.10-16	Jacoby, Fragment 29 of Cleitarchus Hamilton Cleitarchus & Diodorus 17 Hammond THA 71, 156	Cf. Nearchus in Strabo 15.2.12 and Arrian, Indica 30.4-5 on whale spoutings. The use of trumpets to frighten the whales in Diodorus & Curtius matches the accounts in the fragments of Nearchus.

Summary	Sources	References	Comment
Alexander orders ship construction at Babylon using Lebanese timber to support a campaign around the eastern sea coast (Arabia?) & across N Africa to the Pillars of Heracles then back through Spain and Italy – letters from Porus & Taxiles	Curtius 10.1.17-21	Hammond THA 156-7	Was this from Cleitarchus?
Bagoas prosecuted & hanged Orsines at Parsagada (perhaps included mention of the execution of Baryaxes, who had worn the tiara upright and was brought to Parsagada by Atropates – Arrian 6.29.3)	Curtius 10.1.22-38	Hammond THA 157, Brown, Clitarchus p.153-4	Brown concludes that Cleitarchus was not unfavourable to Alexander, so C's emotive treatment of this story probably reflects his own spin on the matter. A large lacuna begins at Curtius 10.1.45 after an account of the defeat of Zopyrion by the Getae
Alexander and the army progress to Susianê. Self-immolation of Calanus (Caranus in Diodorus) on becoming ill: the disdain of the Indian gymnosophists for death	Diogenes Laertius 16 Aelian VH 5.6 Diodorus 17.107.1-5	Jacoby, Fragment 6 of Cleitarchus Hammond THA 71	Diogenes Laertius attributes this to the 12th book of Cleitarchus
Calanus would greet Alexander at Babylon	Arrian 7.18.6 Plutarch 69.3-4	Hammond Sources 132-3 & 301	
The marriages at Susa	Diodorus 17.107.6 Justin 12.10.9-10		Hammond THA 72 thinks D is Diyllus
The 30,000 Epigoni arrive	Diodorus 17.108.1-2 (Plutarch 71.1)	Hammond Sources 134-5	Hammond THA 72 thinks D is Diyllus - Curtius had mentioned the instigation of their formation and training at 8.5.1
Καὶ τὰ μὲν περὶ Ἀλέξανδρον ἐν τούτοις ἦν ("These were the concerns of Alexander")	End of Diodorus 17.108.3		This seems to indicate the end of Book 12 of Cleitarchus: the same formula is found at Diodorus 17.83.3, where Cleitarchus' Book 7 closed. This is also the boundary between chapters 12.10 and 12.11 in Justin.

Book 13: July 324BC – June 323BC

Summary	Sources	References	Comment
Destruction of Zopyrion and his army in Europe	Curtius 10.1.43-45		Cf. Justin 12.1.16-17
The extravagance of Harpalus towards his courtesans – his flight to Athens & bribery of the demagogues – his ejection from Athens and his murder by Thibron	Athenaeus 586C-D Diodorus 17.108.4 8 Curtius 10.2.1-3 Plutarch, *Demosthenes* 25-26	Jacoby, Fragment 30 of Cleitarchus	Cleitarchus commonly began (or ended) his books with news from elsewhere. Curtius emerges from a major lacuna in the midst of the Harpalus story. Hammond THA 72 & 157 thinks this is Diyllus, but this is confuted by a close match between the Cleitarchus fragment in Athenaeus and D's version

Alexander the Great and the Conquest of the Persians

Summary	Sources	References	Comment
The Exiles Decree	Diodorus 17.109.1 Curtius 10.2.4-7	C10.2.4,8-12,30=D17.109.1-2 Schwartz	Hammond THA 72-3 thinks D is Diyllus
Paying of troops' debts at 10,000 talents (20,000 in J & A) on planning to send 10,000 veterans home to Macedon	Diodorus 17.109.2 Curtius 10.2.8-11 Justin 12.11.1-3 (Arrian 7.5.3?)	Hammond Sources 285; C10.2.4,8-12,30=D17.109.1-2 Schwartz	Hammond THA 72-3 & 157-8 thinks D & C are both from Diyllus, but I assert that all matches between versions in D & C are overwhelmingly likely to be from Cleitarchus – Hammond is probably wrong to suggest that Arrian used Cleitarchus
The Mutiny (at Opis) - troops taunt Alexander for claiming to be the son of Ammon – drowning of ringleaders of the mutiny in the river – Craterus to lead the veterans home – Antipater to come to Babylon with a force of fresh recruits	Plutarch 71.2-5 Justin 12.11.4-12.10 Diodorus 17.108.3 & 17.109.2-3 Curtius 10.2.12-10.4.3	Hammond Sources 134-6; C10.2.4,8-12,30=D17.109.1-2 Schwartz	There is no evidence that Cleitarchus located the mutiny at Opis – Diodorus implies that it took place at Susa - Curtius enters a further long lacuna during events at Opis - Hammond THA 72-3 & 157-8 thinks D & C are both from Diyllus, but I assert that all matches between versions in D & C are very likely to be from Cleitarchus
Arrival of Persian reinforcements; 20,000 archers and slingers arrive with Peucestes	Diodorus 17.110.1-2		This occurred nearly a year later in 323BC in Arrian - Hammond THA 73 thinks D is Diyllus
Arranges for the upbringing of 10,000 children of his veterans by captive women	Diodorus 17.110.3		Hammond THA 73 thinks D is Diyllus
March from Susa to Ecbatana via Karai, Sambana and the Kelones, where he saw a settlement of Boeotian Greeks	Diodorus 17.110.4-5		Hammond THA 73 thinks D is Diyllus
Quarrel of Hephaistion with Eumenes	Plutarch, *Eumenes* 2 Arrian 7.13.1		The only hint that Cleitarchus may have mentioned the quarrel between Hephaistion and Eumenes is that Arrian mentions their reconciliation as a "story", which usually means he did not find it in Ptolemy or Aristobulus (the main source on the quarrel is Plutarch's Life of Eumenes) – there is a similar dearth of evidence for the quarrel between Hephaistion and Craterus in India, so perhaps Cleitarchus avoided this topic
Sightseeing trip to Bagistane - 60,000 horses where once there had been 160,000 - Atropates gives Alexander 100 Amazons	Arrian 7.13.2-3 Diodorus 17.110.5-6	Hammond Sources 293	Strabo 505 Hammond THA 73 thinks D is Diyllus
Arrival at Ecbatana – holds a drama festival - the Death of Hephaistion and Alexander's mourning – orders Perdiccas to conduct the corpse to Babylon for a magnificent funeral	Plutarch 72.1-3 Diodorus 17.110.7-8 Justin 12.12.11-12	Hammond Sources 136-140 & THA 107-8	Hammond THA 73 thinks D is Diyllus, but that J is drawing on Ephippus, perhaps via Cleitarchus and "P's much more sensational account" is Cleitarchus

Alexander the Great and the Conquest of the Persians

Organisation & Sources

Summary	Sources	References	Comment
Unrest in Greece fuelled by dissolution of Satrapal armies of mercenaries on Alexander's orders	Diodorus 17.111.1-3		Hammond THA 73-4 thinks D is Diyllus
Against the Cossaeans	Diodorus 17.111.4-6 Plutarch 72.3		January-February 323BC - Hammond THA 73-4 thinks D is Diyllus
To Babylon – ill omens – warnings from the Chaldean scholars	Plutarch 73.1-4 Diodorus 17.112 Justin 12.13.3-5	Hammond Sources 141-3 Hammond THA 108	March-April 323BC - Hammond THA 74 thinks D is Diyllus
Embassies at Babylon including the embassy of the Romans	Pliny NH 3.57 Diodorus 17.113 (cf. Arrian 7.15.5, Livy 9.18.6) Justin 12.13.1-2	Jacoby, Fragment 31 of Cleitarchus Hammond THA 108	Possibly suggestive that Cleitarchus wrote after campaigns of Pyrrhus made Romans famous in the Greek world, but could simply be true. Livy attacks "frivolous Greeks" who harped on about Romans bowing to Alexander in his digression on Alexander vs. the Romans - Hammond THA 74 thinks D is Diyllus
Hephaistion's pyre at 12,000 talents - anecdotes of Hephaistion's status in Alexander's affections – response from Ammon brought by Philip that Hephaistion should be worshipped as God-Coadjutor (Paredros)	Diodorus 17.114-115 Arrian 7.14.8 Plutarch 72.3 & 75.2, Jacoby Fragment 41	Hammond Sources 139 & 296 Hamilton Plutarch Alex liii	Cf. Lucian, Slander 17, Aelian, VH 7.8 - Hammond THA 74-5 thinks D is Diyllus & Ephippus (however, there are grounds to suspect that Cleitarchus used Ephippus' book on the Death of Alexander & Hephaistion)
Episode of the prisoner who sat on the throne	Diodorus 17.116.2-4, Jacoby Fragment 52	Hammond THA 76-7	Cf. Plutarch 73.3-4
Visit to the marshes – Alexander's boat becomes lost for three days – diadem catches on a reed, retrieved by oarsman	Diodorus 17.116.5-7	Hammond THA 76-7	
Drinking party hosted by Medius the Thessalian following a ceremonial banquet in honour of Nearchus - Cup of Heracles – Alexander falls ill	Plutarch 75.3 Justin 12.13.6-10 Diodorus 17.117.1-3	Hammond Sources 151 & THA 77-8 & 108-9 Hamilton Plutarch Alex liii	Cf. Ephippus in Athenaeus 434A-B
Death in Babylon (After 3 days troops filed past, Where to find a worthy king? Body to Ammon, Funeral Games, On 6th day voice failed and gave ring to Perdiccas, "To whom do you leave your kingdom?" - "To the strongest", Divine honours when happy)	Diodorus 17.117.4 Curtius 10.5.1-6 Justin 12.15 Arrian 7.26.3	Hammond Sources 309& THA 77-8 & 108-9	Towards evening 10th June 323BC – Hammond THA 158-9 thinks C did not draw on Arrian's sources, but he is unsure of the identity of C's source
Reaction in Babylon	Curtius 10.5.7-17		
Death of Sisygambis (D: Sisyngambris)	Diodorus 17.118.3 Curtius 10.5.18-25 Justin 13.1.5-6	C10.5.21-25=D17.118.3, J13.1.5-6 Schwartz	Hammond THA 78 & 159 thinks D & C are both from Diyllus, but all matches between versions in D & C are very likely from Cleitarchus
Obituary for Alexander	Curtius 10.5.26-37		

Alexander the Great and the Conquest of the Persians

Summary	Sources	References	Comment
Accession of Philip III: the dispute between the cavalry and the infantry and its resolution in the elephant parade	Curtius 10.6-9 Justin 13.2-13.4.8 Diodorus 18.2 & 18.4.7-8		
First Division of the Satrapies	Curtius 10.10.1-8 Diodorus 18.3 Justin 13.4.9-25		Cf. Metz Epitome 116-122
Preservation of Alexander's corpse	Curtius 10.10.9-13 Plutarch 77.3		
The Last Plans	Diodorus 18.4.1-6	Jane Hornblower, Hieronymus of Cardia, pp.80-97	The lengthy geographical review starting at Diodorus 18.5 probably marks his switch to his next source, Hieronymus of Cardia
Conspiracy of Antipater and his sons, Cassander and Iollas (and Philip) – poison from the Styx brought in a mule's hoof - the rumour was suppressed, because of the subsequent power of Antipater and Cassander; restoration of Thebes and murders of Alexander's family by Cassander; fate of Cassander and his family	Diodorus 17.118.1-2 Justin 12.14 Val Max 1.7 ext2 Curtius 10.10.14-19 Pausanias 9.7.2	C10.10.14,18-19=D17.117.5& D17.118.2 cf. J12.13.10 Schwartz	Cleitarchus may have given this as an alternative as in Diodorus – cf. Ampelius 16.2, which Seel thought a fragment of Trogus: it says it was thought unclear whether Alexander died of drunkenness or poison (cf. Pliny NH 30.16.53) – Hammond THA 78 thinks D's version inspired by Hieronymus and THA 109-111 thinks J's version is from Satyrus and does not identify C's source, but it is more likely (e.g. Heckel LD&T) that Cleitarchus took this rumour from the *Liber de Morte* – NB D & C 10.10.18-19 say this story was suppressed until Cassander died in 297BC
Entombment in Memphis and transfer to Alexandria by Philadelphus	Curtius 10.10.20 Pausanias 1.6.2-3	Jane Hornblower, Hieronymus of Cardia, p.93	There is reason to suppose Cleitarchus extended so far as to mention the entombment in Memphis and perhaps the move to Alexandria (how could he ignore it, if it had just happened when he wrote in Alexandria ~280BC?) The clues are that Curtius ended his history with this information and that Pausanias mentions the Memphite entombment and the transfer to Alexandria in the context of his having noted some Cleitarchan stories (e.g. Ptolemy's birth and Alexander's wound among the Malli/Oxydracae). Pausanias uses Cleitarchan phraseology in speaking of "burial with Macedonian rites" (cf. Curtius 7.9.21). This implies that most of the information in Curtius on the aftermath of Alexander's demise was taken from Cleitarchus.

7. Bibliography

Modern References

1) Atkinson, JE, "A Commentary on Quintus Curtius Rufus' Historiae Alexandri Magni, Books 3 & 4", Amsterdam 1980.

2) Atkinson, JE, "A Commentary on Quintus Curtius Rufus' Historiae Alexandri Magni, Books 5 to 7.2", Amsterdam 1994.

3) Atkinson, JE, "Quintus Curtius Rufus' *Historiae Alexandri Magni*", *ANRW* II (H. temporini ed., Aufsteig und Niedergang der römischen Welt, Berlin), 34.4: 3447-83, 1998.

4) Atkinson, John E, "Curzio Rufo: Storie di Alessandro Magno. Volume I (Libri III-V) & Volume II (Libri VI-X)", tr. Virginio Antelami and Maurizio Giangiulio, Milan: Fondazione Lorenzo Valla/Arnoldo Mondadori Editore, 1998 & 2000.

5) Atkinson, JE, "Originality and its Limits in the Alexander Sources of the Early Empire" in *Alexander the Great in Fact and Fiction* (editors: AB Bosworth & EJ Baynham), Oxford 2000, pp. 307-25.

6) Atkinson, JE, & Yardley, JC, "Curtius Rufus: Histories of Alexander the Great, Books 10", Oxford 2009.

7) Badian, E, "The Date of Clitarchus" *Proceedings African Classical Associations* 8 (1965): 5-11.

8) Bardon, H., "Quinte-Curce: Histoires", Paris, Tome I (1947) & Tome II (1948).

9) Baynham, Elizabeth, "Alexander the Great: The Unique History of Quintus Curtius", Ann Arbor 1998.

10) Baynham, Elizabeth, "An Introduction to the *Metz Epitome*: its traditions and value", *Antichthon* 29 (1995) 60-77.

11) Berve, H, "Review of W I", *Gnomon* 5, 1929.

12) Billows, Richard, "Polybius and Alexander Historiography" in *Alexander the Great in Fact and Fiction*, ed. A.B. Bosworth and E.J. Baynham, Oxford 2000.

13) Borza, EN, 1968, "Cleitarchus & Diodorus' Account of Alexander" *Proceedings African Classical Associations* 11:25-45.

14) Bosworth, AB, "A Missing Year in the History of Alexander the Great", *Journal of Hellenic Studies*, Vol. 101, pp. 17-39, 1981.

15) Bosworth, AB, "From Arrian to Alexander", Oxford, 1988.

16) Bosworth, AB, "Conquest & Empire: The Reign of Alexander the Great", Cambridge, 1988.

17) Bosworth, AB, "Commentary on Arrian's History of Alexander I", Oxford 1980.

18) Bosworth, AB, "Commentary on Arrian's History of Alexander II", Oxford 1995.

19) Bosworth, AB, "The Historical Setting of Megasthenes' Indica," *Classical Philology* 91, 1996.

20) Bosworth, AB, "In Search of Cleitarchus: Review-Discussion of Luisa Prandi: Fortuna è Realtà dell'Opera di Clitarco" in *Histos* (University of Durham, electronic journal of historiography), Vol. 1, Aug. 1997.

21) Bradford Welles, C, "Diodorus Siculus: Library of History", Vol. 8, Loeb, Harvard, 1963.

22) Brown, TS, 1949, "Onesicritus", Berkeley.

23) Brown, TS, 1950, "Clitarchus" *American Journal of Philology* 71: 134-55.

24) Brown, TS, "The Merits and Weaknesses of Megasthenes," *Phoenix* 11, 1957.

25) Brunt, PA, "Arrian: History of Alexander and Indica", Loeb, Harvard, 1976 & 1983.

26) Chesney, F. R., "The Expedition for the Survey of the Rivers Euphrates and Tigris, Carried on By Order of the British Government, In the Years 1835, 1836, and 1837", Vol. I, London, 1850.

27) Chugg, AM, "The Journal of Alexander the Great", *Ancient History Bulletin*, 19.3-4 (2005) 155-175.

28) Chugg, AM, "The Sarcophagus of Aleander the Great?" *Greece & Rome*, Vol. 49.1, April 2002.

29) Chugg, AM, "The Tomb of Alexander in Alexandria", *American Journal of Ancient History*, New Series 1.2 (2002) [2003], pp.75-108.

30) Chugg, AM, "The Quest for the Tomb of Alexander the Great", AMC Publications, 2007 (2nd Edition 2012).

31) Chugg, AM, "The Lost Tomb of Alexander the Great", Periplus – Richmond Editions, London 2004.

32) Chugg, AM, "Alexander's Lovers", Lulu & AMC Publications, 2006 and revised 2012.

33) Chugg, AM, "Alexander the Great in India: A Reconstruction of Cleitarchus", AMC Publications, 2009.

Bibliography

34) Chugg, AM, "The Death of Alexander the Great: A Reconstruction of Cleitarchus", AMC Publications, 2009.

35) Chugg, AM, "Alexander the Great in Afghanistan: A Reconstruction of Cleitarchus", AMC Publications, 2011.

36) Depuydt, L., "The Time of Death of Alexander the Great: 11 June 323 BC, ca. 4:00-5:00 PM," *Die Welt des Orients* 28 (1997) 117–135.

37) Engels, Donald W, "Alexander the Great and the Logistics of the Macedonian Army", University of California, 1978.

38) Errington, RM, "Bias in Ptolemy's History of Alexander", *Classical Quarterly* 19, 1969, 233-242.

39) Errington, RM, "From Babylon to Triparadeisos, 323-320BC," *JHS* 90 (1970) 72-75.

40) Fontana, M, "Il problema delle fonti per il XVII Libro di Diodoro Siculo," *Kokalos* I (1955), 155-190.

41) Fraser, P. M., "Ptolemaic Alexandria", OUP, 1972.

42) Goralski, Walter J., "Arrian's Events after Alexander," *Ancient World* 19, 1989.

43) Goukowsky, P, 1969, "Clitarque seul? Remarques sur les sources du livre xvii de Diodore de Sicile" *Revue des Etudes Anciennes* 71: 320-6.

44) Grzybek, E., "Du calendrier Macédonien au calendrier Ptolémaïque", Basel, 1990.

45) Gunderson, Lloyd L, "Quintus Curtius Rufus: On His Historical Methods in the *Historiae Alexandri*" in *Philip II, Alexander the Great and the Macedonian Heritage*, eds. WL Adams & E N Borza, Lanham, 1982, pp.177-196.

46) Hamilton, JR, 1961, "Cleitarchus & Aristobulus" *Historia* 10: 448-59.

47) Hamilton, JR, "Plutarch, Alexander: A Commentary", Oxford 1969.

48) Hamilton, JR, 1977, "Cleitarchus and Diodorus 17" in *Greece & the Ancient Mediterranean in History and Prehistory*, ed KH Kinzl, Berlin, 126-46.

49) Hammond, NGL, "Three Historians of Alexander the Great", Cambridge 1983.

50) Hammond, NGL, "The Miracle that was Macedonia", London 1991.

51) Hammond, NGL, "The Regnal Years of Philip and Alexander," *Greek, Roman and Byzantine Studies*, Vol. 33, 1992, 355-373.

52) Hammond, NGL, "Sources for Alexander the Great", Cambridge 1993.

53) Heckel, W, "The Last Days & Testament of Alexander the Great", *Historia Einzelschriften*, Heft 56, Stuttgart 1988.

54) Heckel, W, "The Marshals of Alexander's Empire", Routledge, 1992.

55) Heckel, W, "The Earliest Evidence for the Plot to Poison Alexander" in *Alexander's Empire: Formulation to Decay*, California 2007.

56) Heckel, W, "Who's Who in the Age of Alexander the Great", Blackwell 2006.

57) Holt, Frank, "Alexander the Great and Bactria", supplement to *Mnemosyne* 104, 1989.

58) Holt, Frank, "Alexander the Great and the Mystery of the Elephant Medallions", California, 2003.

59) Hornblower, Jane, "Hieronymus of Cardia", OUP, 1981.

60) Howard, CL, "Review of the Teubner Edition of the *Metz Epitome*", *Classical Philology* 58, pp. 129-131.

61) Hunt, JM, "An Emendation in the *Epitoma Metensis*", *Classical Philology* 67, pp. 287-288.

62) Hunt, JM, "More Emendations in the *Epitoma Metensis*", *Classical Philology* 80, pp. 335-337.

63) Jacoby, F, "Kleitarchos", *FGrH* 137.

64) Karageorghis, V, "Cyprus", London, 1969.

65) Koldewey, R, "The Excavations at Babylon", London, 1914.

66) Markle, Minor, "A Shield Monument from Veria and the Chronology of Macedonian Shield Types", *Hesperia* 68.2, 1999.

67) Marsden, E. W., "The Campaign of Gaugamela", Liverpool, 1964.

68) Meeus, Alexander, "Some Institutional Problems Concerning the Succession to Alexander the Great: Prostasia and Chiliarchy", *Historia*, Band 58, Heft 3, 2009, pp. 287-310.

69) Merkelbach, Reinhold, "Die Quellen des Griechischen Alexanderromans," *Zetema Monographien zur Klassischen Altertumswissenschaft*, Heft 9, Munich 1954.

70) Miller, Stephen G, "The Date of Olympic Festivals" *MDAI(A)* 90, 1975, pp.215-31.

71) Müller, Konrad & Schönfeld, Herbert, "Q. Curtius Rufus: Geschichte Alexanders des Grossen", Tusculum, Munich, 1954.

72) Oldach, David W. & Richard, Robert E., "A Mysterious Death", *The New England Journal of Medicine*, June 11, 1998, Volume 338, Number 24.

Bibliography

73) Palagia, Olga, "Hephaestion's Pyre and the Royal Hunt of Alexander", pp. 167-206 in *Alexander the Great in Fact and Fiction*, edited by A. B. Bosworth & E. J. Baynham, Oxford, 2000.

74) Pearson, Lionel, "The Lost Histories of Alexander the Great", American Philological Association, London and New York, 1960.

75) Pédech, P., "Deux campagnes d'Antiochus III chez Polybe," *Revue des Études Anciennes*, 60 (1958), 67-81.

76) Prandi, Luisa, "Callistene. Uno storico tra Aristotele e i re macedoni", Milan, 1985.

77) Prandi, Luisa, "Fortuna è Realtà dell'Opera di Clitarco" in *Historia Einzelschriften* 104, Steiner, Stuttgart 1996.

78) Pritchett, W. Kendrick, "Postscript: The Athenian Calendars," *ZPE* 128 (1999) 79-93.

79) Reames, Jeanne, "Hephaistion Amyntoros: Éminence Grise at the Court of Alexander the Great", *Thesis*, Pennsylvania State University, December 1998.

80) Rolfe, John C, "Quintus Curtius: History of Alexander", Loeb, Harvard, 1946.

81) Romm, James, (ed.), "The Landmark Arrian: The Campaigns of Alexander", Pantheon, 2010.

82) Samuel, Alan E., "Ptolemaic Chronology", Munich, 1962.

83) Samuel, Alan E., "Greek & Roman Chronology", Munich, 1972.

84) Schachermeyr, F, "Alexander der Grosse", Salzburg, 1949

85) Schachermeyr, F, "Alexander der Grosse: Das Problem seiner Persönlichkeit und seines Wirkens", Vienna, 1973.

86) Schachermeyr, F, "Alexander in Babylon und die Reichsordnung nach seiner Tod", Vienna, 1970.

87) Schwartz, E, *Paulys Real-Encyclopädie*, Vol. 4, 1901, s.v. Q. Curtius Rufus, cols. 1871-1891, & Vol 5, 1905, s.v. Diodoros, cols. 682-684.

88) Smith, William, (ed.), "The Dictionary of Greek and Roman Geography", 1854.

89) Steele, R. B., "Quintus Curtius Rufus", *AJP* 36, 1915.

90) Stein, Aurel, "Limes Report", *Geographical Journal*, Vol 92, 1938, pp.62-66

91) Stein, Aurel, *Geographical Journal*, Vol 95, 1940, pp. 428-438

92) Stein, Aurel, *Geographical Journal*, Vol 100, 1942, 155 ff.

93) Stein, Aurel, "Old Routes of Western Iran", London, 1940

94) Streck, *Paulys Real-Encyclopädie*, Vol. 7, cols. 861ff.

95) Tarn, WW, "Alexander the Great, Vol II, Sources and Studies", Part One, The So-Called 'Vulgate' and its Sources, pp. 1-133, Cambridge 1948.

96) Thomas, PH, Editor, "Incerti Auctoris Epitoma Rerum Gestarum Alexandri Magni cum Libro de Morte Testamentoque Alexandri" (The *Metz Epitome*), Teubner, Leipzig 1966.

97) Wood, Michael, "Footsteps of Alexander", BBC, 1997.

98) YardleyC & Heckel, W, "Quintus Curtius Rufus: The History of Alexander", Penguin Classics, 1984.

99) Yardley, JC & Heckel, W, "Justin: Epitome of the Philippic History of Pompeius Trogus, Vol I, Books 11-12, Alexander the Great", Oxford 1997.

100) Zeller, Eduard, "Die Philosophie der Griechen", 4th ed., Part II, Leipzig, 1889.

Selected Ancient Sources

Aelian, Varia Historia, N.G. Wilson, Loeb, Harvard, 1997

Aelian, On The Characteristics of Animals, trans. A.F. Scholfield in 3 volumes, Loeb, Harvard, 1958

Agatharchides, Agatharchides of Cnidus on the Erythraean Sea, Stanley M. Burstein, Translator and Editor, Hakluyt Society, London, 1989

Arrian, Anabasis Alexandrou and Indica, P.A. Brunt, Loeb, Harvard, 1976 and 1983

Arrian, Discourses of Epictetus

Arrian, Epitome of the History of Events After Alexander, *Photius* 92, Photius, Bibliothèque, vol. II, René Henry, Paris, 1960

Athenaeus, Deipnosophistae, Charles Burton Gulick, Loeb, Harvard, 1927-41

Cicero, Ad Familiares

Curtius, The History of Alexander, John C. Rolfe, Loeb, Harvard, 1946; The History of Alexander, trans. John Yardley, Penguin Classics, 1984; Historiae Alexandri Magni, ed. E. Hedicke, Teubner, 1908; De Rebus Gestis Alexandri Magni, Freinshem et al., Petrus vander Aa, Lugduni Batavorum, 1696; Konrad Müller & Herbert Schönfeld, Geschichte Alexanders des Grossen, Tusculum, Munich, 1954; H. Bardon, Quinte-Curce: Histoires, Paris, Tome I, 1947 & Tome II, 1948

Bibliography

Dexippus, *Photius* 82, Photius, Bibliothèque, vol. I, René Henry, Paris, 1959

Diodorus Siculus, Library of History, vol. VII, Charles L. Sherman, Loeb, Harvard, 1952; vol. VIII, C. Bradford Welles, Loeb, Harvard, 1963; vol. IX, Russel M. Geer, Loeb, Harvard, 1947

Diogenes Laertius, Lives of Eminent Philosophers

Dio Cassius, Roman History, Loeb, translated by Earnest Cary, based on translation by H.B. Foster - reprints of the editions published from 1914-1927

Ephemerides, FrGrHist 2.117

Hegesias, FrGrHist 2.142

Herodotus

Homer, Iliad, trans. A.T. Murray, revised William F. Wyatt, Loeb, Harvard, 1999

Itinerarium Alexandri, Didericus Volkmann, Naumburg 1871

Justin, Epitome of the Philippic History of Pompeius Trogus, Books 11-12, J.C. Yardley and W. Heckel, Oxford, 1997; Justin, Cornelius Nepos and Eutropius, Rev. John Selby Watson, London, 1853

Livy, History of Rome, Loeb Classical Library in 14 Volumes

Lucian, Dialogues of the Dead, XIII, vol. 7, M.D. MacLeod, Loeb, Harvard, 1961

Lucian, Essay on How to Write History, vol. 6, K. Kilburn, Loeb, 1959

Lucian, Calumniae non temere credendum, Lucian: Vol. I, A. M. Harmon, Loeb, 1913

Macrobius, Saturnalia, Macrobius: Opera: Band I Saturnalia, Saur Verlag, 1994

Martial, Liber de Spectaculis, De Spectaculis Liber, Shackleton Bailey, Loeb, 1994

Metz Epitome & Liber de Morte, P.H. Thomas, Ed., Incerti Auctoris Epitoma Rerum Gestarum Alexandri Magni cum Libro de Morte Testamentoque Alexandri, Teubner, Leipzig 1966

Nepos, Eumenes in Justin; Cornelius Nepos and Eutropius, Rev. John Selby Watson, London, 1853

Pausanias, Description of Greece, vol. 1, W.H.S. Jones, Loeb, Harvard, 1918

Pliny the Elder, Natural History, H. Rackham, W.H.S. Jones, D.E. Eichholz, Loeb, Harvard, 1938-62 and the 1855 translation by John Bostock and Henry Thomas Riley

Plutarch, Agesilaus, Lives vol. 5, B. Perrin, Loeb, Harvard, 1917

Plutarch, Alexander & Caesar and Cicero & Demosthenes, Lives vol. 7, B. Perrin, Loeb, Harvard, 1919; Plutarch: The Age of Alexander, trans. Ian Scott-Kilvert, Penguin 1973

Plutarch, Camillus

Plutarch, Eumenes, Lives vol. 8, B. Perrin, Loeb, Harvard, 1919

Plutarch, Demetrius, Antony & Pyrrhus, Lives vol. 9, B. Perrin, Loeb, Harvard, 1920

Plutarch, Moralia, vols. 3 and 4, Frank Cole Babbitt, Loeb, Harvard, 1931 and 1936

Pollux, Onomasticon

Polyaenus, Stratagems of War, trans. Peter Krentz & Everett L. Wheeler, Ares, Chicago, 1994

Polybius, The Histories, W.R. Paton, Loeb, Harvard, 1922-7

Pseudo-Callisthenes, Alexander Romance, e.g. Guilelmus Kroll, Historia Alexandri Magni, vol, 1, Weidmann, 1926

Claudius Ptolemy, Geographia, ed. C.F.A Nobbe, Leipzig, 1843-1845 and Claudius Ptolemy: The Geography, trans. Edward Luther Stevenson (1932), reprinted by Dover Publications, London, 1991

Stephanus Byzantinus, Augustus Meineke, Stephani Byzantii, Ethnicorum, Berlin, 1849

Strabo, Geography, H.L. Jones, Loeb, Harvard, 1917-32

Suidae Lexicon (a.k.a. The Suda), Ada Adler (ed.), Leipzig, 1928-35

8. Acknowledgements

I would like to express my particular gratitude to the following for their assistance in the research reported in this book:-

Matthew Wofinden and Centonex for website support

Visitors to the Cleitarchus Reconstruction pages at www.alexanderstomb.com

The readership of the earlier volumes in the reconstruction for its support and encouragement

C. Bradford Welles for recognizing the usefulness of a reconstruction

A. B. Bosworth for endorsing the feasibility of reconstruction

9. Index

Index

Index

Index

S

www.ingramcontent.com/pod-product-compliance
Lightning Source LLC
Chambersburg PA
CBHW031249090426
42742CB00007B/373